Good Practice in Primary Religious Education 4–11

11.95

D0308595

Good Practice in Primary Religious Education 4–11

Edited by

Derek Bastide

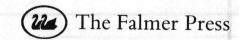

The Falmer Press

(A member of the Taylor & Francis Group)
London • Washington, D.C.

UK   The Falmer Press, 4 John St, London WC1N 2ET
USA   The Falmer Press, Taylor & Francis Inc., 1900 Frost Road, Suite 101, Bristol, PA 19007

First published 1992

British Library Cataloguing in Publication Data a record of this title is kept by the British Library

Library of Congress Cataloging in Publication Data is available upon request

ISBN 1 85000 634 2 cased
ISBN 1 85000 639 3 paperback

Jacket design by Caroline Archer

Typeset in 10.5/12 pt Bembo by
Graphicraft Typesetters Ltd., Hong Kong

Printed in Great Britain by Burgess Science Press, Basingstoke on paper which has a specified pH value on final paper manufacture of not less than 7.5 and is therefore 'acid free'.

Contents

Contents

1   Introduction

Derek Bastide

There can be no doubt that the Education Reform Act of 1988 has caused a revolution in the educational system of England and Wales. The educational tradition and practice of more than 100 years was swept away and schools found that the system of which they were part and which had been one of the most decentralized in Europe was now one of the most centralized. A National Curriculum emerged with profile components, attainment targets, programmes of study and statements of attainment along with a requirement for formal assessment at the end of four key stages in a pupil's educational career. Within these new requirements were embedded a number of concerns for clearly identified skills, knowledge and understanding, for development and progression.

RE has a unique position within the curriculum framework of the Education Reform Act. It forms part of the basic curriculum — indeed, it is listed first — but is not part of the National Curriculum. Because it is not part of the National Curriculum it is not subject to the same requirements as the subjects which form the National Curriculum, though it is still a legally required part of the school curriculum (and has been since 1944). The Act has much to say about religious education and collective worship and this is looked at in some detail by the editor in chapter 3.

There is much evidence to suggest that as well as quickening the pulse and increasing the blood pressure of many schools, the Education Reform Act has breathed fresh energy into an RE which had in places become tired and weary. It seems a good time as the Education Reform Act is becoming part of the thinking of primary schools and the time of teacher panic is passing to take a fresh look at RE in the primary school curriculum.

The contributors to this book are all practitioners in the field of primary RE, either in schools, in training institutions or in advisory positions. All have much to offer which is thoughtful, informative and appropriate to primary aged children — in fact, what is good practice in primary RE. All the contributors write as individuals from their own experiences but at the same time all display a considerable unity of view. All would subscribe to the view that the role of the school in matters of religion is different from that of the religious or faith community and that attempts to proselytize in the county school are inappropriate. All are agreed, too, that RE must transcend the informative. Cold, hard facts are not enough! RE must foster *understanding* of religions at both a cognitive and at an affective level. There is a shared concern, too, that the pupils' understanding of religion should progress and develop and, in so doing, keep pace with the growing child.

Chapters 4 and 5 focus closely upon the RE syllabus in two schools: an infant school and a junior school. Both Hazel Waddup and Liz Collis recognize that RE must be planned across the whole school and that there is need for an agreed policy. Both are alert to the dangers of haphazard and individual approaches to RE — the odd story arising out of the class topic, for example — and Liz Collis makes special provision of RE mini-topics to guard against this. Hazel Waddup is particularly concerned about the spiral nature of the curriculum and the consequent need for planned integration. They both ask the question at different stages: 'What ought the children to know and understand?' and there is the emerging recognition that RE must be defined in terms of its subject content and its key concepts.

Comparatively little has been written about making RE special in the primary school and this is an unfortunate omission. Erica Musty has the advantage of a background which includes both religious education and the education of children with special needs and she applies her wide experience in the preparation of an appropriate approach to RE in chapter 6. At the heart of her concern is the philosophy that all children have individual needs in learning and that schools can manage classrooms to meet those needs. Because of their learning difficulties children often spend a disproportionate amount of time in acquiring basic knowledge and skills, with the result that their cultural and spiritual development may be neglected. Arguing from the position that pupils' learning should include aspects of the curriculum which they enjoy and in which they are able to progress and develop, Erica Musty presents a range of practical approaches designed to meet this situation.

Planning implies a planner and RE seems to flourish best in primary schools where there is a curriculum consultant who will coordinate RE and oversee the planning, unless, as in Hazel Waddup's case, the head-teacher takes personal charge. Elaine Bellchambers is a lively RE consultant who describes her work in chapter 7. In this autobiographical chapter, full of good sense, she discusses the problems encountered in the staffroom and describes in detail the strategies she used to establish RE as an important element in the curriculum of her school. It should prove to be essential reading for newly-appointed and established RE consultants alike.

A crucial issue which pervades all thinking about RE in the primary school is its place in class topics. Such a concern underlies the chapters from Hazel Waddup, Liz Collis and Erica Musty. Dennis Bates tackles the question head-on in chapter 8 'Developing RE in topic-based approaches to learning'. It is a contribution which requires particularly careful reading. In an incisive way he analyzes the approaches which have been adopted to RE since the work of Goldman and the popularity of 'depth' theology in the 1960s and urges that the core of RE work within a topic-based approach in primary schools must be the *subject* content of religion and the *concepts* which underlie it. Readers who are familiar with the changes and developments both in RE and in approaches to topic work over the past twenty-five years will enjoy reading the chapter from the beginning. Those less familiar may find it more helpful to read the last part first, beginning at 'Good practice in topic work in RE'.

Having considered curriculum planning issues, the next three chapters examine three different strategies in teaching RE: the use of artefacts, story and drama.

Artefacts — objects used in the life and practice of religions — can be a powerful way of providing children with first-hand experience of religion in the classroom. Vida Barnett emphasizes the importance of the visible and tangible in the understanding of religion. Aware that artefacts out of context can be completely dead objects, she demonstrates ways of using them creatively in the classroom. She looks carefully at ways of using artefacts which do not give offence and gives helpful guidance on acquiring them inexpensively.

Carole King discusses the importance of *story* in the educational experience of children, and not just of young children. She identifies a number of the functions of story and discusses in some detail the significance of a variety of stories for developing an awareness of religious ideas and symbols. In a very practical chapter, Carole King discusses a number of helpful books for teachers to read with children and then goes on to show the importance too of the children writing their own stories. The chapter concludes with a detailed consideration of the role of story in assembly — a useful cross reference with Alan Brown in chapter 12.

From the rare position of being both a highly experienced teacher of drama as well as a primary education specialist, Kate Fleming argues in a tightly written chapter for the importance of *drama* as a tool in the development of children's religious understanding. She leads the reader firmly away from the notion of drama as a simple straightforward enactment of religious stories to an approach based on thinking from within. Using the symbolic language of drama to interpret abstract concepts into a concrete form she takes, as an exemplar, the parable of the Good Samaritan and demonstrates in a detailed way how she would develop it over four workshops. By experiencing from the inside, she argues that children are able to discover the implications of a role which could lead to a change in understanding.

It is impossible to look at the clauses on religious education in the Education Reform Act without giving some consideration to *collective worship* in the primary school. Alan Brown addresses himself to this controversial area. He acknowledges that the provisions of the Education Reform Act are detailed and therefore intricate; it is this complexity, he argues, which has led to poor and inaccurate reporting in the media, leading in turn to considerable misunderstanding among many teachers. He spends time looking closely at the provisions of the Act, exploring in particular the notion of worship as an educational activity. He offers a helpful and constructive framework within which primary schools can approach and plan their assemblies. He does not 'spoon-feed' — planning assemblies is an activity which staffrooms must work through themselves in detail. However he does include an extensive annotated bibliography which should prove to be of considerable use in the task.

One of the most significant current issues in RE is attainment and assessment. Since the framework of profile components, attainment targets, programmes of study, statements of attainment, assessment and so on has been established to deal with the foundation subjects of the National Curriculum, there has been extensive discussion as to whether RE ought to conform to the same framework. The editor considers the issues involved and proposes a way in which a familiar foundation model of RE — Ninian Smart's seven dimensions of religion — can fit into the National Curriculum framework with advantage both to the teacher and the pupil. There is, of course, risk here as this is, as yet, a largely uncharted sea and it may well be that the process used in the chapter is more important ultimately than the product. However, SACREs around the country are giving active consideration to this issue and no treatment of the contemporary RE scene can ignore it.

The intention of this book is that to assist headteachers and teachers in primary schools, teachers in training and members of SACREs to plan RE in the 1990s. Not only has RE itself been developing and changing but the whole system in which it is inevitably embedded has also been subject to change — and a change which has been swift and in ways revolutionary. Schools have been forced to examine their practices and to reorder their priorities and these have inevitably had implications for religious education. The following chapters seek to address these implications.

2   The Aims of Religious Education[1]

Derek Bastide

A number of primary school teachers attending courses at a teachers'
centre were asked the following question: 'What do you think ought to
be the aim of religious education in school?' Here is a sample of their
replies.

(a)   To get the children to know something about God. Hardly any
       of them seem to go to Sunday school these days so it's the only
       opportunity they'll have to learn about Him.
(b)   I don't know. I never teach it myself. I'm not religious.
(c)   To give the kids some knowledge of their religious back-
       ground. After all they've got to know something to understand
       Milton and Shakespeare.
(d)   To help the children to have some understanding of how other
       people live and what they believe. To make them more tolerant
       I suppose.
(e)   To make children Christian.
(f)   To make children better behaved. I guess — though it doesn't
       seem to work!

It is this wide range of answers which shows how much confusion
there is about the aims of RE. Views certainly do differ though it is
possible to detect three broad — and differing — approaches:

(i)   the 'confessional' approach;
(ii)   the 'giving them the facts' approach;
(iii) the 'understanding religion' approach.

Briefly, these mean:

The 'confessional' approach sees the aim of religious education as leading
pupils into Christian commitment — replies (a) and (e) above fit neatly

into this approach. The approach assumes the truth of the Christian religion and would seek to initiate pupils into it over the period of compulsory education. In practice, this aim is little different from that of the Church or the Sunday school. Sometimes it has been called the 'missionary' approach. It is interesting that reply (b) might also subscribe to this view of the aims of religious education — although she does not agree with it!

The *'giving them the facts' approach* rejects completely the 'confessional' approach with its desire to teach children to be Christians. It adopts a completely neutral view of whether religions are true or false; they are around and children ought to know about him. Reply (c) above fits well into this approach.

'The understanding religion' approach rejects both these approaches. It starts from an uncommitted position but does not feel that just giving children information is sufficient. Children need to be helped to understand religion. Reply (d) fits partly into this approach.

How Did All This Come About?

Historically in England there has always been a close link between school and church. Most schools before 1870, the date when compulsory education for all was agreed, were founded by religious bodies and transmitted their religious teaching. Most of the schools built as a result of the 1870 Act continued the practice of giving religious instruction although of a non-denominational kind. In the 1944 Butler Education Act, when religious instruction was made compulsory, it was only making mandatory what was universal practice.

The 1944 Education Act required the following with regard to religion:

  (i)   that religious instruction should be given in every county school;
 (ii)   that each day should begin with an act of worship;
(iii)   that there should be a right of withdrawal for both pupils and teachers on the grounds of conscience;
 (iv)   that each local education authority should formulate its agreed syllabus for religious instruction (or adapt that of another authority).

This clearly implied a 'confessional' approach to religious teaching. The name of the subject, religious *instruction*, the daily act of worship, the provision for parents to withdraw their children from both the teaching and worship and of non-believing teachers to refuse to enter into this part of the curriculum on the grounds of conscience all showed that what the Act intended was that children should be inducted into the Christian religion. Agreed syllabuses, written at this time, make this abundantly clear. Here is an example from the Surrey Syllabus of 1945:

> The aim of the syllabus is to secure that children attending the schools of the county ... may gain knowledge of the common Christian faith held by their fathers for nearly 2000 years; may seek for themselves in Christianity principles which give a purpose to life and a guide to all its problems, and may find inspiration, power and courage to work for their own welfare, for that of their fellow creatures and for the growth of God's kingdom.

This approach to religious teaching reflected the sort of society at the time. Most people identified in some way and at some level with the Christian religion. A large majority turned to the churches for the rites of passage — for baptism, for marriage and for burial, though the majority were not regular church attenders. There were, of course, groups within society which clearly rejected the Christian religion, bodies like the British Humanist Association and the National Secular Society. They were persistent campaigners for the removal of this sort of religious teaching from the schools but they made little headway with the vast majority of parents and teachers.

However changes were afoot both in school and in society. During the 1950s and 1960s there was immigration into Britain on a large scale from the Caribbean, Africa, Cyprus and from the Indian sub-continent. Practically all those from India and Pakistan practised religions other than Christianity. Mosques began to appear in Bradford, Hindu temples in Manchester and Gurdwaras (Sikh temples) in Middlesex. These new residents had children who attended local schools alongside indigenous children and it was not unusual in many of our cities for a teacher in a primary school to find that she had within her class adherents of four or more religions.

This, of course, raised the question of whether it was right given a class containing practising Muslims, Sikhs and Hindus to present Christianity as *the* religion. Some people saw no problem but many others did.

In a wider way too within the general population there were changes taking place — attitudes towards Christianity were changing. The 1960s saw a rapid decline in church attendance. People felt freer about admitting religious doubt — certainly in public opinion polls on religious allegiance the number of professed agnostics and atheists increased. The change was inevitably reflected in the teaching profession and a number of teachers felt unable to teach religious education in this way: 'How can I teach RE if I don't believe in God — it would make me a hypocrite'.

7

Within schools, too, there were changes. Visitors walking round primary classrooms noticed that teachers spent less time standing in front of their classes and talking to them and more time moving round the children as they worked. Children were being encouraged to learn from practical activity, to discover things for themselves. In mathematics they were being encouraged to attempt to solve problems, in creative writing to express themselves through poetry and story. Above all they were being encouraged not to accept things merely on authority but to question and then to challenge and to think for themselves. The confessional approach to RE did not seem to fit in. Although religious education as it was conceived seemed to be very much out of joint, there were still persistent and massive demands for its continued presence in schools. In surveys of parental opinion, around 90 per cent were in favour of RE in schools. Commentators put it down to many causes — guilt, a desire to offload on to the school an unpalatable part of parenthood (rather like sex education), a feeling that it might encourage good behaviour. Whatever the reasons the demand still seemed to be there.

All this led many of those involved in religious education to seek out a different approach. Religion would still figure in the school curriculum but its *aims* would be different.

One which appeared attractive to many was the straightforward 'giving them the facts' approach. The argument for it goes thus: children live in a world surrounded by religion: the church on the corner, brothers and sisters baptized, aunts and uncles married, monarchs crowned, the Bible permeating much of literature. They need to know all about this as part of understanding how the world works. This can be developed: on their TV screens children see and hear about mosques, Muslims, Sikhs in turbans and so on. They should have some knowledge of other religions and ways of living so as to enlarge their understanding of the world — and with some luck — learn greater tolerance through knowledge. The teachers' role is clearly not to foster belief or to encourage commitment to any particular religion nor even to commend a religious view as opposed to a non-religious view of life. They are there to provide information that will help the child to make more sense of the world in which he/she lives.

On first sight this view seems ideal. It respects the plurality of society; it is seen by most people as a valuable exercise; teachers of any religious persuasion or of none can teach it without conflict of conscience. They can make statements like 'Christians *believe* that Jesus is the Son of God' or 'Muslims *believe* that the Qur'an is the Word of God' — factual statements which any teacher can convey to any class of children — they are not required to evaluate them or to examine them for truth.

It was this very openness and neutrality, this insistence upon keeping to the *facts about* religion, to being always descriptive that led to numbers of people being unhappy about this approach to the teaching of religion.

It would be likened to certain approaches to the teaching of music, in which pupils learn about the lives of great composers, the name of every musical instrument, where each one is positioned in the orchestra but never hear a symphony or make a note of their own music. In what sense could this approach be called a musical education? In the same way the 'giving them the facts' approach to religious education was seen as arid and as avoiding the heart of the subject. There was no real place for *appreciation* or *understanding*.

Advocates of the third approach, that of *'understanding religion'* reject both the confessional and the 'giving them the facts' approaches, the confessional on the grounds that they do not want to persuade children to commit themselves to a particular religious stance and the 'giving them the facts' approach because it avoids the central questions of religion. The key term they use is to 'understand' and by understand they mean to empathize. They want, as far as is possible, to get children to step into the shoes of other people and to see things from their stand-point. So, understanding in this sense involves appreciation. For example, it is a fact that devout Muslims fast during the hours of daylight in the month of Ramadan. Children can be told this as a simple fact but if they are to have some understanding of it they need to have some glimmering of *why* devout Muslims fast. In this way they can begin, even if only in a very small way, to enter inside a religion. In this sense it is often said that religious education should transcend the informative.

Alongside this emphasis of looking with sensitivity at religions, and to a small extent from within them, comes the notion of *personal search*. This underlines the idea that children (and many adults too for that matter) are on a personal quest for meaning, trying to make sense of such insistent questions as 'Is this all there is to life or is there more?' or 'What happens when we are dead?'. It is to these deeper questions that religions address themselves and this approach to religious education can be helpful in this personal search. It might be argued that this is more a concern for the teenager than for the 5-year-old or the 9-year-old. As an emphasis this is almost certainly true but it would be a mistake to overlook younger children's less sophisticated attempts to make sense of some of these religious questions for themselves.

This approach is reflected in a number of influential publications. *The Fourth R* (the Church of England Commission on Religious Education in Schools, usually referred to as the 'Durham Report') states:

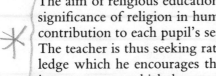

> The aim of religious education should be to explore the place and significance of religion in human life and so to make a distinctive contribution to each pupil's search for a faith by which to live ... The teacher is thus seeking rather to initiate his pupils into know-ledge which he encourages them to explore and appreciate, than into a system which he requires them to accept. To press for

acceptance of a particular faith or belief system is the duty and the privilege of the churches and other similar religious bodies. It is certainly not the task of the teacher in a county school. If the teacher is to press for any conversion, it is conversion from a shallow and unreflective attitude to life. If he is to press for commitment, it is commitment to the religious quest, to that search for meaning, purpose and value which is open to all men. (p. 103)

Discovering an Approach, (The Schools' Council Project on Religious Education in Primary Schools) indicates that:

Religious education can build upon the desire to make sense of life. It tries to help pupils to enter imaginatively into the experience of a believer so that they can appreciate the importance to him of what he believes and does. It can provide a basis of understanding and appreciation upon which reasoned assessments and informed decisions can be made. In short, religious education is helping pupils to understand religion. However, such an understanding is not quickly acquired; for many it is a life-long process. So, in the primary school, teachers are concerned with laying foundations, with the question of the extent to which we can equip children with the tools of understanding.

It is this approach which informs the thinking of the contributors to this book.

Note

1 The material in this chapter appears in part in Bastide, D. (1987) *Religious Education 5–12*, London, Falmer Press.

3 Religious Education and the Education Reform Act

Derek Bastide

Historically there has been a close link between church and school in England. Before 1870, the date when Parliament approved the notion of compulsory education for all, most schools had been founded by religious bodies and promulgated the appropriate religious teaching. Most of the 'Board schools' provided as a result of the 1870 Education Act to fill the gaps in the previous voluntary provision taught religion, though subject to the Cowper-Temple clause, the form of religious teaching was not to be given 'by means of any catechism or formulary which is distinctive of any particular religious denomination'. In 1944, when the Butler Education Act made Religious Instruction mandatory, it was, in fact, only requiring what was already universal practice in English maintained schools.

The 1944 Education Act required the following with references to religion

(i)   that religious *instruction* should be given in every county school;
(ii)   that each day should begin with an act of worship;
(iii) that there should be a right of withdrawal for both teachers and for parents on behalf of their children;
(iv)   that each local authority should formulate its agreed syllabus for religious instruction (or adopt that of another authority)

Although the 1944 Education Act did not lay down what it considered should be the aims of religious instruction, there seemed to be an implicit assumption that the teaching should be, to use the technical term, *confessional* (that is, to attempt to lead pupils into a commitment to the Christian faith). This is suggested by the use of the term *instruction* and by the right of withdrawal on the grounds of conscience for both teachers and parents on behalf of their children.

Over the years since 1944 many changes have taken place in practice. Acts of worship soon began to take place at different times of the day and not always at the beginning. The large size of many schools made it impractical for all the pupils to gather together at the same time and so the act of worship took place in smaller groupings such as year groups or houses. Research into the ways in which children understand religious concepts made teachers think very carefully about the appropriateness of much of the traditional content of religious teaching. Social change, not least the growing presence in the country of significant groups of people who practised religions other than Christianity, made teachers and educators question the confessional approach to religious education. In its place there began to develop the idea, sanctioned by such significant publications as *The Fourth R* and the two Schools' Council Working Papers 36 and 45, that the principal aim of religious education should be to help children and young people to *understand* religion. An example of this is the general aim for religious education placed at the beginning of the Hampshire Agreed Syllabus, one of the most influential of the Agreed Syllabuses:

> The principal aim of religious education in schools within the public sector is to enable pupils to understand the nature of religious beliefs and practices and the importance and influence of these in the lives of believers.

This notion of *understanding* involved moving *beyond* a merely *factual* approach to religion — just telling children, for example, about the furniture of a church or that Jews and Sikhs cover their heads in a place of worship — to one which involved *empathy*, often described as 'standing in other peoples' shoes'. Here there was a real attempt to deal not only with the questions of how and what but also of why. This approach also necessitated a variation in the content of RE. Increasingly material from a range of religious traditions was beginning to appear in the classroom: stories, festivals, customs, religious buildings, sacred books entered into the repertoire of RE. Needless to say not everybody liked this approach but it began to gain wider and wider acceptance.

Alongside this newer approach the more traditional approach still continued. Sometimes a whole primary school had considered its policy to RE and had adopted the 'understanding' approach, sometimes it had reaffirmed its commitment to the traditional way. Sometimes in a school which left such decisions to individual teachers there might be adjoining classrooms where totally different approaches were being adopted. In addition to this there were primary school teachers who were quietly ignoring the legal requirement to teach RE. It was against such a varied background that the Education Reform Act of 1988 was introduced.

RE in the Education Reform Act

Contrary to many reports in the media at the time of the publication of the Act, the requirements on RE are not an attempt to move the educational clock back to the period of the 1944 Education Act but rather they reflect and enshrine in law the thought and practice which had developed in the intervening years. In its attempt to give coherence and balance to the overall curriculum, the Education Reform Act has given religious education a firm if slightly idiosyncratic place in its plans. In general, the Education Reform Act continues the religious settlement of the 1944 Education Act but introduces some helpful clarifications and modifications.

The Education Reform Act introduces the notion of a *basic* curriculum which is the entitlement of all pupils and will be provided in all schools. This shall be a 'balanced and broadly based curriculum which promotes the spiritual, moral, cultural, mental and physical development of pupils at the school and of society' (section 1:2). It consists of RE and the ten foundation subjects which form the National Curriculum (English, mathematics, science, technology, history, geography, music, art, physical education and, in key stages 3 and 4, a language plus Welsh in schools in Wales where Welsh is not spoken). Of these foundation subjects English, mathematics and science (and Welsh in Welsh speaking schools) are described further as core subjects.

With the core and other foundation subjects, the Secretary of State for Education and Science is given the power to specify 'attainment targets', 'programmes of study', and 'assessment arrangements' for each subject within each of the four key stages, 5–7, 7–11, 11–14 and 14–16. These will have a national currency and will provide a minimum educational experience for pupils in maintained schools in England and Wales. In all this the Secretary of State is advised by the National Curriculum Council (NCC) and he is free to accept, reject or modify this advice. He may, if he wishes, introduce new foundation subjects and drop others.

From this it is clear that religious education is unique in the basic curriculum. The DES Circular 3/89 expresses this uniqueness thus:

> The special status of religious education as part of the basic curriculum but not of the National Curriculum is important. It ensures that religious education has equal standing in relation to the core and other foundation subjects within a school's curriculum, but is not subject to nationally prescribed attainment targets, programmes of study and assessment arrangements.

This means that the Secretary of State has little power over religious education. He cannot remove it from the basic curriculum as he could with any of the foundation subjects and he cannot make changes to its content as this is not prescribed nationally. Responsibility for RE is placed firmly in the hands of the Local Educational Authority.

That RE is not part of the National Curriculum with all that entails seems to result from a number of reasons. Firstly it is no doubt partly due to the longstanding responsibility that LEAs have had for the content of RE through the Agreed Syllabus. Secondly, the fact that parents are able, under the law, to withdraw their children from RE seems to be an important factor as it would be odd to the make part of the National Curriculum voluntary. A third factor would seem to be the position of RE in voluntary-aided schools (for example, Church of England and Roman Catholic schools) where it is the responsibility of the Governing Body and subject to the Trust Deeds. There can be little doubt too that to reach agreement on national programmes of study and attainment targets for RE would be a very controversial process! By not being part of the National Curriculum RE is free of government control. Being the responsibility of a Local Education Authority means in practice that it comes into the hands of its Standing Advisory Council for Religious Education, known widely as SACRE.

SACRE

The establishing of a Standing Advisory Council for Religious Education in each Local Education Authority was a discretionary power under the 1944 Education Act but under the 1988 Education Reform Act it became mandatory. The 1988 Act lays down in detail the composition of the SACRE, a composition which reflects those groups which are perceived to have an interest in the provision of religious education in maintained schools: the LEA itself, the various teachers' associations and various religious bodies. The Act lays down that a SACRE shall be made up of four representative groups (or three in Wales): Christian and other religious denominations, the Church of England (except in Wales), teachers' associations and the LEA. It is interesting to note that these four groupings were those which the 1944 Act laid down as the constituents of the Standing Conference which was to draw up an Agreed Syllabus. It is further interesting to note that in the first named grouping there is a useful clarification in the wording. This was, in the 1944 Act, always referred to as the 'other denominations' group for the Agreed Syllabus conference and controversy always existed as to whether 'other denominations' referred only to Christian denominations other than the Church of England. This new wording removes the ambiguity and now members of non-Christian religious traditions can belong to a SACRE on equal terms with those of Christian denominations if, in the opinion of the LEA they 'appropriately reflect the principal religious traditions of the area' (11:4(a)). This is significant because it underlines the intention of the

Act that religious education should take account of the teaching and practices of the other principal religions represented in Great Britain. In one LEA, not noted for the multiracial or multicultural composition of its population, the 'Christian and other religious denominations' group consists of representatives of the Baptist Union, the Methodist Church, the Orthodox Church, the Religious Society of Friends, the Roman Catholic Church, the Salvation Army, the United Reformed Church and representatives from Islam and Judaism.

It is perhaps surprising to note that there is no requirement that a SACRE should include any teachers of religious education though the Secretary of State 'believes that there would be advantage in ensuring that members representing associations of teachers include teachers of religious education' (*Circular 3/89*). Although it is technically possible for there to be a SACRE without such membership, in practice it is highly unlikely. In the SACRE referred to in the paragraph above, the Church of England, for example, made a special point of ensuring that its nominated members were not only Anglicans but also specialists in religious education. A SACRE can also coopt other members, including representatives from grant-maintained schools, if there are any in the authority area. Some SACREs have coopted representatives of non-religious philosophies of life, such as humanists.

The *chief function* of the SACRE is to 'advise the authority upon matters connected with religious worship in county schools and the religious education to be given in accordance with an agreed syllabus as the authority may refer to the Council or as the Council may see fit' (ERA, 1988, 11.1.(a)). These matters of concern are likely to focus upon such items as teaching methods, the choice of teaching materials and the provision of in-service training for teachers. To fulfil this function the SACRE is required to publish a report each year on its activities and this report should be distributed to schools, local teacher training institutions and the National Curriculum Council. This report should describe the matters upon which the SACRE has advised the LEA, the advice which was given and if advice was given upon matters not referred to it by the LEA, the reasons for so offering it.

In addition to this advisory role, the SACRE does have two very specific responsibilities. *Firstly*, it can require the LEA to review its Agreed Syllabus. In reaching such a decision the LEA group on SACRE does not have a vote; this decision is taken by the other groups. If such a requirement is made, the LEA must constitute a Standing Conference to review the syllabus. *Secondly*, SACRE can consider requests from schools for a variation in the legal requirements for the Act of Worship. There are, for example, schools which have significant numbers of pupils from religious backgrounds which are not Christian. It may be that the headteacher and/or the school governing body applies to the SACRE for an exemption from the requirement that school assemblies should be 'wholly or mainly of a broadly Christian character', or alternatively, that this should be so for certain pupils in the school. Such a decision by a SACRE is called a 'determination'. A SACRE is permitted to make a determination for a particular school but it can only do so within certain laid-down limits. It cannot, for example, allow a school to discontinue worship nor allow a group of pupils to discontinue worship (unless, of course, the pupils have been withdrawn by their parents) nor permit an act of Christian denominational worship. Within constraints such as these, SACRE has the power to enable all schools to fit in with the spirit of the Act.

Clearly the Education Reform Act is laying upon the SACRE the responsibility for seeing that the provisions for religious education and collective worship are implemented sympathetically and effectively in schools. The Act, however, does not invest SACREs with much real power; their role is largely advisory and they have little power to make sure that their advice is heeded. There is no provision for a SACRE to appeal to an authority above its LEA should it feel that it is not being allowed to do its work and it is very difficult to see what could be done about an LEA which was determined to ignore the advice of its SACRE. However it is very likely that whatever the attitude of any individual LEA, SACREs will have influence through their membership and their reports. As these arrangements have only recently been established, it will be interesting to see how influential and effective SACREs will become.

The Content of Religious Education

With regard to the content of religious education, the Education Reform Act continues the general tradition of the 1944 Education Act but makes three modifications and clarifications, two of them small but the third very significant. The two small modifications can be mentioned briefly.

Firstly, the name of the subject is changed from the religious *instruction* of the 1944 Education Act to religious education. This is a timely change as the former term had virtually disappeared from usage. The change to the almost universal use of religious *education* reflected the broadening role of religion in the school curriculum. That this change of terminology has been made in law, overdue as it is, must be a matter of satisfaction to all those involved in RE as it represents official acknowledgment of how the subject has been developing over the past forty-four years.

Secondly, there is the modification to the Cowper-Temple clause of the 1870 Forster Act, already referred to, which prohibited the use of 'any catechism or formulary which is distinctive of any particular religious denomination'. This reflected very deep controversy at the time about financing any form of denominational teaching on the rates which were, of course, paid by people of all denominations and of none. It is difficult nowadays in comparatively ecumenical times to appreciate the depth of feeling about this denominational teaching in Board schools (now County schools) and by putting in its place the possibility of a syllabus upon which most Christian denominations could agree averted a very serious clash which might have marred the birth of the notion of universal education. The Cowper-Temple clause has been in force since that time and still remains in force in the 1988 legislation. While the Education Reform Act does still prohibit the teaching of denominational formularies it does permit the study of such formularies: if, for example, a class of children is investigating Roman Catholicism, it is clearly very important to know what its distinctive formularies are. The 1988 Act recognizes this: 'this provision is not to be taken as prohibiting provision in such a syllabus for the study of such catechisms or formularies'.

The major change, however, is that all new Agreed Syllabuses must 'reflect the fact that the religious traditions in Great Britain are in the main Christian whilst taking account of the teaching and practices of the other principal religions represented in Great Britain'. This is extremely interesting for a number of reasons. Firstly, it is the first time that any educational legislation dealing with RE has laid down any indication of its content in this way. Over the years since the 1944 settlement, as we have seen, RE has been developing in such a way as to include in its content material from a number of religious traditions. This trend now receives the seal of approval from Parliament: an acceptable syllabus for RE must include some study of the teaching and practices of a number of religious traditions. Secondly, it is important to note the reference to the religious traditions (in the *plural*) being in the main Christian; thus, by placing Christianity as one, albeit the main one, of the religious traditions removes the Christian monopoly in what is seen as a religious pluralism. Thirdly, Agreed Syllabuses must take account of the presence of other major religious faiths in Great Britain. Here the geographical context is extremely important: it is Great Britain and not the immediate locality. As Hinduism, Islam, Judaism and Sikhism are major religious faiths present in Great Britain, their teaching and practices should be taken account of in the Agreed Syllabuses of areas such as Cornwall even though their presence in that particular county is not significant as it is in those parts of the country where their presence is strong. It is interesting to see this alongside the general approach of the Act which is to make RE primarily a matter for local, as opposed to national, concern: this is a limitation upon the power of local decisions. Fourthly, the verbs used in the Act 'reflect' and 'take account' do not give any indication of the balance there ought to be in an Agreed Syllabus nor of the weightings which ought to be given to the different religious traditions. This is presumably a matter for local agreement. Presumably, a Standing Conference revising an Agreed Syllabus could, if it wished, produce a syllabus which gave equal weighting to Christianity, Hinduism, Judaism and Sikhism or it could, if it wished, allocate 75 per cent of the time to Christianity and divide the remainder between the other religious traditions. Both positions would be allowed by the Act. Fifth, although the Act does not anywhere discuss the *aims* of RE, it would seem that, by its reference to an agreed syllabus reflecting and taking account of a variety of religious traditions, it is implicitly supporting an approach to the teaching of RE which encourages understanding rather than one which is confessional.

A closer look at the provisions of the Education Reform Act does confirm the generally progressive nature of its clauses concerning RE. While it does continue earlier requirements that RE should be given in all county schools, that it should be based upon a locally determined Agreed Syllabus and that there should be a right of withdrawal on the grounds of conscience for both teachers and pupils, it does also build in modifications and clarifications which reflect and give approval to those developments of thought and practice which have been happening in the subject over the intervening years. By renaming the subject officially it has acknowledged its wider role and by making a specific requirement that new Agreed Syllabuses must pay attention to religions in the country other than Christianity, the Act has built into law what has become widespread practice since the late 1960s and early 1970s. Perhaps even more importantly, through this requirement in conjunction with another modification referred to earlier in the chapter that a SACRE may contain representatives from non-Christian religions, the Education Reform Act seems to have accepted implicitly that the principal aim of RE is to encourage understanding of religions rather than to be confessional.

Collective Worship

The 1988 Education Reform Act makes a large number of requirements concerning collective worship and it seems useful to list them before considering their significance. They are:

    (i)   a daily act of worship must be provided for all pupils in school and also in sixth-form colleges (6(1));

   (ii)   this act of worship must occur in school time, though unlike the requirement of the 1944 Act, it may be at any time of the school day;

  (iii) collective worship must normally take place on school premises (6(4));

  (iv) collective worship may be organized for the whole school at one time or for smaller groupings, provided they are natural school groups (for example, forms, houses, years) (6(2));

(v)   collective worship should be 'wholly or mainly of a broadly Christian character' (7(1)) and it 'is of a broadly Christian character if it reflects the broad traditions of Christian belief without being distinctive of any particular Christian denomination' (7(2));

(vi)   not all acts of collective worship in a school need to be broadly Christian provided that a majority of them are so (7(3));

(vii)   responsibility for the arrangements for collective worship lies, in a county school, with the headteacher, after consultation with the governing body and in a voluntary school, by the governing body after consultation with the headteacher (6(3)). In all cases the head teacher is responsible for seeing that the requirements are met (10(1));

(viii)   teachers, including headteachers, continue to have the right to withdraw from collective worship on the grounds of conscience;

(ix)   parents retain the right to request the their child be excused from attendance at religious worship in school (9(2));

(x)   all acts of collective worship must have regard to any relevant considerations relating to the pupils concerned, namely (a) any circumstances relating to the family background of the pupils concerned; and (b) their ages and aptitudes (7(5));

(xi)   parents who have withdrawn their child from religious worship and/or religious education at a school may arrange for the child to receive religious education of a different kind elsewhere providing that the responsible authority is satisfied that the child cannot with reasonable convenience be sent to another maintained school where religious education of the kind desired by the parent is provided, that the LEA is satisfied that arrangements have been made and that no cost falls on the authority (9(4));

(xii)   the Standing Advisory Council on Religious Education of each LEA has a statutory responsibility to advise the LEA on matters connected with religious worship. It can grant a 'determination' to vary the requirements for a majority of the acts of collective worship in a particular school to be of a broadly Christian nature (12).

The clauses on religious worship are undoubtedly of all the requirements in the Education Reform Act concerning religion, the area which causes most anxiety and controversy. Early interpretations of the clauses tended to see them as an attempt to turn the clock backwards and to impose a rigid pattern of Christian worship upon pupils, even, it was said, to introduce an agent of Christian indoctrination. As with the clauses on religious education such an interpretation was premature and did not arise from a careful study of the wording of the clauses themselves.

In effect, the clauses on religious worship have considerable flexibility and are supportive of the ways in which thinking and practice in schools has been developing. It is worth noting that in the 1944 Education Act worship was required to take place at the beginning of the school day. Many schools over the years have placed it at a different time of the day for all sorts of good educational reasons. The Education Reform Act acknowledges this and allows the act of worship to take place at any time of the school day. The 1944 Education Act required the whole school to assemble together for the act of worship. Many large schools found this impossible as there was no room, hall or gymnasium on the school premises which would hold all the school at the same time! The Education Reform Act acknowledges this situation and allows for the organization of a school community into smaller groupings for the purposes of worship provided that these are natural school groupings such as a house, a year group or a form and not one specially created for the purpose. Safeguards are retained in the Act: parents can withdraw their children from the act of worship, teachers may opt out of attending as also may headteachers though they still have responsibility for the arrangements for collective worship in the school.

What perhaps is the cause of all the concern which has arisen is the fact that the 1988 Act has attempted to do something which the 1944 Act never did, and that is to define the content and the nature of the acts of worship. Collective worship, it says, should be 'wholly or mainly of a broadly Christian character'. Such a description is difficult to interpret without further guidance and the Act gives us this. A 'broadly Christian character' would reflect 'the broad traditions of Christian belief without being distinctive of any Christian denomination.' It does not, however, define 'broadly Christian character' any more closely than this and this, in turn, leaves much to the creative imagination of teachers and there continues to be considerable professional discussion as to what constitute the 'broad traditions of Christian belief'. 'Broadly Christian' has been further defined in DES *Circular 3/89: Religious Education and Collective Worhip*: an act of worship, it says, which is 'broadly Christian' 'need not contain only Christian material provided that, taken as a whole, it reflects the tradition of Christian belief.' This would suggest that it would be well within the intention of the Act for a 'broadly Christian' act of worship to include material from other religious traditions provided that this material is in sympathy with the 'broad traditions of Christian belief'. This raises all sorts of possibilities especially when we remember, for example, that Christianity, Islam and Judaism share a considerable portion of the Bible. This understanding of the term 'broadly Christian' could be very significant, particularly in a multifaith school.

Collective worship may be wholly Christian according to but it need not be. The description Christian of acts of worshi modified by the adverb 'mainly'. This is further elucidated in the ~~~. not all acts of collective worship in a school need be broadly Christian provided that a majority of them are so. 'Majority' is nowhere defined but it has been pointed out that 51 per cent is a majority and that, if out of 100 acts of worship, fifty-one are of a 'broadly Christian' nature then the law has been fulfilled!

Such a consideration of the actual wording of the Act does not seem to support the early view that the clauses of the Act represent a narrow and restrictive approach to collective worship. On the contrary it seems to provide for considerable flexibility. This view is reinforced by further provisions in the Act which require all acts of collective worship to 'have regard to any relevant considerations relating to the pupils concerned, namely (a) any circumstances relating to the family background of the pupils concerned; and (b) their ages and aptitudes'. It is strengthened even further by the provision in the Act for the headteacher of a school in which the majority of the pupils come from religious backgrounds which are not Christian to apply to the local Standing Advisory Council for Religious Education (discussed earlier in the paragraphs concerning SACREs) for a determination to exempt the school from the requirement to provide acts of worship which are 'wholly or mainly of a broadly Christian character'. The provisions and safeguards of the 1988 Education Act should make it clear that this is no attempt at Christian indoctrination. In fact collective worship is seen as an *educational* activity.

There is already evidence appearing from the reports of SACREs in their first year of operation under the 1988 Act that a number of schools have applied for determinations on religious worship under the provisions of the Act. In some Local Education Authorities there have been no applications but in others, mostly with a multiracial composition, there have been a number — the London Borough of Ealing, for example, has so far had a number of schools which have successfully sought determinations. In such a case, the headteacher and/or the Governing Body makes a case to the local SACRE for permission to vary the statutory requirements for their particular situation for a period of five years. The SACRE cannot grant a determination to allow a school to cease to provide religious worship but it can permit a different sort of worship. So far permission has been given by SACREs to individual schools to provide separate worship for individual religious groups and also, more frequently, to provide multifaith worship. The following case study illustrates the process. The headteacher of an infant school whose 150 children on roll contained only two children of Christian background and tradition, the rest being composed of Hindu, Muslim and Sikh children in roughly equal numbers, felt that the religious worship provisions of the 1988 Act were completely inappropriate to the situation in her school. After discussions with the RE adviser for the authority, she and her governors submitted a case for a determination. In place of the 1988 requirements they requested leave to provide what she called 'multifaith worship'. The governors deliberately rejected the solution of arranging separate acts of worship for children of different faiths because they felt that to be divisive. Their argument for 'multifaith worship', at least at the infant stage of schooling, was that as there are so many themes which cross all religions which are appropriate to the development of religious under-standing in young children, then it would be most helpful in their situation to keep all the children together and not to focus upon any one religion predominantly. No doubt other governing bodies will argue differently for their own school and this is a strength of the 1988 Act, that it permits schools to make proposals which would suit their own situations.

The reasons for unease are probably much deeper than this and reflect the question asked by many people of all religious persuasions and of none about the appropriateness of worship as an activity in a county school. This is an extensive debate argued by people of good faith on both sides but this chapter, seeking as it does to explore the the terms of the 1988 Education Reform Act, is not the place to pursue it. Reference has been made to the flexibility of the provisions for collective worship and it seems clear that the Act intends that this flexibility should be exploited to the full so that each school can devise within the defined limits an approach to collective worship which is most appropriate to its own constituency. Alan Brown's chapter on worship shows ways in which some schools have developed this.

What of the Future?

While it lays down the basic ground rules for the teaching of religious education in all county schools, the Education Reform Act does within that framework permit considerable development. While there will be no 'attainment targets', 'programmes of study' or assessment arrangements laid down nationally as in the foundation subjects of the National Curric-ulum, there is nothing to prevent each LEA, through its SACRE, from either writing its own or adopting those of another LEA. There is evidence that this is already happening at the level of 'attainment targets' and 'programmes of study'. Most existing agreed syllabuses were written in the form of aims and objectives. What content is recommended tends to come in the guise of backup booklets often called 'Suggestions for teachers'. The National Curriculum with its strong emphasis upon laid down content has tended to make these 'process' type approaches seem out of kilter. There is much evidence of rethinking of agreed syllabuses to bring them into line with the approach of the National Curriculum working parties. It may well be that over a period of time that by a process of sharing and adoption there may be considerable unanimity across the country. In the more contentious issue of the assessment of RE, there have been several research projects, some of which have produced findings which have been distributed nationally. This again may be the beginning of a national approach to the planning and assessment of RE, but this would be by voluntary agreement rather than by legal requirement. This issue is looked at more closely in the chapter on Attainment and Assessment.

These are early days after the introduction of the Education Reform Act but already there is no doubt that the strengthened legislation on RE has resulted in a higher level of interest and enthusiasm. SACREs are being set up and are reviewing provision for RE in schools and colleges; more primary schools are appointing curriculum leaders and the number of posts for RE inspectors, advisers and advisory teachers within the Local Education Authorities has increased. The signs are all present for a resurgence of RE in the curriculum of county schools.

References

Cox, E. and Cairns, J.M. (1989) *Reforming Religious Education*, London, Kogan Page.
Hull, J.M. (1989) *The Act Unpacked*, London, CEM.

4   Planning RE Across an Infant School

Hazel Waddup

What RE needs now is 'an inflow of bridled enthusiasm' wrote the poet
Roger McGough in *The Guardian* in December 1988, when describing the
significance of religious education to his own development. My hopes are
that this chapter will convey enthusiasm and make explicit some of the
ways in which RE can be planned and be implemented within a whole
curriculum, as well as give a flavour of some of the more implicit
influences of RE on the content, methodology and ethos of the school.
Whilst I am inevitably going to put emphasis sometimes on staff activities
and sometimes on pupil activities, my current thinking is that the dualism
between teaching and learning can do a disservice. The Taoist symbol of
Yin and Yang, the 'Diagram of the Supreme Ultimate', is an arrangement
of dark and light pattern in a circle. It suggests dynamic rotational
movement rather than two parts that are static and separate, as the dots in
the diagram indicate that the seed of the opposite is always contained in
the part that is currently dominant. Thus, in the darkness and bleakness
of winter is the seed of spring and new life, which as it develops to
fullness of summer contains the seed of the autumn. Each segment is
valued, significant and a necessary part of the growth and development of
the other. Any teacher who has led or taken part in an educational
workshop will be able to recognize afterwards the points where learning
takes over from teaching, and vice versa. The control of the ideas can
change hands and directions many times during the session in a dynamic
way. For me the Yin/Yang symbol is then a good model for the staff
development programme which is a significant part of the work of the
school in RE, as in other subject areas. The aim is that process should
mirror process, and that the learning skills which surface as appropriate to
a content area will need to be examined, experienced by the teachers at
the planning stage, if these skills are to be fostered and monitored among
the pupils in a classroom setting. Because of this pattern it is quite
difficult to review and differentiate what has led to the current practice in
religious education in the school, as it has various contributory strands

and has developed in a partly structured and partly organic way (the seed of one way being always in the other). I would hope to do some justice to each of the contributions.

The School

My school is a large infant school of some 270 children aged between 4 and 7, situated in a pleasant residential area in East Sussex between the sea and the Downs. I have been here for seven years, previously having been head of a town school. The children come from mainly private housing with a fairly constant population, and there are few children of ethnic origins. These few are mainly Muslim. However, Hove has traditionally had a large Jewish population with five synagogues and some of these Jewish children are nearly always in the school. The local churches represent a range of Christian practice from 'charismatic', to a more traditional Anglican, and we have among parents, those who are active members of their local congregations. In nearby Brighton there are active Muslim, Sikh and Hindu groups and multifaith activities and services are beginning to emerge as part of the Diocesan calendar. As teachers in the school we are closely involved with two training institutions, the University of Sussex which has a PGCE course and the Brighton Polytechnic which has PGCE and BEd (Hons) four-year training courses, and some staff contribute to teaching in these institutions. Thus the RE curriculum is more than what is planned by teachers in the school.

Initial Considerations

Following a working party on RE, within the county, of which I was a member, I began to lead curriculum development in this area using our pilot documents, but now it seems that the strength, the commitment and interest in RE belong to the staff, parents and governors and children as much as to me. Staff represent a variety of different faiths, philosophies and backgrounds, but what is significant is their professional attitude and willingness to discuss and teach openly, and to learn from each other in a curriculum area where there has been much fudging and muddle over the past forty years and even a misunderstanding of the 1944 Act. Recent in-service sessions with teachers in other schools and with students still indicate that the myth prevails in some staffrooms and amongst some parents that religious *education* is firmly rooted in, and best served by, assemblies. The new Act clarifies the situation. Assemblies may no doubt form the basis for good learning experiences for the children within a large group situation, especially if the said assemblies are planned and are complementary to the religious education in the classroom. Teaching RE in this way only in assemblies, may have denied to children, historically, the experiential learning in such small groups as the handling and dividing of the dough in bread making and the questioning of the symbolism of yeast, the sharing of the dilemma of the lost coin or the lost sheep in a piece of drama, the informal discussion of the symbolic patterns of Hinduism and Islam whilst the children are decorating hand-made artefacts. Even the mathematical problem solving involved in making a curved roof for a mosque from a Eurocentric constructional toy kit can be the basis for discussion of a religious nature, for example the relationship of the design and decoration on such a building to the practice and belief of those who use it. I owe much of my enthusiasm for developing RE within the school to County RE Advisers, and from my involvement in a County Primary Working Party which split into two groups, Infant and Junior, and worked on producing some guidelines for classroom use. Previously to this we had used, and still use, the Hampshire Syllabus Publications, *Paths to Understanding* and *Following the Paths*, which provide firm foundations. What concerned us at the time was that much of the integrated topic work in schools, planned by spider charts or similar models led to a frustration in many teachers in not knowing or losing sight of the religious aspect of the topic. We attempted in our guidelines to give some pointers in this direction, by extrapolating and making explicit what we thought could be the religious aspect in a number of 'life' themes, and there are indications that some teachers have found it helpful. This is a source of debate in many staffrooms and the editor has discussed this in his book *Religious Education 5–12*. As so many schools work through themes and topics in an integrated way, it is vital to encourage staff to help each other with this aspect of planning and to give guidance oneself and I will return to this later, when describing our life themes and their interpretation.

Considering Available Resources

Whilst some teachers may say they have little interest in religion, few can deny it is part of their physical and cultural landscape, through buildings, art, music, literature and travel. This is a good starting point in schools in using people's interests as a valuable resource. Teachers that I know, who have been brought up in India, although with a predominantly Christian family background, have been able to interpret for us through childhood memories, family artefacts and souvenirs and photographs, some of the beliefs and practices of religions in that sub-continent. Those interested in development education, parents and teachers, have access to a wide variety of posters, photographs and quality resources for RE through such organizations as Oxfam, Christian Aid and Traidcraft. They may also know speakers who can visit the school. Friends and staff in environmental and conservation groups also can provide photographs of animals and natural landscapes that can make a worthy display for work on our stewardship of the planet. Enthusiastic travellers can bring back postcards of stained glass windows, Celtic patterns, church sculptures and photographs of mosques and other religious buildings that dominate the landscape on Mediterranean holidays. We have an excellent collection of 'mother and child' images which derive from art galleries, church postcard shops, charity Christmas cards and calendars, and our own collection of photographs and drawings. Staff who are active in local churches have access to artefacts, and events of outside interest in the town such as festivals and multifaith services, to which the school can be linked. Through such groups we have expanded our collection of music for circle dancing, drama and listening, with tapes of different masses from Africa, South America and Europe. It is important of course to find at least one person on the staff who will be responsible for mounting, sorting and cataloguing these resources in some way to keep them in circulation. One of the most useful of 'resources' for myself was participation in the Open University Course, 'The Religious Quest'. I took this two years ago as part of my degree and it provided a good discipline for examining belief and practice within the six main religions of this country. Such a short course can only provide a basic introduction to a wide content area. From the course, I was encouraged to be more adventurous in my visiting of places of worship, and in my encouragement of visitors to the school, which now include local rabbis, the Imam, Buddhist monks and nuns, and representatives from the Hindu community. Through this course I also extended my own reading, being introduced for the first time to the *Bhagavad Gita*, Jewish short stories, the poems of Tagore, and a wonderful find, the Conference of Birds, a Sufi parable. To conclude this section on resources, I should mention the excellent selection of RE magazines and material by such groups as the Christian Education Movement that come into the school staffroom. From such magazines one can send away for selections of artefacts, but many LEAs like ours have a museum collection of articles, for example a Jewish box, a Hindu box, which can be borrowed for educational purposes. This provides a good source of material for drawing, modelling, handling, drama, display, and for supporting work on rites of passage and festivals.

When one is considering reshaping an area of the curriculum it is important to look honestly at the way the school works, and at its existing structures to find a receptive base. By 'structure' I mean planning and organization structures, such as year group meetings, guidelines, lists of topics, forecasts, and explicitly documented aims of the school, as well as considering the hidden 'structure' or ethos. We were able as a staff to agree on the following aims for our religious education:

(i) To help the children to understand what it is to be human and to be alive and to understand themselves in relation to the natural world.

(ii) To help children to develop a loving and responsible relationship to other people, friends, family and community, and to develop care for their environment, as stewards of the planet.

(iii) To help them to raise and consider questions about the significance of religion in people's lives.

(iv) To share with them experiences that show the contribution religion has made to cultural traditions through art, music, literature and landscape.

As a school we have a strong commitment to 'experiential learning', which means that as much of the curriculum as possible is to be learning at first hand, using materials and modes that are most appropriate to the age and development of the children. Story, particularly myth and legend through drama, plays a large part in this, and music making and poetry are interwoven with the teacher and children together exploring and constructing meaning. Artefacts, which can be handled and used as a basis for creative and scientific investigation, are collected and borrowed from museums and friends. As Sybil Marshall says in *An Experiment in Education*, 'Some materials and objects often satisfy unclassifiable cravings in many a child!' A wildlife garden provides us with a rich source of plants and creatures, whose existence can be marvelled at, all round the year. We also have established a strong multicultural curriculum, with a range of resources including books, music, dolls, artefacts, pattern designs, posters and photographs from many countries and cultures. Thus the RE curriculum fits well into the existing structures and working organization of the school and underpins the objectives we have in other curriculum areas. Many teachers have traditionally used story as the main medium for RE with infant children. We do this too but it is not unusual for the RE to be carried out through CDT, cookery or art. Recent visitors to the school were surprised and delighted to find children in the 7-year-old classes making 'Jewish' and 'Hindu' scarves with silk-screen printing using patterns and symbols from those cultures.

A Spiral Approach

All good curriculum work has planning as a basis, and I endorse the statement quoted from *Following the Paths*,

Any topic which develops children's opportunity to reflect on experience has relevance for religious understanding.

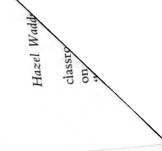

After my involvement on the County Working Party
at our thematic approach to the whole school curri
religious education would map into this structure. T
call them, arose organically over a period of time ;
main influences are the work of Goldman, some of
have seen in Steiner schools and topic work that has b
in county schools where I have worked. Basically the
framework of the whole school year, taking in elements, the natural and
man-made environment, people and aspects of friendship and community, life and death and polarities such as light and dark. They are all used
across the curriculum, and operate *spirally*, for example the theme *Myself*
is operational in the first term of each year, for all three year groups. I
will use this theme as an example of the spiral, progressive curriculum.

Myself

For children in the reception classes this would mean for the child the first
separation from his family, so we look at babyhood to see how the child
has arrived at four years in a state of independence. We work on the
importance of food and bodily care.

For year 1 children (5–6 years) this develops into the child and the
school community — those who look after and interact with the child
regularly during the school day. We work on a greater understanding of
the human body, looking at our dependence on good food, and our joy
in movement. We begin to look at friendship.

For year 2 children (6–7 years) we work on more concepts of
identity and difference, on making passports or family trees, on exploring
friendships and loyalty, and examining our dependence on commitment
and trust within the group situation, and with our teachers. There is
work linked with health education on good food choices, the sharing and
conserving of scarce resources, and some examination of handicap and
sensory deprivation.

Within each theme, work is planned across the curriculum, with
teachers in each year group meeting together to discuss details. They then
make a forecast at the beginning of each term in which the RE element of
the theme is identified. Stories from the Old and New Testaments,
fiction and factual topic packs from the library service and the school's
own resources are selected to augment the chosen theme. Artefacts are
very important, and we use the County RE boxes, museum exhibits, and
those collected in the school and lent by friends. It is very important to
have items that children can handle such as scrolls, prayer beads, vestments, and items for ritual and worship such as Menorah and Diwali
lamps that children can draw and, if they wish, make their own versions.
From the forecasts that I receive, I am able to check that resources are
ordered, and I can suggest visits or visitors and can plan to link my own
assemblies and corridor displays which I collate, to the work in the

ms. Where the curriculum for young children is very dependent
ncrete experiences, it is very useful to record events and informal
ppenings' in photographs. This has a very positive effect by giving
children lots of opportunity to discuss the 'event' from their own perspective, and photography can be used as a basis for written work or
drama later. Staff who are keen on photography are encouraged by
having the camera always ready with a supply of films and we are
making our own developing laboratory in a stock cupboard to facilitate
this side of our work. The school works on a rotational groups basis,
whereby each class is divided into five or six groups and a major part of
the day's work takes place within these set groups. The group activities
usually are planned over two days, so that on the second day the new
groups have the previous day's work as a reference point. Any RE that is
done in the way of making and sharing bread, constructing Sukkot
shelters, writing and drawing about babies' visits, making clay shepherds,
would all take place in a small group situation, even if there had been an
input for the whole class to start it off.

Skills

With RE, as with any other planned area of the curriculum, we try to
evaluate the learning and the outcome, sometimes informally and sometimes more formally. The National Curriculum requires teachers to pay
more attention to these aspects of assessment and evaluation. At present
we find a skills model one useful frame for looking at the learning
process, and staff are asked to identify, when planning, which key skills
they consider to be most needed and most in evidence in the activity.
Sometimes a new skill may be introduced, and sometimes the children
are practising or experiencing a known skill in another context. There are
some skills which seem to me to be more significant than others in RE
and I will identify them briefly.

(i) *Observation*: This is most appropriate to any work which requires interpretation of signs, symbols and rituals, and also for
looking at artefacts.

(ii) *Questioning*: Within RE we need to question and discuss attitudes, behaviour, stereotypes, differences in order to construct
our meanings.

(iii) *Manipulating*: Under this heading I put all the manual skills,
drawing, modelling, designing, printing, all the ways in which
the young child learns and makes things his own.

(iv) *Experiencing through the body*: Here I mean dance, drama, mime,
rituals, singing, chanting.

An excellent list of analytic, reflective and expressive skills are given in
Following the Paths.

As all of these skills help us to understand behaviour of all kinds,
religious practices, written texts, stories and myths, pattern and shape,
historical actions and their interpretation in pictorial and linguistic form,
they are of great importance in helping children to be open to ideas and to
be tolerant. It is essential for RE that time and value is given to each
child's contribution, and that children practice the key communication
skills of presenting information thoughtfully and of listening with respect. One of the reasons for including drama in the curriculum for
young children is that it is one of the few areas of the curriculum where
these skills can be isolated and practised in a cause and effect situation —
the drama cannot move forward if the dialogue has not been listened to,
or is misinterpreted through carelessness. All of my drama sessions in the
school begin with affirmations saying that within the group we will trust
each other and listen carefully. Here is an example of how one theme,
'Myself', was planned for the youngest age group, 4–5-year-olds.

Autumn term   *Theme: Myself*   *Reception classes*

Topic: Babies

RE content: The wonder of being alive and of growth.
Babies (brothers and sisters) of 1–3 months to be brought into school
during an assembly. Mothers and fathers to be asked to bring examples of
clothes, foodstuffs and toys appropriate to the age. The babies will be
weighed and hopefully fed and even bathed in front of the children. The
aim is that children will see via siblings how the baby begins its journey
from helpless dependence towards physical independence. Comparisons
will be made between eye and head movements at various stages, and
each baby will have a toy moved across its line of vision. The children
will be asked to choose songs that the babies will like, to help them go to
sleep. Photographs to be taken.

It is hoped that the same babies will visit later in the term just before
Christmas, so that their growth and development can be monitored, and
for the parents to tell us of preparations for the baby's first Christmas.
The information will be recorded in class books, with photographs and
graphs of weight. Baby toys to be collected and investigated.

The naming of children is discussed and children are asked to bring
in birth certificates. The naming of children in different cultures is also
considered, possibly with an example. Christening is acted out by the
teacher with a doll. The children are encouraged to build churches with
constructional toys with the Village of Three Corners Materials. Fictional
christenings and birth certificates to be made for the villagers' babies and

for the children, for example Billy Blue Hat. There might be a visit from the vicar to look at the church buildings and for the children to ask questions. Stories through picture books will be chosen which emphasize family life and the concept of each individual having separate worth and identity. This will lead to a further exploration of the baby's community, for example, the clinic. A role-play clinic will be set up in the resource area with scales, baby food, baby toys and a bathing area. All children will be encouraged to bath and handle toys carefully. Family photographs will be collected in a class album. There are many stories for young children which deal with adapting to new brothers and sisters, dealing with jealousy, sleeplessness and all the feelings that arise during the first separation from the home on going to school.

The excitement of babies coming into the family can be explored through the story of Abraham and Sarah, and the preparation for the special babies of Elizabeth and Mary in the New Testament. Rites of passage, birth, christening, and going to the school if celebrated and discussed can help the young child come to terms with his feelings at this age, that is the ambivalence of being loved and separated at the same time whilst he is at school.

This then leads into the story of the special baby Jesus, at Christmas, and it is hoped to involve as many families as possible in the Christmas celebration with parents taking part in the telling of the story and singing of carols, culminating in a family coffee morning afterwards, involving grandparents as well. This topic runs concurrently with the other autumn term themes of Harvest and Seasonal Change, and each teacher may choose to develop in her individual class other aspects of the topic. What is important for the continuity of the curriculum is that all the children in the year group have a foundation introduction to the topic that is planned and agreed upon. This obviously leads to good use of shared resources as well as individual work.

Significant Aspects of RE in this School

Before I give more detailed evidence of planned work using the life themes, I would like to define what I preceive to be the most significant aspects of RE in this school, and then it will be clearer what our criteria are for choosing certain materials and ways of working.

The Need for Children to Have Quiet Reflective Time in the School Day

As a foundation for building self-esteem and identity, the child needs time in a very cluttered and exciting home and school environment, to be as a French teacher described it, 'sans domination'. There must be space in the school day for the child to feel secure by him/herself, to sit quietly either singly or in a group and to be led to feel safe with silence. Whilst we encourage children to establish and value friendships and to work in groups, there is a need to develop the 'internal' curriculum. Just as we in our adult lives find quiet places for meditation, prayer and reflection, then we must respect the child's need for this. Within assemblies, in drama, and at other times, teachers can encourage children to be still for a few minutes either sitting or lying, and to examine or centre their thoughts. Children also need opportunities to be able to sit by themselves in a library or garden without being considered 'solitary'. We can look back to the Christian mystics as well as to Eastern religions for evidence of the contribution that reflection and contemplation make to wholeness. We can encourage 7-year-olds to write about a special place they like, where they can be by themselves and be quiet. Children write about what adults might consider to be unlikely places, sheds, under tables, attics, cupboards, in the bath, in bed, places where they can get away from the demands of family. Most of us can probably remember as children the great yearning and pleasure felt, to be out of hearing of the domestic scene, but tucked comfortably somewhere with a book, toy or even just one's thoughts.

The Relationship Between Equal Opportunities and the RE Curriculum

As this school has an equal opportunities policy, and attempts to provide a gender-friendly curriculum, RE must take this into account. This is not easy as the founders of most of the main religions are men, and many of the Bible stories are about the patriarchs. Alongside these, it is possible to find material which represents the contribution that women make; to find examples of women choosing the spiritual life by inviting women deacons and nuns into the school. The feminine side of RE can be developed using the stories of Ruth, Esther, Martha and Mary, and in particular the role that the women played during Jesus' last days during and after the Crucifixion. Myths and legends can be chosen carefully, and material about African and Asian tribes and villages used for drama can feature women farmers, and wise women as well as mothers in the nurturing role. Drama can be chosen where values are more important than gender stereotypes. It is important for teachers to check that in RE, as in other areas of the curriculum, posters, photographs and illustrated materials represent a wide variety of lifestyles, cultural backgrounds, skin colours and family types.

The Use of Stories from Non-European Cultures as a Contribution to RE

Within Christianity there is a whole range of interpretations of different stories and the use of a wide variety of texts can lead to understanding through discussion. This year we have used the publications by Oxfam of the birth of Jesus and stories of saints from Ethiopia (*The Miracle Child, Story of St Tekla Haymanot*). These books, with their vivid, unusual illustrations, combined with other material from Africa, helped to make the Christmas story less European, and our 7-year-olds looked at it with new eyes. Taoist and Buddhist stories have a different view of animals, and the story of the monkey king is one I use to illustrate the kind of sacrifice a monarch may make on behalf of his/her people. There are many African stories of how a ruler or head of a tribe behaves when confronted by a collective group. Some of these stories take us back to a time when crops and rainfall affected people's lives in a more direct way than they do for children in England, and lead us to understand the role which food production and harvesting plays in celebrations and rituals. A favourite story for RE drama with us is a Japanese folk tale, *Taro and his Grandmother*, where the headman in the village orders the people to put their older relatives on the mountain to fend for themselves in order to save enough food for the breadwinners and children of the village. This always has a profound effect on the children when acting it out and leads to much debate and reflection. One rather 'tough' boy was found crying after putting his grandmother on the mountain.

'Next time', he confided, 'I'm going to play the gran, it doesn't make you feel so cruel.'

I had actually thought he was crying because there had been some unseen bullying between members of the class rather than as a direct result of the dramatic action! There is a legend of *Hares and Elephants* where a bunch of elephants suffering from drought stumble and take over the territory of some hares, which includes a sacred lake. The lake then becomes muddied, as it is put to more pedestrian use by the elephants for washing and drinking. This always provide an excellent base for working on the significance of religious rituals in people's lives, and what happens when your neighbour does not respect these and has more immediate needs. Cambridge University Press provide a good range of these stories in their publications, *Legends of Sun and Moon* and *Legends of Air, Fire and Water*.

The Use of Rituals such as Dance, Chanting and Ceremonies

Jean Liedloff in her book *The Continuum Concept*, after observing young children in South American tribes over a number of years, says:

Ritual is another form of relief from the burden of choice-making. During the ritual, especially if one has an active part such as dancing or chanting, the organism is run under a flag far older than that of the intellect. The intellect rests.

This may be a deeper definition of the 'sans domination' phrase of my French teacher friend. Certainly we find an intuitive and joyful response amongst our children to circle dancing, chanting, sung prayers and invented ceremonies. Circle or sacred dancing was a part of religious practice before worship became formalized in more recent centuries. Much medieval music was played on simple instruments for celebratory and respectful dances, and there is a revived interest in this type of dance throughout Europe. It is interesting to note how strange we Westerners find the use of the body in other religions. We can be embarrassed by the Sufi dancing and the prostrations and bowing in Islam and the Eastern religions, as mostly our body movements in the Christian church are confined to discreet bowing and kneeling and crossing ourselves. Sometimes it is this frightening and unusual behaviour of another religious group that gets in our way before we can understand and appreciate universalities. As a convert to Buddhism some years ago, I certainly found the bowing the most difficult part of the ceremony, being used to the more restrained Anglican practices in worship. Chanting has also played a key part in both Eastern and Western religions for hundreds of years. Buddhist chanting opens the chest and voice, and so the heart allows the mind to centre and focus with great reverence. We find that children enjoy very simple chanting either from such sources as the '*Taize*' masses, or using simple mantras either in English or other languages.

'Jesus remember me, when you come into your kingdom', is a favourite sung chant in our school, from *Laudate Taize*. We adapt songs and music to dance for our own purposes, when we want to have an informal celebration, as well as for calendar events such as Christmas and the Harvest Festival. Children seem quite willing to work on some of the more difficult rhythms of Jewish and Indian dances, especially when they are made more colourful by addition of scarves and instruments.

The Importance of Visitors and Significant 'Others' as Part of the RE Curriculum

In an attempt to help children to develop moral attitudes, we can in school offer them models other than ourselves from the local religious community. Teachers from other religious groups have visited the school, the rabbi and members of the local synagogues, the imam, Hindu and Sikh teachers, Buddhist monks and nuns, and representatives from a whole range of Christian denominations in the town. It is important to have women as well as men, in order to show that the spiritual life is open to all. When Buddhist friends visit from the Theravāda Monastery, I always spend some time in preparation, explaining about the privations and discipline of monastery life and the choices they have made. I also tell some stories of the early life of the Buddha, *Prince Siddhārtha*, using the book by Jonathan Landaw and Janet Brooke. Preparation and respect are important in arranging such visits, as it seeems wrong to invite people in to compare their differences with ourselves — it can just end up in critical gawping! It must be because we believe they have some wisdom to share or a spiritual dimension to their lives that is worth hearing about. The children find it fascinating to see the saffron robes and the shaven heads, and always ask a variety of likely and unlikely questions. The main surprises about the monks and nuns seem to be human ones — where did they get their glasses, as I had told them they carried no money. Because our children are infants, we find it more appropriate to bring visitors into the school rather than to take children out to places of worship, which can be more beneficial when they are older. We are able though to visit the nearby parish church with its lovely flint walls, and ancient features, and so this is a chance to meet the vicar in context. Other visitors to the school have been a group of mentally handicapped people who came to spend a day with us, sharing a puppet show. Despite the children finding the visitors in strange places such as stock cupboards and the home corners, the children treated them with love and respect, although they became worried when one lady seemed to think the home corner toy telephone was real. We played parachute games to round off the day. The next day their reactions and questions were interesting and thoughtful but the main impression was, 'Don't they have fun!' One child said, 'I've always been frightened of people who looked like that when I've seen them on the bus'.

The Centrality of the Garden

When I came to the school, there was a small paved garden in the centre of the building that was undeveloped. With keen staff I set to work to create a garden and sanctuary which would be quiet and would be a reservation for plants that smelled and looked beautiful such as herbs. Putting in new plants has created ecological change and we have many nesting birds and butterflies and a pond and abundance of minibeasts. The garden has been featured in the BBC radio series for schools, *Special Places*, and the children were interviewed about how they saw the garden as part of the school. Now we also have a wildlife meadow at the front of the school with long grass and hedges planted, and there is evidence of new wildlife there. I cannot desentangle RE from environmental education, and I cannot put words better on this subject than James Lovelock.

To see and feel the earth in this way and to think of it as a living organism gives substance to the Christian concept of stewardship and turns our hearts and minds towards what should be our prime environmental concern, the care and protection of the earth itself.

This is from *Stand up for Gaia*, the Schumacher lecture of 1988 and expresses what I can only describe as grass roots reverence. During the year most of the classes have the opportunity to do some gardening either with a small plot or a gro-bag on the patio. In autumn we ask children to bring two daffodil bulbs each and are making extended bulb gardens which give more delight each year. It may be very important for the health of the planet to let children learn respect for all living things; plants can be shown as vital to the ecosystem as well as being useful for medicine, pot pourri and for decoration. I particularly like the story of the Buddha and the tree spirit to emphasize the link between our responsibility as spiritual beings and our care for the earth and living organisms. We have our own calypso hymn about the school garden.

Themes Across the Age Groups

Here is the basic list of themes for the year for all three age groups.

Theme	Main RE elements
Autumn term	
Myself	Identity and self-esteem.
	Growth and the wonder of being alive.
	Friendship and community.
	Differences and handicaps.
Seasonal changes and harvest	Our reliance on food.
	Animals' and humans' need to store food.
	Our opportunities to share resources and our need to preserve them.
	Famine, drought.
	Making bread from various cultures.
	Food as part of religious practice.
	Ramadan and Sukkot, Christian Harvest Festival.
Festivals of Light (Year 2)	Diwali.
	Hanukah.
	Advent.

Christmas and the special baby
    Epiphany   Giving to other people.

Spring term
Polarities:
    Day and night   Creation and creation myths.
    Hot and cold   Hot and cold feelings.
                                     Wonder of planets and constellations.

Stories of saints   People of courage with vision (men
                                     and women.)

Parental love   Love and respect for parents,
                                     grandparents, respect for old age.

New beginnings   Growing things from seed, looking at
                                     bulbs planted in autumn.

Chinese New Year (Year 2)
Spring and Easter   Death and new life (the cycle).
                                     Making Easter gardens.

Summer term
Planet Earth and the elements   God as creator.
    which sustain us   People as caretakers.
Water   )   Our dependence on these three
Earth   )   elements for life and health.
Air   )

Journeys   Moving on, looking back at the school
                                     community, trust and friendships,
                                     before going to new schools and on
                                     holidays.

Autumn Term: *Seasonal Change and Harvests*

For the *reception children* who are 4–5-years old the children usually start with examining the food of human babies, and then make autumn collections of ripening foods and fruits for humans and animals. Apples and other fruits are cut open, examined and drawn in pastels, chalk, or painted and the seeds carefully planted afterwards. Bird seed, nuts and conkers are looked at and then restored to the earth. Bulbs are planted in anticipation of spring. All first-year children make wholemeal bread and experience yeast and the wonderful smell and excitement of rising dough. The bread is cut and shared out in the classroom sometimes with home-made butter, and jam or nut spread. Prayers and poems are written about our dependence on our daily bread and giving thanks for our favourite foods.

The *year 1 children* take a closer look at some fruits and vegetables with more detailed drawings. They may visit the greengrocer to buy and taste ordinary and out of the ordinary produce, mangoes, pineapples etc. Foods are looked at for their contribution to good health. Some are allowed to rot to see change and seeds picked and counted. Stories of harvest from the Old Testament are popular here, Abraham and the Visitors, Joseph and the brothers, Ruth and Boaz, and stories of fishermen and the sea of Galilee to illustrate the harvest of the sea. Sometimes jacket potatoes are cooked with sea salt.

Year 2 children: There are three parallel classes who each take a religion and follow through some of the food rituals as part of their study. Those taking Judaism hear the story of the tabernacles and make Sukkot shelters with Craft, design and technology (CDT) materials and matzos, and learn Jewish celebratory dances, and quite often make challah bread for Hanukkah. The class studying Hinduism make Indian sweets and chapatis full of curried, spicy vegetables as part of their understanding of the significance of food in puja and on special festivals such as Diwali. One year a third year class concentrated on the harvesting of English fruits and vegetables, collected tomatoes and apples, and added ginger and dates from abroad to make a chutney that was sold for Christian Aid. Songs, poems, prayers, accompany this work and there are often visitors from the non-Christian groups. There are many story books published now of family life at the time of the various festivals and these add to children's understanding.

> Food is heaven,
> As you cannot go to heaven alone.
> Food is to be shared,
> Food is heaven.
> As we share the sight of the heavenly stars,
> So food is something which must be shared.
>
> Food is heaven,
> When food passes your throat,
> You accept heaven in your body.
> Food is heaven,
> Ah. Food is something that must be shared.
> (source unknown — believed Korean or SE Asian)

The Tinsel-Free Christmas

Christmas as a Christian festival deserves our very best educational practice and attention, and the most worthy of images and artefacts. Yet it seems to have become for many teachers a time of great stress and continuous joyless effort as children are turned into what one art adviser succinctly calls 'little makers'. There are very beguiling Christmas craft catalogues containing a plethora of shiny materials, and there are the prescribed Nativity plays which can become over-rehearsed. Whole staffs complain of Christmas beginning at half-term, and yet seem unwilling to reconsider their practice at this time and expect competition and exhaustion to rule. Ground rules need to be negotiated for a better time at Christmas for all concerned. I will give some of my suggestions for this agenda.

(i) That whatever art, music and drama is done, it should be of the best of its kind, and it should be organic starting from the child and the content of the Christmas message, rather than the materials available.

(ii) That simplicity in style, content and materials is better than abundance. We concentrate on one card being made per child, beautifully drawn or painted, with best handwriting and attention to mounting. Then it can be taken home and treasured as a work of art. No other artefacts, decorations, are made to take home, unless it be a clay shepherd or candle holder for the Diwali lamp.

Each year we choose an *emphasis* for Christmas and the story of the birth of the special baby is told through this medium. This year it was dance and music and each class in the school was asked to take one or two English carols, or pieces of dance music, and use them for a part of the Christmas message. From the reception children who did a simple meditation dance to a French shepherd's tune, via the Sussex Carol and *Ding, Dong, Merrily on High* from the year 1 children, to Jewish and Indian music with handprinted scarves and hats, and a candle dance to Sidney Carter's *Every Star Shall Sing a Carol*, the Christmas message rang out in rhythm and song with instrumental accompaniment. We finished with a meditation dance with eyes closed, and the lights down to Pachelbel's Canon, dancing in front of the crib in homage. Historically we know that there were sheep and cattle on this site in the last century so at various points through the year, but particularly at Christmas, we tell the story of shepherds and make flocks of sheep with clay and try some spinning and weaving. We decorate the school with natural materials, the plants of Christmas, mistletoe, holly, ivy, poinsetta, and make masks and stables with withies, cook traditional foods and make candles and candleholders from old wax crayons and clay. We make a menorah for our Jewish children and learn a Hanukkah dance. The school pot-pourri, made on the site from our rose petals and herbs is the only home-made gift for parents. The school nativity clothes are put into the home corners so that first years can dress up and experience what Joseph and Mary and the shepherds looked like. Sometimes realism takes over as in the case of a surprised visitor finding a 5-year-old Joseph in the toy phone booth calling for an ambulance for Mary. Thus Christmas is experienced through all the normal curriculum modes of art, music, drama, avoiding the commercial and inconsequential mounds of tissue paper and cotton wool snowmen. We have three celebrations, one for parents of each year with a coffee morning at the end of the first year's event for grandparents and visitors. Sometimes a sustained piece of drama is tackled, but this arises out of our drama lessons or club and we use a variety of trust games for voice and body as a basis for organically developing dialogue and action so it is the children's own work. I have used very successfully the story of *Amahl and the Night Visitors* and the Russian folk tale of *Baboushka* for such pieces. What always shines through for me is the joint respect of both children and parents for the simple story of Christmas.

Spring Term

Work on the polarities such as darkness and light is very fundamental to the young child. It is the time of beginning to learn of life's cycles, of day and night, winter and summer, birth and death and to experience and explore the concept of the earth and the person needing rest in order to revitalize. Provided that children feel safe, they can explore through drama, creative writing, and art, some of these themes, and can confront some of their fears about pets dying and not wanting to go to sleep at night. We use blind and trust games to lead into drama, and have theatre lights in the hall, so that we can work on night themes and dark land-scapes for such stories as Persephone, in *The Night Kitchen* (Sendak); parts of *Watership Down* where the animals move at night towards a place of safety, are useful. Ted Hughes stories, *How the Whale Became*, and some of the stories of Krishna for Holi continue to develop the theme. Buddhist stories are useful for helping children with difficult friendships, they need to be encouraged to let things be, to try to maintain 'metta' or loving kindness towards people they find awkward and annoying. We write poems and prayers about those who work at night, not forgetting mothers with sleepless babies. We show slide shows of the planets and constellations with appropriate music. Chinese legends can illustrate the Yin and Yang principle and there are stories with night as a background in the Old and New Testament. A particular favourite is the one of the neighbour who knocked on the door at night for bread. Sometimes we make a night home corner, with teddybears and a bed inside and a torch, and stories are illustrated by shadow puppets. Writing on dreams and the bedroom as a special place is encouraged. Mothers' day during this term is seen as a time for celebrating family love and caring relationships, with the community and of the strengthening of links with grandparents. This helps to give children a sense of historical place. Stories of their own grandmothers and grandfathers are put into large books and the book *Grandpa and Me* is popular. As the bulbs in the pots and school gardens emerge, some classes make Easter gardens, or grow cress in egg shells to take home. Hot cross buns are made with yeast by all the first years, and palm crosses are shown. Stories such as *The Selfish Giant* and the *Ugly Duckling* are used for drama and for celebrating new life. Easter poles and hats are made and the children have a home-made version of Easter egg rolling, an obstacle race, transporting an egg over various hurdles, through tunnels, sailing it along the toy canal in boats and finally rolling the egg and themselves down the school bank. I find this an exciting time to be in school, as the spring sunshine and flowering bulbs are symbols of the whole school community organically recharging its life forces.

Summer Term

Much of the summer term is given over to working across the curriculum on three elements, earth, air, and water. Staff choose to use them in whatever order suits their planning and sharing of resources. The overriding aims are to use as much of our own school environment as possible for the first hand experience required. For example we have large grounds, the aforementioned gardens, indigenous trees, a hill for kite flying, a view of sea and downs, and the beach is a bus-ride away. We have patios for sand and water play and grass and willing parents for parachute games. In RE terms we are at this time of year celebrating the planet in all its awe and wonder, restoring to children their links with elemental forces. For the youngest children, they learn to respectfully observe and leave unharmed the minibeasts that are part of the science curriculum. I use some of the Buddhist stories here. Particularly good are those versions of the *Jataka* tales by John Snelling (Jataka meaning rebirth) where it is thought that in previous lives of the Buddha he had been an animal or bird who had a lesson to teach its peers. Other stories are used from folk sources of various cultures that question our dependence on healthy plant and animal life, and whether we should needlessly destroy tree and plants. The dump in Russell Hoban's story of *The Mouse and His Child* can be a basis for discussing creative reuse of our own resources. Year two children visit Arundel Wildlife Park to see the water birds and breed moths and silkworms. Some work is often done in this term on the lives of the shepherds at the turn of the century and this is well documented in books by local authors and folk tunes. In this term we often have a home-made celebration making a banner or a flag for the planet, each class choosing one element or one species to centre on. This year we are making prayer flags. In circle dances our summer favourites are The King of the Fairies which celebrates the four elements, in turn, to a lively Irish tune, and The Bee Dance, which is a home-made dance about bees and hives using a Playford tune called *All in a Garden Green*. We have garlands for dance and last year made up a rose dance which attempted to simulate patterns in roses and rose windows. There are wonderful elemental stories from all sources to use at this time, stories of Jesus and friends by the sea of Galilee, stories of the river Jordan in both Old and New Testament, the story of Hagar and the well (Muslim). Whilst Jonah is regarded as a difficult story for infants, I have used part of it for drama, working on some aspects of feelings and fears. I began from the viewpoint of the sailors and their families on shore, and then as the crew on the ship and their terror of the storm but their ambivalence towards Jonah. Stories representing Air are myriad, some from the Hindu traditions, Icarus, *Jonathan Livingston Seagull* by Richard Bach, to which I will refer later. *Don't Go Near the Water Shirley* invites writing and drawings of the child/parent ambivalence of allowing children to take risks and explore their environment. Poetry and literature on the theme of Water are abundant. *Le Petit Prince* by Antoine De St Exupery is a good text to use in short extracts to examine some of our attitudes to the planet.

From this chapter, it will be clear that I believe the arts and particularly drama, play a fundamental part in helping children understand what it means to be human. Drama is the most lifelike of the art forms, as it takes place in the 'now', with people moving in time and space constructing meanings from a variety of language and symbolic forms. Dramatic forms encourage us to work on an everyday item or event, and then to inject a disturbance into it which then encourages us to find a solution. The teacher in role as the woman, sweeping her house, searching everywhere in nooks and crannies for the coin she has lost from her wedding headdress, can invite the children as villagers and friends to look and search and share her sadness at losing something of value. Thus the particular can become the universal and this simple work can lead on to the consideration of why people in exile or on journeys carry symbols of their faiths such as the ark with its scrolls. Drama frames can be from the very simple such as depictions, sculptures, snapshots, mimes, to longer sustained plays. I find that drama has a very liberating effect on children of all ages, particularly if they are encouraged to take some ownership and responsibility and develop their own dialogue and songs rather than from reading from a ready-made script. This does not come about by accident but requires 'skill' based work from an early age, developing listening, and questioning and learning to respond in a variety of modes using voice, body and space. Each of our drama sessions in the school begins with an affirmation, holding hands in a circle, we say, 'I trust you, I want to work with you, I will be careful'. Once this promise has been made, and a reminder given from time to time, the teacher can begin to encourage her pupils to take risks in the secure knowledge that they will be respected and trusted. It is worthwhile spending time on the language of touch, using blind games. A lovely exercise is for the children in groups to create an interesting garden for a blind person, using their own bodies and voices. Blind 'visitors' are then led through the arches and across stepping stones to feel moving sculptures and listen to waterfalls. Blind earth walks round the school garden are nice, feeling the texture of trees and walls, and smelling different plants.

The story of *Jonathan Livingston Seagull* by Richard Bach is one of my favourites. It is a story on many levels, of a seagull who chooses to be different, to concentrate on higher flying skills at the expense of being isolated from family and flock, and distancing himself from the pedestrian daily activities of the other seagulls, such as eating. It is a good vehicle for exploring differences, and for investigating the sense of self and separation that can arise with some enlightening experience, and there are parallels in religious writings that some of the children recognized. I have used it alongside stories such as St Paul on the road to Damascus, and Jesus in the temple being chided by his parents and replying, 'Can't you see, I was about my father's business'. It is very appropriate for using for depictions, or sculptures in family groups taking such titles as — 'Why can't you be like us?' On the last production I acted as narrator/reporter, asking Jonathan and other seagulls in role how they felt about certain situations, — 'How do you feel Jonathan now you are banished by your friends?'

The whole production came from trust and blind games and group work as before described. A great deal of trust needs to be developed before you can allow one seagull to crash head-first into a flock and scatter all asunder. In the end Jonathan finds like friends on a higher plane, and returns to teach higher flying skills to the flock, but his gifts are misunderstood, and only valued retrospectively. A considerable amount of sensitive art and writing accompanied this project. The production began and ended with a musical version of some of Martin Luther King's words,

> We have flown in the air like birds and swum in the sea like fishes, but have yet to learn the simple act of walking the earth like brothers and sisters.

At the end of the school year, journeys are topical because of transition to other schools, and holidays. There are many good narratives for journeys, Old Testament travels, *Pilgrim's Progress* for older children, St. Paul's journeys, and many modern stories of transformation and search (see references). For older children, leaving the school is a rite of passage, and is well served by the learning and singing of Sydney Carter's hymn, *One*

More Step Along the World I Go. We try to encourage children to write about the value they have placed on this time with their infant teachers and friends and other staff in this school without resorting to sentimentality. I believe this affirmation to be valuable to children's spiritual development; to have space and time to articulate their feelings at a time of change, without losing face. Pieces of writing entitled 'Who do you trust in this school?' or 'Who can you trust on your journey as you leave it?', have shown that children have developed and valued very trusting relationships with many diverse people in the school. It opens up the question, which can be tackled as the child grows older, 'Is there something or someone greater you can trust in, besides friends, family and teachers?'

References

BASTIDE, D. (1987) *Religious Education 5–12*, Lewes, Falmer Press.

GOLDMAN, R.J. (1964) *Religious Understanding from Childhood to Adolescence*, London, Routledge and Kegan Paul.

GOLDMAN, R.J. (1965) *Readiness for Religion*, London, Routledge and Kegan Paul.

HAMPSHIRE EDUCATION AUTHORITY (1980) *Paths to Understanding*, London, Macmillan.

HAMPSHIRE EDUCATION AUTHORITY (1986) *Following the Paths*, London, Macmillan.

LIEDLOFF, J. (1986) *The Continuum Concept*, London, Penguin Books.

LOVELOCK, J. (1988) *Stand up for Gaia*, Schumacher Lecture, Oxford, Oxford University Press.

McGOUGH, R. (1988) 'Praying with energy', *The Guardian Weekend Newspaper*, 24–25 December.

MARSHALL, S. (1966) *An Experiment in Education*, Cambridge, Cambridge University Press.

OPEN UNIVERSITY (1978) *The Religious Quest Course AD 208*.

Books That Are Helpful to Use with Children

Buddhist Stories

LANDAW, J. and BROOKE, J. (1984) *Prince Siddhārtha*, London, Wisdom Press.

BARKER, C. (1985) *Ananda in Sri Lanka*, London, Hamish Hamilton.

SNELLING, J. (1986) *Buddhist Stories*, Hove, Wayland Publications.

Christmas

LAIRD E. WITH ABBA AREGAWI WORLDE GABRIEL (1985) *The Miracle Child*, London, Collins for Oxfam.

Attitudes to Elderly People

ALEX, M. and ALEX, B. (1983) *Grandpa and Me*, Oxford, Lion Books.
EAST, H. (1986) *Taro and his Grandmother*, London, Macdonald.

Elemental and Environmental Themes

ADAMS, R. (1986) *Watership Down*, London, Puffin Story Book.
BACH, R. (1972) *Jonathan Livingston Seagull*, London, Pan Books.
BURNINGHAM, J. (1988) *Come Away from the Water Shirley*, Oxford, Picture Lions.
EAST, H. (1986) *The Emperor and the Nightingale*, London, Macdonald.
HADLEY, E. and T. (1983) *Legends of Sun and Moon* and *Legends of Air, Fire and Water*, Cambridge, Cambridge University Press.
HOBAN, R. (1969) *The Mouse and his Child*, London, Faber and Faber.
HUGHES, T. (1963) *How the Whale Became and other Stories*, London, Young Puffin.
MORIMOTO, J. (1985) *Mouse's Marriage*, Glasgow, Blackie and Son.
TROUGHTON, J. (1988) *Who Will Be the Sun*, Ginn Library Corner Books.
WILDE, O. (1978) *The Selfish Giant*, London, Picture Puffins.

Journey or Exploration Stories

ATTAR FARID-UD-DIN (1985) *The Conference of the Birds*, London, Arkana Press.
CARLE, E. (1988) *Rooster's Off to See the World*, London, Hodder and Stoughton.
DE SAINT EXUPERY, A. (1974) *The Little Prince* (trans Katharine Woods), London, Heinemann.
HOWELL, M. (1973) *The Mouse Who Wanted to be a Man*, London, Longman.

Night Themes

SENDAK, M. (1970) *In the Night Kitchen*, London, Bodley Head.

Love and Generosity

ZOLA, M. (1981) *Only the Best, A Story for Sukkot*, London, Julia McRae Books.

5   Planning RE Across a Junior School

Liz Collis

Education is concerned with the *quality* of growth and religious education in the junior school and with the growth of the child's spiritual understanding and experience. Its function (except in the church school) is neither to nurture the child in a faith nor merely to pass on a body of knowledge but to help the child to develop spiritually. Religious education in the junior school is concerned therefore with providing activities and experiences for the child which will help him to engage with the concepts, with the development of religious understanding and hence the development of a child who is *religiate*.

Topic-based Approaches

Flexibility in the curriculum is an important part of the primary ethos. Young children learn most readily when engaged in exploring through themes that which is related to their own experience. The recognition of the artificiality of rigid subject barriers for the young child means that most schools adopt a topic-based cross-curricular approach to the curriculum. It is essential to incorporate religious education within the topic-based approach and interrelated to other aspects of the curriculum rather than existing only as a discrete subject. Often subject areas overlap, the one informing the other. For example, some understanding of Jewish history will illuminate the meaning of the Passover for the older child. Furthermore religious education needs the other subjects as vehicles for its expression. Through literature and role play particularly the child's religious understanding can be developed. It is useful therefore to see where, within the class topic, it is possible to extend the child's spiritual understanding and to capitalize on it using active learning approaches.

Planning is a vital important part of topic work and it can be useful for teachers to work together in small groups at the planning stage to decide what activities the children will be engaged in and what skills will

47

be developed. Whilst it is not always desirable to integrate all the disciplines into a topic, a cross-curricular approach offers the most fruitful opportunities for children's learning. It is important that religious education only be included in the topic in a way which is legitimate, otherwise the links can become contrived. However most topics offer some potential for thematic links which are real.

In order to support the development of the spiritual dimension adequate *resources* of quality are essential. Topic resources to support themes such as 'bridges' or 'water' are a good starting point and the Christian Education Movement termly mailings provide a useful basis in developing thematic approaches. As wide a range of resources as possible is desirable so that a variety of materials and methods may be used. Charts, slides, videos, sets of pictures and books are all useful in this context, providing materials also for interactive resource based learning and use of study skills. In particular it is useful to build up a collection of *artefacts* for each major faith, such as, for example, a Jewish prayer shawl, a menorah, seder plate, skull cap and matzos. It is also useful to collect resources for each major festival.

The development of communication skills is an important part of the young child's growth. How children show what they have been learning about to others reinforces the child's own learning, develops communication skills and celebrates the child's work and achievement. In most schools a variety of opportunities is provided for the child to share the work they have been doing. It is also a way of increasing the understanding and experience of those who are the audience. For example, in one upper junior class assembly children explained the work they had been doing over the term on the topic *'Light'* demonstrating their science tasks and other aspects of the theme. The assembly then concluded with a shadow puppet play of the story of Rama and Sita. The approach of the teacher had been through story, the children had then written their own ballads of Rama and Sita and made their own puppets. Similarly, a lower junior class engaged in a topic on *'food'* included in their assembly presentation, along with observational drawings of fruits and reports of scientific experiments, information they had found out through research work about symbolic Jewish foods. An integrated approach to learning includes religious education.

Another form of communicating to a wider audience and celebrating children's achievements is through *display*. For example, a year 3 class as part of their topic on 'Our school' worked on 'belonging' writing and drawing about their membership of other groups and communities outside school included family, Sunday school and other clubs. The way in which the spiritual area of learning and experience relates to the main theme is shown by the planning web on the facing page. Sometimes display will be in the classroom but usually the entrance hall or a common area provides a place for topic work to be shared.

SUMMER TERM

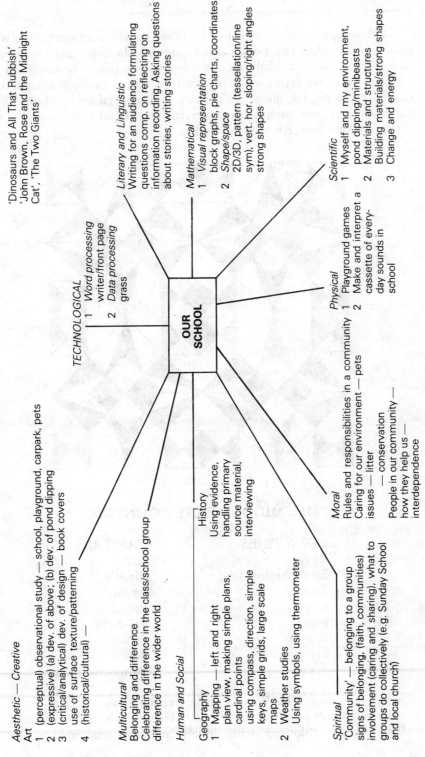

OUR SCHOOL

Aesthetic — Creative
Art
1 (perceptual) observational study — school, playground, carpark, pets
2 (expressive) (a) dev. of above; (b) dev. of pond dipping
3 (critical/analytical) dev. of design — book covers
use of surface texture/patterning
4 (historical/cultural) —

Multicultural
Belonging and difference
Celebrating difference in the class/school group
difference in the wider world

Human and Social

Geography
1 Mapping — left and right
plan view, making simple plans,
cardinal points
using compass, direction, simple
keys, simple grids, large scale
maps
2 Weather studies
Using symbols, using thermometer

History
Using evidence,
handling primary
source material,
interviewing

Spiritual
'Community' — belonging to a group
signs of belonging, (faith, communities)
involvement (caring and sharing), what to
groups do collectively (e.g. Sunday School
and local church)

Moral
Rules and responsibilities in a community
Caring for our environment — pets
issues — litter
— conservation
People in our community —
how they help us —
interdependence

TECHNOLOGICAL
1 Word processing
writer/front page
2 Data processing
grass

'Dinosaurs and All That Rubbish'
'John Brown, Rose and the Midnight
Cat', 'The Two Giants'

Literary and Linguistic
Writing for an audience formulating
questions comp. on reflecting on
information recording. Asking questions
about stories, writing stories

Mathematical
1 Visual representation
block graphs, pie charts, coordinates
2 Shape/space
2D/3D, pattern (tessellation/line
sym), vert. hor. sloping/right angles
strong shapes

Scientific
1 Myself and my environment,
pond dipping/minibeasts
2 Materials and structures
Building materials/strong shapes
3 Change and energy

Physical
1 Playground games
2 Make and interpret a
cassette of every-
day sounds in
school

49

Often topic work is presented in a *book* in which all the child's work on a theme is put. The book can be made by the child and bound with each piece of work carefully mounted before insertion. The cover may be simple or a more elaborate press print or tooled rubbing design. One class in exploring the theme of 'pattern' looked at Islamic patterns. They made up their own symmetrical patterns and found out about the way Islamic people live. An example follows:

THE MIDDLE EAST COUNTRIES

COUNTRIES	CAPITALS
Egypt	Cairo
Saudi Arabia	Riyadh
Turkey	Ankara
Iraq	Baghdad
Israel	Tel-Aviv
Iran	Tehran
Lebanon	Beirut
Syria	Damascus

The Way Islamic People Live
Islamic people pray five times a day. They each have a mat which is brightly coloured with lovely patterns that are usually

symmetrical.If Islamic people came to England and got their little mat out in the street and prayed the English would think it strange because they all face east wherever they are because that is where Makkah is. In Makkah there is gigantic stone. To make a pilgrimage you have to walk round the Ka'aba stone seven times until you reach the Ka'aba stone chanting TAL-BI-YAH. There are lots of people who go to Makkah. When you reach Makkah you have to bend down and kiss the Ka'aba stone and then work your way out.

The approach to religious education was explicit — the children became more familiar with aspects of a major world faith increasing their knowledge and understanding. By contrast children in another class working on the same topic 'pattern' looked carefully at natural things making detailed drawings and descriptions. The approach was implicit, increasing the children's perceptions of the world around then arousing their awe and wonder at it:

The Fossil

Smooth is the rock the fossil lies,
Ready to be found by anyone,
The sand and mud waits to engulf a dead creature,
It hardens and dries and melts into the ground,
The fossil awaits to be uncovered from the dark depths,
Of the ground,
The fossil is a reminder of the creatures that lived
millions of years ago,
Before our time!!

Fungi

It is like ...
A dull rainbow arching in colours of beige, brown,
black and green,
A rose petal, a frilly heart
without the dip,
It feels rough, like a dry towel
On the back it is ...
White at the tip running down to beige
Ending with a brown brim,
It looks soft and spongy like a mushroom
But it is a rock, small and dry
Turn it over and the tip of the front
has a velvety touch.

A mini-topic on 'eggs' undertaken by an upper junior class in the last few weeks of the spring term. As well as lending itself to egg decorating, strength tests and mathematical work, it also provided a way in to Easter story. Simple 'express' topic books were made and the work was presented in an assembly:

THE EASTER STORY

1 *The Last Supper*

As Jesus and his twelve disciples were eating the Passover meal, Jesus said, 'one of you is going to betray me,' and he took bread and said, 'eat this, it is my body,' and he took wine and said, 'drink this, it is my blood,' 'Who of us would betray you?' the disciples asked. 'Whoever I give the first piece of bread to is going to sacrifice me', and he handed the bread to Judas Iscariot, son of Simon. Jesus said, 'do what you must do and do it quickly.' Judas went out quickly.

2 *Farewell to the Disciples*

Jesus said, 'Farewell my friends, I will have to go where you cannot and one of you will deny me three times before the cock crows in the morning'.

Another upper junior class presented their work on the theme 'difference' in class books in which art work on investigating difference in texture through unit printing was incorporated alongside written work on 'The Diddakoi' which had been used as the initial stimulus for the theme.

Specific RE Topics

Whilst topic work offers considerable opportunity for developing children's religious understanding, in considering the school as a whole there must be some planning also to ensure that children have access to experience in certain key areas of religious education. Despite the skills-orientated curriculum of recent years, it must be acknowledged that religious education is a content-related subject and that children need to be given access to it. Some sort of school structure needs to be organized to ensure that children develop key concepts in religious understanding and that adequate provision is made for progression. There is a danger that adequate provision for religious education cannot be made solely within the class topic structure.

It can be achieved by planning a programme of termly *mini-topics* which children encounter in both lower and upper school but at different levels of complexity and growth. Based on Bruner's *spiral* curriculum this allows older children to explore in greater depth those themes touched on more simply in their earlier years. Through studying six topics, 'worship', 'signs and symbols', 'buildings', 'festivals', 'people', and 'writings', children study fundamental aspects of religious belief.

It is useful to have a list of resources to support each theme available in addition to the main school inventory. Some of the best 'resources' will of course be human rather than material. A year 4 pupil from a Jewish family wrote of the Passover festival:

The Story of Passover

As I have said before, Passover celebrates Pharaoh freeing the children of Israel, led by Moses. Here is the story in better detail.

Pharaoh didn't like all of the Jews that were living in Egypt. Over the years, more Jews had come to Egypt, hearing how nice it was there, so there were quite a number of Jews living there. Anyway, Pharaoh thought that he would make them his slaves. He captured them, and set them to work. Now God disapproved of Pharaoh, making the Jews work for him, so he sent ten plagues to destroy Egypt. These were the plagues:

1	BLOOD	6	BOILS
2	FROGS	7	HAIL
3	VERMIN	8	LOCUSTS
4	BEASTS	9	DARKNESS
5	CATTLE DISEASE	10	SLAYING OF THE FIRST BORN

After all ten, Pharaoh let them go back to Egypt. Moses led them. Pharaoh gave them five minutes to pack and go. They did not have enough time to put yeast in their bread, so the bread was flat. We call it Matzos, and we eat it at the Passover celebration to remind us. At Passover we have a Seder Plate, with an egg, shank bone, bitter herbs, parsley and haroseth. The shank bone is a lamb bone. When God passed over the houses to slay the first born, he did not do it to the Jews. He knew Jewish people lived in a house, because lamb blood was on the door. The bitter herbs were to remind us of bitter times. The haroseth reminds us of better times. The egg is life, and parsley, growth.

The most well-known Passover ceremony is 'The Last Supper'. It is the Passover ceremony when Judas betrayed Jesus to the Roman soldiers. It was the last Passover ceremony Jesus took part in.

So, that is the story of Passover. It has been celebrated for thousands of years. Over those years, Passover has changed. Now I will tell you about Passover as we celebrate it now.

Modern Passover

I have already told you the story of Passover in as best detail as I can. Now I will tell you how Passover is celebrated nowadays.

As far back as I can remember we have driven up to London. London is where my Jewish grandparents live. (Booba is the Jewish name for Granny and Zieder is the Jewish name for Grandad). We sometimes have Passover at my Auntie Jan's but as far as I can remember we have gone to my Booba and Zieder's. The Passover ceremony is quite long so you have to stay up late. I find it hard to stay up so late, so I take a little nap. Remember, we still have to drive to Hook. It's a good thing Passover occurs only once every year, a little while after Easter. Passover is celebrated in two parts. Part 1 and Part 2. At the end of Part 1, it's supper time. We normally have chicken (my favourite), roast potatoes, parsnip and greens. We also have red wine, which we keep refilling. We can drink our wine only at certain times. During the ceremony bits of Matzos are passed round. The Matzos is quite big so it is broken up into smaller bits. I like Matzos with butter and blackcurrant jam. In one part of Passover we dip our little finger in our wine. We then take our finger out and shake a little drop of wine on to a little cup-size tray, put underneath our cup. For the last two or three years, I have read out the four Passover questions. My sister didn't want to do it and the youngest person is supposed to read them out. I was the second youngest, so I read them out. Here are the four questions:

Why Is This Night Different From All Other Nights?
1 On all other nights we eat either leavened bread or unleavened; on this night why only unleavened bread?

2 On all other nights we eat herbs of any kind; on this night why only bitter herbs?

3 On all other nights we do not dip our herbs even once; on this night why do we dip them twice?

4 On all other nights we eat our meals in any manner; on this night why do we sit around the table together in a reclining position?

The rest of the service is spent answering how Passover came about. Briefly the Israelites were slaves in Egypt and Moses, Pharaoh's adopted son, led the Israelites out of Egypt as quickly as possible after the ten plagues and because of this the Israelites had no time to let their bread prove (or leaven) which meant that the bread when it had baked was still flat and this is commemorated in the eating of Matzos on Passover.

A simulation of the Passover meal in which the children can taste the Matzos and haroseth can also provide a helpful experience. The programme of mini-topics provides structure but allows also for flexibility and a variety of approaches.

Core Bible Stories

Planning a core programme of Bible stories for lower school and upper school (ten stories for each), is useful in ensuring that all children have experienced the central stories of the Bible. Such a list is skeletal of course — each story in itself may take several sessions. Resourcing is an important consideration here as the quality of books of Bible stories is very variable. Often it can be useful, especially with older children, to link a Bible story with another story from the children's experience. For example, the story of 'The Good Samaritan' has parallels with Rumer Godden's 'The Diddakoi' in which Kizzy was not helped by those whose assistance seemed most appropriate.

Festivals

Whether or not a set plan is agreed upon it is important that children encounter the major Christian festivals each year at a level meaningful to their stage of development. One lower junior class teacher used drama as a way of developing children's understanding of the Easter story. She used the beautiful illustrations of Jan Pienoslab's 'The Easter Story' with the text which is the authorized version as a way in to explore the symbolism of the cross and the Easter story. The children designed crosses and wrote poems each taking the part of a character in the story.

Mary Magdalene's Song

'If only he were, if only he were', I cry. 'But if he was, it would only happen again'. 'Who on earth do I mean?' Why Jesus of course! 'If only he were here now'! 'He came alive but is dead now I fear'. 'Do not cry dear lady'. 'For he is not dead, but all the pain of carrying that cross, and, oh! the thorns in that crown'. 'Who could that have been'. 'Oh gardener'. 'Oh, it is Jesus, my lord'.

John's Song

The day John looked after Mary while Jesus was crucified was pulled up the hill and being whipped all the way to the cross. He had holes in his hands. Three hours later he was dead.

Easter Song

Barrabus feels sorry. Yes he does. He is sorry now that Jesus is crucified. He will be sorry for the rest of his life. He hated to watch Jesus up the hill.

Sometimes a whole school approach to a festival is appropriate. For example, a whole school approach to Harvest was developed around the themes of Harvest from the fields, Harvest from the sea, Harvest from the hedgerows and Harvest from other countries. Each class chose one theme and developed it in their own way. Representative pieces of work from each class were assembled in a display at the rear of the local church together with harvest contributions for the children's service. Work included corn dollies, plaster casts of wheat and barley, pastel drawings of fruits, clay models of fish, baked bread and sketches. Most of the work was based on first-hand experience, careful observation and investigation, extending the children's skills and understanding and putting 'harvest' into a meaningful context.

Church Visits

Planning a regular programme of church visits can also extend the children's religious experience, particularly if the child has little or no experience of church going. Whether the whole school visit together or whether separate upper and lower school visits need to be arranged will depend on the size of school. After a visit by the upper school to the nearby church at which the lay reader had talked about the church and its environment one child wrote:

St Johns Church

St Johns Church is fifty years old. On the top of the porch it says Venite Exultemus Deo. That means O Come Let Us Sing Unto The Lord.

On the wall outside the porch there is a notice board. Public notices are put on it and official ones were put on by law. When you go inside there is a font that water is put in it and when babies are Christened they have water put on their forehead three times and they are signed with the sign of the cross. The dove represents when Jesus was baptized. The pews and the aisle make the nave. All the kneelers have crosses on them and were all made by hand.

In other churches they probably would be different. Other churches have wooden pews but in St Johns there are chairs forming pews. At the back of each chair there is a slot. In the slot you put the hymn and prayer books that you would have been given on the way in.

The aisle is the passage between the chairs and leads to the Chancel. The Chancel is in between the choir stalls. It goes up to the rail where you receive bread and wine. Behind the rail is the sanctuary. The Altar is in the sanctuary. A meal is prepared of bread and wine. You go up to the rail and receive a small bit of wafer and a sip of wine. The sacristy is a room off the side of the church.

The vestry is where the vicar and choir put on their cassock and surplice.

The choir comes out led by the crucifer who carries the processional cross.

On special services they parade down the aisle and Sharon and Lindsay are Acolytes and walk either side of the crucifer and carry torches to light the darkness. If the Rector visits an ill person he takes some bread and wine so that they can share.

There is a banner with a black angel and white angel with a candle in the middle of them and it represents Jesus as the light of the world. There is another banner with Mary the mother of Jesus holding him in the shape of a cross. If you go out of the side door near the Chancel then you see some black steps going up. They lead up to the organ. The organ has twenty-nine sound pipes.

The cord you can see if you carry on along the passage. If you pull it the bell rings.

On the tower there is St George's flag. It is a white flag and has a red cross on it. It is flown on special Saints days.

On the top of the tower there is a chiro. It is made from copper. It acts as a lightning conductor that saves lightning striking the tower.

A regular programme of church visits provides a basic structure whereby children can become familiar with the church building and its aspects and gain some understanding of the significance of, for example, ecclesiastical dress. They can understand that churches are rooted in history and tradition, that the colour of the clergy's robes, the carving on the font, the shape of the church itself are all things invested with meaning. It provides a basis which individual teachers will develop variously, perhaps by inviting a member of the clergy to talk to the children or by taking the children to visit another place of worship such as a synagogue.

A structured programme of termly mini-topics, a core programme of Bible stories, the teaching of major festivals each year and a regular programme of church visits ensures that children have access to experience in the key areas of religious experience. They will have opportunity to become familiar with the forms and rituals of Christianity and gain an appreciation of the significance of religious belief in the lives of people of other faiths.

Encountering Other World Views

Enabling children to encounter and understand other world views requires planned provision. It requires a commitment on the part of teachers to find ways of developing themes which encourage children to encounter material related to other cultures in an authentic way, to provide glimpses of other world views and faiths.

If such approaches are to be authentic and avoid tokenism the context in which learning takes place is of particular importance.

One year 6 pupil, on the arrival of a Buddhist prayer wheel in the classroom, looked at it curiously and then examined it carefully. He wondered what it was and what it was used for. The answers were not readily apparent. When informed that it was Buddhist he went to collect a book on Buddhist customs he had looked at some time previously and found a picture of a prayer wheel and some accompanying information. 'It helps to focus the mind', he said. His sketch and notes are below.

In school we have a Buddhist prayer hand wheel. It says:

'Om — mani — padme — hum', which means:
'Hail — to the jewel — in the lotus — welcome'

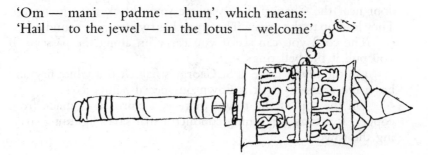

Of course not all pupils are so competent or motivated and didactic as well as inductive methods are sometimes appropriate. Nevertheless, if stereotyping and tokenism are to be avoided, finding ways of developing understanding which spring from the natural context of the classroom work is important.

Within the main class topic this will be to see what opportunities exist within the theme. A teacher whose class/topic was on 'bridges' explored the idea of bridges and barriers in human relationships. The following essay was one child's response.

John's Journey of Barriers

There was a new boy at school, his name was Pritpal, and he was a Sikh. He had to wear his long dark hair in a bun with a cloth on his head. Pritpal also wore a silver bangle around his wrist. This was all part of his religion. All the other boys teased him and wouldn't let him join in their games. They said he was a girl and couldn't play football. The girls who were able to play football were very annoyed at this and resented Pritpal even more, when he told them how the girls in his country were not allowed to play football or such sports at all!

One boy was nice to him, he was called John. He felt sorry for Pritpal and tried to play with him. But Pritpal was sullen and miserable, no fun at all. Eventually John managed to persuade his classmates to let Pritpal join in. So next playtime they invited Pritpal to play football. His face lit up in a sudden smile, his teeth looked surprisingly white against his yellowish-brown face. Although Pritpal was last to be chosen when they picked teams, he did not seem put off. He beat them all at football, he scored the most goals and didn't boast. All the boys admired him, they realized that just because he was a different colour it didn't mean Pritpal was dumb or abnormal. They got to like him and stuck up for him when stupid juvenile little idiots jeered and said Pritpal was brown because he never washed. John noticed that Pritpal never fought back, just ignored their cruel remarks. Except when his family or customs were insulted. There was always a 'scrap' then!

When John went to Pritpal's house for tea, it smelt of curry and spices. Pritpal's family spoke a different language. They were all very nice and knew that Pritpal probably thought that his food and language was weird.

John went on holiday the next week. He went to South Africa. He was very angry and surprised to find that there were two playgrounds, with fencing in between. In one were a lot of black children, and in the other were white. There was more playing equipment in the white playground but John wanted to

[handwritten in margin: children don't see barriers, they are made by adults!]

59

get to know the black kids, for a school project. He ran into the black playground and spoke to them. Most of them spoke another language, but some understood.

A man roughly hustled John out, he pushed him towards the other playground. His parents explained that black and white people were separated here. From his experience with Pritpal he knew this was wrong. They are a different colour but all human! John whispered to the children he had a plan. They all rushed into the other playground ignoring the man. He could not control them all. A lot of parents wrote to the British government and was so disturbed that they spoke to the African government. They agreed to take down the fence and integrate the people. But a lot is still separate.

Similary a teacher engaged on a topic on 'time' encouraged the children to draw personal time lines. The children then identified which events occurred only once, (for example, starting school) and which events were repeated (for example, birthdays). She then explored with them the notion of linear and cyclical time and how it relates to Buddhism.

Within the mini-topic structure to examine other faiths would be a natural progression from looking at the Christian faith. So for example a starting point for a topic on 'signs and symbols' could be to look at signs and symbols in everyday life. With older pupils it may be relevant not only to discuss the difference between 'sign' and 'symbol' but also how 'image' also differs. From more explicit work on Christian symbols, their origins and significance, children could then look at signs and symbols in other faiths.

The Role of Story

In developing children's religious understanding teachers help to foster the growth of the child's inner world, his/her inner reality. Developing children spiritually is about developing the quality of growth of the child's inner experience. An approach through *literature* is a particularly appropriate one. Stories of different kinds embody moral or universal truths. Through story children can explore their feelings and emotions in a way which is safe and secure. For example, the story 'The Owl Who Was Afraid of the Dark' allows children to acknowledge their own feelings of fear in a safe way. Similarly 'Henrietta Goose' the story of a goose who strays through the hole in the fence allows children to identify securely with the experience of getting lost.

Story can also be a means of helping children to gain greater under-standing and insight into the world in which they live. Hence 'Dinosaurs and All That Rubbish' allows them to reflect on important issues about this world.

Story also fosters the child's imagination and sense of wonder. For example the poetic quality of Ted Hughes 'The Iron Man' with its powerful description has a magic for young children.

Sometimes just reading the story, and allowing the children to take what they will is sufficient. However one or two carefully selected questions may enable the children to look beneath the surface and explore the layers of meaning. Other ways of drawing out meaning are through using role play, dramatization or the overhead projector or the flannelgraph.

Even if suitable books are in the library of the classroom it is still useful to have separate copies in the RE resource area. A small sheet of notes can be attached to the front page describing the story, theme and which topics it would be appropriate for.

One teacher having read '*I am David*' suggested to the class they might write a sequel. Here is one of them:

I Am David (A Sequel)

David awoke. He was in a small white washed room. There were blue curtains and a green bedcover. The room was bare except for a table and a chair. The room was bright and cheerful and reminded David of Maria.

Downstairs David heard voices. He turned over and looked at his clock. It was nearly 9 a.m. David quickly dressed and grabbed his shoes. He stumbled down the stairs and entered the living room. His mother had his breakfast ready and was singing in time to the radio. As David walked into the room his mother kissed him on the cheek and said 'Good morning, how are you?' David replied that he was very well. The two people still felt uneasy with each other and David's experience.

David ate his breakfast and packed his bag. Today David was going to start school. David's mother asked if she could walk David to his new school but David said it didn't matter and that he could ask someone directions. His mother kissed him on the cheek again as he opened the front door.

David started walking in the direction he knew the school was and only turned to wave. This was a dream come true for him, going to school, going somewhere where he could learn things. He just didn't understand why Maria and Andrea had groaned when David had mentioned school, and because of that David knew he would never be a normal boy. As David's thoughts dissolved he noticed that he was passing 33b Strandvejen Street.

David turned. He saw, out of the corner of his eye, one of

them patrolling the streets! The man was accompanied by a large dog and it was definitely one of *their* dogs. The beast had a large shaggy coat, big ears, terrifying fangs, and worst of all he had black staring eyes. Thoughts flashed through David's mind. What if the man saw him and looked into his eyes? He would surely guess he had come from one of their camps. David disappeared into the crowd as the man walked past. David remembered what he had been told 'Denmark is a free country'. Wasn't it true then? If *they* were there, Denmark *couldn't* be a free country.

David walked in a trance. His thoughts were jogging in his mind. 'Why don't you look where you're going?' a voice called loudly as a small boy ran by, knocking David and making all his books spill out of his bag. 'Oh, I'm so sorry', said the boy, 'but you'll have to come with me', he added and took David's hand. David, puzzled by the boy's actions, stared at him spellbound. As David stared at the boy, he noticed he had sharp features, light blue eyes and red hair.

Suddenly and swiftly the boys turned a corner. The red-headed lad roughly pulled away a dustbin which was resting on a wall. There in the wall was a large hole. A trap, it must be a trap. The boy was probably one of *them* and there was probably one of their camps on the other side of the wall. David squirmed, trying to find a way out his predicament. The boy climbed through the hole. David followed through, clenching his teeth. David started to pray 'God of the green pasture, if this is a trap please let me die now because I would die in one of their camps anyway. I am David'.

David suddenly found himself in a large room and it wasn't a camp. The boy turned to face him. 'My name's Arnold. Call me Arnie. I'm sorry I had to bring you here but I'll explain later'. The children went into a sloping corridor which led down into the ground.

The boys walked down the corridor into another room filled with machinery. Children were rushing around pushing buttons. What was this place? David politely asked Arnold where he was. Arnold replied, 'The CSA, the Children's Spy Association'. 'You see' Arnold explained, 'We spy on *them* and send the information to headquarters. Anyway who would think of a child being a spy?' David considered and agreed with Arnold. 'But', David said, 'Why did you bring me here?'

Arnold walked over to a girl who was writing something on paper and she scurried off. 'Come and sit down', said Arnold. 'Tell me your name first'. David, surprised at the outburst, said 'David'. 'Well, David' said Arnold, 'I was running away from the enemy and because I knocked you over, they might have thought that you were one of us and I had given you a secret David was terrified at this suggestion. How could he g 'But on the other hand,' Arnold continued hopefully, '*th* see you.' David let out a sigh of relief. 'Anyway', Arn 'you'd better go now. You'll probably be missed.'

The boys sprang up and walked out of the room back up the corridor into the smaller room. David pushed away the dustbin and clambered through the hole. 'Goodbye David,' said Arnold. 'Goodbye', replied David. 'I'll keep in touch'.

In Conclusion

In planning religious education across a junior school, provision needs to be made whereby children can become aware of the *key concepts* related to religious understanding. They need to become familiar with aspects of religion within contexts that are meaningful and appropriate. They need also to understand that stories, rituals and symbols are associated with deeper meaning. Religious education must be an integral, not a separate part of the curriculum.

Similarly the place of worship in the school community is central, a focus of the values and philosophy of that community and a forum for the celebration of what is considered to be of worth. It is important for children to be able to share their work and communicate what they have done to a variety of audiences. The School Assembly is a time when the talents and achievements of children can be celebrated and themes which are drawn from the curriculum or the community are as relevant as those drawn from explicit religious tradition.

The pattern of assembly can be organized in such a way that it incorporates both routine structures and allows for a variety of approaches in both the content and delivery of the theme. Some assemblies will be class assemblies, others taken by the headteacher or a member of staff or a visiting speaker. The assembly may relate to a theme. For example an assembly taken by the local rector on 'The rectory as a working home' linked with one class topic on 'homes'.

Finally, in planning religious education across a junior school the key question for teachers must be what is it that the religiously educated 11-year-old should know and understand? Religious education is about the nature and practice of belief and its significance in our world both past and present. Ultimately the framework, the structures that are created to ensure that adequate provision is made for religious education in the curriculum are dependant for their success on those who deliver the curriculum. This exists as the relationship between the planned curriculum and the received curriculum, not merely for religious education but for the whole curriculum. Our concern in developing religiously educated children is not with the transference of knowledge or a nurture faith but with developing, thinking, questioning open-minded young people and with enabling each child to fulfil spiritually its present stage of growth. Our concern is with *quality* of growth.

6   Making RE Special in the Primary School

Erica Musty

In every class, no matter how the allocation of pupils has been made, streamed, unstreamed or vertical grouping, there will always be those children whose progress is slower than most. These children, who are the exception to that which would normally be expected from any particular group of pupils, present difficulties to their teachers concerning the type and level of curriculum they should be following. The ages from 5 to 11 in the primary phase are particularly important if children are to remain confident learners and to develop a positive self-image of themselves in school. Many children with physical, sensory, emotional or cognitive disorders are being educated with skill and devotion by teachers in mainstream schools. Some schools have already developed methods of helping such children to achieve their potential. Others are seeking help and guidance. At the heart of the pages that follow lies the philosophy that *all* children have individual needs in learning and that schools *can* manage classrooms to meet those needs. The chapter is also written in the belief that the needs of pupils cannot be seen in isolation from those of their teachers. The fact that we all have learning difficulties when we are acquiring new facts or skills is a deliberate reminder that learning is a continuous and continuing process.

The challenges which I face as Coordinator for RE and Special Educational Needs are in no way unique. Others have shared my concerns and have developed their own responses. Sometimes they have been similar and sometimes different and more effective. My task is to attempt to describe the more important concerns which are facing teachers and to offer some solutions that have been instituted.

The Way Forward for Pupils with Special Educational Needs

It is more than a decade since the committee chaired by Mary Warnock published its report, *The Education of Handicapped Children and Young*

People (1978). If teachers in primary schools were asked what they knew about the Warnock Report and the 1981 Education Act which implemented most of its recommendations, almost all would know that they dealt with special education. If questioned about the recommendations of the reports they would probably be less confident, although many would know that it has been estimated that one child in five will require some form of special educational provision during his/her time at school.

The 1981 Education Act recognized a wide range of special educational needs and it stressed that the definition of special needs is not linked to specific causes and therefore it is relative to the needs of *all* children. The Act outlined three major issues concerning special educational needs: firstly, it endorsed the right of all children to education, advocating the pre-eminence of common needs. Secondly, the Act recognized the need for each child to be individually assessed so that where special education was thought to be necessary, it could be planned to meet identified needs. Thirdly, the Act suggested that mainstream schools should be the setting for special education wherever possible.

Integration and Pupils with Special Educational Needs

There has been no shortage of debate about integration. Integration is an international conviction that, as far as humanly possible, those with special educational needs should share the opportunities offered those in mainstream education. But integration means a thousand things. It means being treated like everybody else. It means the right to learn alongside other pupils and to develop into an individual who can make a worthwhile contribution to the community. The principle of integration has made great strides on recent years but it would be foolish to deny that integrating pupils with special needs into the mainsteam classroom does not make great demands on the teacher — it also requires educational reform. And the success of integration depends of the quality of the education on offer.

The Curriculum Requirements of Pupils with Special Educational Needs

The 1981 Education Act had an implicit vision of a better world for those children who are designated as having special educational needs. But during the years which have elapsed since the Act there have been conflicting views about whether these pupils have different curricular needs from other pupils. Because of their learning difficulties children often spend a disproportionate amount of time in acquiring basic knowledge and skills, with the result that their cultural and spiritual development may be neglected. I firmly believe that pupil's learning should include aspects of the curriculum which they enjoy and in which they are able to progress and participate, developing their own learning styles. Achievement in any field can give children self-confidence and assist in their development of self-esteem. More than anything else pupils with special educational needs need to know that they are accepted and given the kind of encouragement which is an expression of other people's faith in them.

Religious Education and Pupils with Special Educational Needs

It is unusual for religious education to be confined to one particular period on the primary school timetable. Indeed it is usually integrated into the whole curriculum allowing teachers to use situations which arise spontaneously as examples of experiences, values and attitudes which they wish to nurture in their children. Thus the lessons which pupils learn at school extend far beyond those things which are taught in the formal curriculum. But if schools are really to open their doors to pupils with special educational needs, there is a need for them to review aspects of their curriculum and teaching methods. It will mean establishing a broad curriculum framework which can encompass the diverse needs of pupils with exceptional talents and those who learn most things with difficulties. Instead of children being seen to 'fail' (for example because they are below average reading age) they will be able to reach realistic and achievable learning goals from a rich and diverse bank of educational experiences. In religious education we aim to give children the paintbox and not the painting — in other words the effective curriculum seeks to give pupils a variety of experiences through which they can develop the skills, attitudes and concepts necessary to create their own beliefs and values.

There are a number of elements on primary education generally which are especially relevant to religious education and pupils with special needs:

— children spontaneously explore their world;
— as part of their spiritual development many children experience a sense of awe and wonder of the physical world;
— children see the world as a whole and not in separate disciplines of knowledge;
— children respond more readily to an environment which is well organized, stimulating and challenging;
— children's awareness of standards and integrity is greatly influenced by the example of adults;
— children are likely to sustain a sense of their own worth and to

appreciate the worth of others when they themselves are valued and encouraged.

It is no accident that the HMI document *The Curriculum from 5–16* takes its statement of the goals of education from the Warnock Report:

> to enlarge a child's knowledge, experience and imaginative understanding and thus his awareness of moral values and capacity for enjoyment; and secondly to enable him to enter the world after formal education is over as an active participant of society and a responsible contributor to it.

It also repeats the observation of the Warnock Report that 'for some children the road they have to travel towards the goals is smooth and easy, for others it is frought with obstacles'. Furthermore the five characteristics of a comprehensive curriculum which the report outlines are essential to religious education curriculum: these characteristics are:

— breadth
— balance
— relevance
— differentiation
— progression and continuity

The curriculum should be **broad** in the sense of bringing all pupils into contact with a range of learning and experience. It should be **balanced**, allowing for adequate development without undue regard for, or the neglect of, any area. It should be **relevant** to pupils' present and future needs. It must be **differentiated** to allow for different pupil ability. Finally, and perhaps most importantly, it must take into account that learning is a continuous process and provide for **systematic progress** from one learning stage to the next. Much modern teaching of religious education is based on the **experiential** approach. It starts with the life and the experience of the children and seeks to help them to explore and to understand this. All teachers should be aware of times, whether in a small group or a large assembly, when something happens which evokes in pupils a sense of awe. Although times like this may be rare they can be fostered and used to develop a capacity for wonder and a real sense of 'otherness' or belonging in creation. Research suggests (Robinson, 1977) that spiritual experiences are not uncommon in childhood and for pupils with learning difficulties, it is important to acknowledge this dimension of religious education.

The children's own development, their ability to discover their own identity and then to 'put themselves into another person's shoes' will be influenced by the relationship with other children which the teacher encourages. Beyond their own families, their teacher may well be the most important person in their lives. This relationship starts with the child's first encounter with him/her and it is one where there is no room for falseness or insincerity but a knowledge that the partnership is based on trust and confidence. He/she will require an intimate knowledge and understanding of the children in his/her care — their strengths and their weaknesses in cognitive abilities; their different levels of emotional, social and physical maturity; the particular effect on them of special educational needs; and the influence of their homes and families. An understanding of the stages and progresses of their religious development is also required although this may be at variance with chronological age.

Providing a range of stimuli and means of expression can help to make an intermediary channel of communication where children may be enabled to grasp truths about religion and to 'internalize' their thoughts. But children respond to people first and foremost. Visual aids can provide a valuable resource but they will not replace the teacher. Neither will they compensate for an inadequately planned curriculum. Preparation is of vital importance. There are no short cuts. The whole pattern of a school's organization, curriculum and educational philosophy, should contribute to children reaching their full potential. Moreover, if the corporate life of the school offers opportunity for responsibility and service, pupils will grow in an awareness of the contribution they can make not only to the school community but in their families and society.

Most local communities provide examples of religious communities. In the context of children with learning difficulties it will be appropriate to study what different faith groups do and the buildings where they do it, in an attempt to develop sympathetic attitudes towards religious beliefs and practices. Meeting people from other faiths and joining in celebrations will also nurture an understanding of the value of myth, ritual, symbol, commitment, responsibility and rules.

Assemblies and Worship

If religious education aims to help all children to deepen their understanding of religion, then the content of assemblies must also be appropriate to their intellectual ability. This includes those which are in a language which the pupils understand, based on themes which arouse their interest and using maximum participation of the children. Assemblies in primary schools are often used to emphasize values such as justice, tolerance and respect for others, They can also help to encourage pupils to reflect on moments of celebration or sadness but they should aim to broaden the horizons of the school by bringing in members of the religious communities.

Assemblies may provide moments away from the bustle of modern life where there is the opportunity to wonder at, to delight in and to celebrate that which is best in the pupils' experiences. But surely the purpose is deeper than this? There should be time to explore the harsher realities of life with its paradoxes and its tensions. Children are increasingly entering into a world where there are choices to be made, where moral decisions cannot be evaded and personal identity needs to be established. We do pupils an injustice if we do not allow them to be at least 'grazed' by some of the perennial human questions and dilemmas.

For less able children the most meaningful feature of worship will probably be the 'atmosphere'. No amount of verbal content can compensate for a lack of this, and no amount of participation in daily ritual will educate sensitively to an understanding of why people worship if the 'feel' is lacking. Therefore 'feeling' experience is essential to a mature concept of worship. The creation of atmosphere may be helped by phenomena such as music, by projecting a slide, using light, flowers or perhaps giving children objects from the natural world or religious artefacts to touch and hold.

Festivals and Celebrations

The whole ethos of a school is reflected in the way in which it celebrates. Festivals and celebrations are an integral part of the culture and religion of civilizations all over the world. There are times when communities express thanksgiving, joy and devotion; they link the past with the present and demonstrate hope for the future. Even children of very limited ability remember festivals long after the everyday events of life have been forgotten because celebration brings a sense of occasion and a break from everyday routine, heightening emotional responses to life. Furthermore life is enriched by celebration and children begin to recognize the pattern of festivals throughout the school year, anticipating them as times of togetherness and sharing.

But to understand the elements which are found in religious festivals it is essential that children experience the anticipation and preparation which precede celebrations and that *they* are encouraged to make the decorations, to sing the songs, to hear the stories and to cook and eat the foods.

The Northamptonshire Agreed Syllabus states 'Christmas activities tend to dominate the life of the school during the second part of the autumn term. This has brought about a number of dangers — the over-familiarity of the children with the story — a sense of duty rather than celebration among teachers; the danger that the simplicity of the announcement of the birth of a child might be lost beneath the cardboard, glue and tinsel!

I suggest that teachers who plan a developmental approach to teaching festivals in their schools will prevent themselves falling into this trap. The wide range of age and ability found in our classrooms prevents the planning of such an approach according to children's chronological age. For this reason I have outlined four suggested stages of religious development which are to be found in the later discussion of curriculum planning. The developmental charts are designed to give scope for development in a variety of ways, taking the individual needs of children into account:

Stage 1 begins with the child's personal experience;

Stage 2 extends the pupil's experience and understanding;

Stages 3 and 4 gives opportunity for exploring the celebration in a wider context so that children begin to question the meaning and purpose behind the festival.

For non-specialist teachers it will almost certainly be necessary to read widely before attempting to use this teaching approach. For this reason suggested resources are included which support the developmental approach charts.

Some General Aims for Festivals

Through experience of celebrating festivals it is hoped that pupils will:

(i)   develop an awareness of the events within a community which are significant to its people;
(ii) develop an awareness of the diversity of peoples' responses to life;
(iii) develop an understanding of how religious beliefs and insights are expressed in symbolism;
(iv) reflect upon their own experience of celebration at home, at school and in the wider community;
(v)   acquire the ability to share with others, nurturing attitudes of tolerance and respect.

Guru Nanak's Birthday — *Some Suggested Resources*

AGGARWAL, M. (1984) *I am a Sikh*, London, Franklin Watts.
BROWN, A. *et al.* (1988) *Religions*, London, Longman.
CHILDREN'S BOOK TRUST *Guru Nanak*, New Delhi.
DAVIDSON, M. (1982) *Guru Nanak's Birthday*, Exeter, RMEP.
DHANJAL, B. (1987) *Sikhism*, London, Batsford.

Guru Nanak's Birthday

STAGE 1	STAGE 2	STAGE 3	STAGE 4
	Possible aspects of Guru Nanak's birthday to be explored		
Getting ready for a party Anticipating 'special days' Giving presents — Why?	Life in a Sikh home — dress — food — prayer Symbols of celebration in Sikhism — new clothes — decorations	Signs and symbols of Sikhism — kesh — uncut hair — kangha — comb — kara — bangle — kaccha — shorts — kirpan — sword Birth celebrations in Sikhism	Religious rituals and customs in Sikhism The foundation of the Khalsa Teachers/leaders in Religions — Guru Nanak — Jesus — Muhammad
	Ways of celebrating Guru Nanak's birthday		
Pictures of Guru Nanak Dressing dolls in shalwar and kameeze Play in home corner using Sikh artefacts/objects	Making birthday cards Stories of Nanak's childhood Making ghee lamps Dressing up in Sikh clothes	Making traditional Sikh foods Stories of the Gurus Listening/moving to Indian music Celebrating Guru Nanak's birthday in school	Visiting a Gurdwara Making and sharing Kara Prasad Exploring Sikhism through art and music
	Possible topics to be explored		
Birthdays Friends Special foods Growth	Birth/new life Parents Gifts and giving Teachers	India/Amritsar Life Light and darkness Special books	Places of pilgrimage Rules and behaviour Thanksgiving Feasting and fasting Courage Spiritual leadership

Christmas

	STAGE 1	STAGE 2	STAGE 3	STAGE 4
Possible aspects of Christmas to be explored	The Christmas story in pictures — using Christmas cards Legends of Christmas — Father Christmas etc. Christmas trees	The Christmas story — told Christmas customs Christmas legends and tales Christmas at home	Signs and symbols of Christmas The Christmas story — read Christmas in the community past and present Charities at Christmas Ancient winter solstice celebrations	The Christmas story told in art, poetry, music, stamps Christmas and the media Christmas customs abroad The history of Christmas foods Old Testament prophecies of Jesus' birth
Ways of celebrating Christmas	Parties and preparations Decorations Party foods and seasonal food Presents Party hats	Seasonal foods Decorations Christmas cards and gifts Christmas songs and carols Pantomime and drama	Christmas messages Other festivals e.g. St Nicholas, St Lucia, St Stephen Decorations Christmas entertainment	Cooking Christmas foods The Christian celebration of Christmas, e.g. Advent, Christingles, blessing of the crib, advent wreaths, midnight services, carols The Christmas story in mime and drama
Possible topics to be explored	Homes and families Babies Birthdays Names Postmen	Growth Colour at Christmas The Twelve Days of Christmas Birth announcements etc.	Gifts and giving Sheep and shepherds Light and darkness Naming ceremonies Journeys; stars Nature at Christmas — holly mistletoe, fir cones etc.	Loneliness, rejection, i.e. 'No room at the Inn' Commercialization of Christmas Christmas in the media. Joy; happiness

Pesach
(Passover)

	STAGE 1	STAGE 2	STAGE 3	STAGE 4
Possible aspects of Pesach to be explored	'Special days' at home Getting ready for a party Wearing special clothes	Preparation for Pesach Israel in pictures Jewish artefacts, e.g. yad, scroll, mezuzah, prayer shawl	Egypt Signs and symbols of Pesach Story of Exodus as told at Pesach	Ritual of Pesach Jewish worship Moses/Elijah Israel/Jerusalem Biblical references to Pesach Dietary laws
Ways of celebrating Pesach	Using the senses to explore Pesach: taste — matzos sight — candles sound — music, song dressing up — capel tefillin	Traditional Pesach foods Re-enactment of Pesach rituals, e.g. light candles, blessings Story of Moses in the bullrushes Pesach songs/music	Laying the Pesach table The Haggadah (order of service) Pesach songs	Preparing and eating a Pesach meal Visiting a synagogue
Possible themes topics	Spring Presents Home/families Special food Losing and finding Saying 'thank you'	Emotions Bread Remembering/memories Journeys Spring cleaning Sheep and shepherds Special stories	Religious headwear Behaviour/rules Promises Torah Temple in Jerusalem Sacred books	Laws Prayer Peace Freedom Famine/plague Punishment Thanksgiving

HENLEY, A. (1979) *Asians in Britain — Sikhs*, Tunbridge Wells, King Edward's Hospital Fund.

MINORITY GROUP SUPPORT SERVICE *Guru Nanak's Birthday*, Coventry.

A. BROWN FOR THE SHAP WORKING PARTY (1986) *Festivals in World Religions*, London, Longman.

SHAP WORKING PARTY (1977) *World Religions in Education*, London, Commission for Racial Equality.

WOOD, J. (1988) *Our Culture: Sikh*, London, Franklin Watts.

Passover — *Some Suggested Resources*

BARNETT, V. (1983) *A Jewish Family in Britain*, Exeter, RMEP.

BRITISH JOURNAL OF RE (1981) 'Teaching Judaism', **3**, 4, summer.

BROWN, A. *et al.* (1988) *Religions*, London, Longman.

CHARING, D. (1984) *Visiting a Synagogue*, London, Lutterworth.

DOMNITZ, M. (1971) *Thinking about Judaism*, London, Lutterworth.

HANNIGAN, L. (1985) *Sam's Passover*, London, A & C Black.

KNAPP, C. (1979) *Shiman, Leah, and Benjamin*, London, A & C Black.

LAWTON, C. (1984) *I am a Jew*, London, Franklin Watts.

LAWTON, C. (1984) *Matza and Bitter Herbs*, London, Hamish Hamilton.

LAWTON, C. (1987) *The Seder Handbook*, London, Board of Deputies of British Jews.

THE LIVING FESTIVALS VIDEO SERIES Section on Passover, Program 1, CEM.

PAULAC, L. *Jewish Tales*, Jewish Education Bureau.

SCHOLEFIELD, L. (1982) *Passover*, Exeter, RMEP.

SHAP WORKING PARTY (1977) *Calendar of Religious Festivals*, London, Commission for Racial Equality.

SHERIDAN, S. (1986) *Stories from the Jewish World*, London, Macdonald.

TURNER, R. (1985) *Jewish Festivals*, Hove, Wayland.

WOOD, A. (1984) *Judaism*, London, Batsford.

Baisakhi — *Some Suggested Resources*

AGGARWAL, M. (1984) *I am a Sikh*, London, Franklin Watts.

BROWN, A. *et al.* (1988) *Religions*, London, Longman.

DHANJAL, B. (1987) *Sikhism*, London, Batsford.

HENLEY, A. (1979) *Asians in Britain — Sikhs*, Tunbridge Wells, King Edward's Hospital Fund.

RE TODAY (1986) 'Developing a topic on Baisakhi', spring.

A. BROWN FOR THE SHAP WORKING PARTY (1986) *Festivals in World Religions*, London, Longman.

SHAP WORKING PARTY (1977) *World Religions in Education*, London, Commission for Racial Equality.

WOOD, J. (1988) *Our Culture: Sikh*, London, Franklin Watts.

Baisakhi

STAGE 1	STAGE 2	STAGE 3	STAGE 4
	Possible aspects of Baisakhi to be explored		
Getting ready for a celebration Anticipating 'special days'	Life in a Sikh home — dress — food — ritual Symbols of celebration in Sikhism — new clothes — decorations	Signs and symbols of Sikhism — kesh — uncut hair — kangha — comb — kara — bangle — kaccha — shorts — kirpan — sword 'Brotherhood and unity in Sikhism'	The Khalsa — the symbols as given by Guru Gobind Singh The first Baisakhi Teachers and leaders in Sikhism Sikh initiation rites
	Ways of celebrating Baisakhi		
Pictures of the Gurus Dressing dolls in the symbols of Sikhism — kangha — kara — kaccha Play in the home corner using Sikh artefacts/objects	Stories of the Gurus Dressing up in Sikh clothes/5 K's The Story of Baisakhi Movement to Indian music	Making and sharing traditional Baisakhi food Stories of the Gurus Dramatization of Baisakhi story	Visiting a Gurdwara Sharing meals in world religions Sharing a meal in the Langar
	Possible topics to be explored		
Friends New clothes Families	Teachers Friendship Beginnings Flags	India Harvest Special books Rules/behaviour Birth/new life	Names Leadership — religions Government — religions 'New Year' in religions Loyalty 'Baptism' in religions Unity

Eid-Milad-Ul-Nabi — *Some Suggested Resources*

ABDUL LATIF AL HOAD (1985) *Islam*, Hove, Wayland.
AGGARWAL, A. (1984) *I am a Muslim*, London, Franklin Watts.
AHSON, M.M. (1985) *Muslim Festivals*, Hove, Wayland.
BROWN, A. *et al.* (1988) *Religions*, London, Longman.
COLE, W.O. (1981) *Five Religions in the Twentieth Century*, Amersham, Hulton.
KHATTAB, H. (1987) *The Muslim World*, London, Macdonald.
REGIONAL RE CENTRE *Islam: Primary Project*, Birmingham, Westhill College.
SARWAR, G. (1980) *Islam: Beliefs and Teachings*, London, Muslim Education Trust.
A. BROWN FOR THE SHAP WORKING PARTY (1986) *Festivals in World Religions*, London, Longman.
SHAP WORKING PARTY (1977) *Calendar of Religious Festivals*, London, Commission for Racial Equality.
TAMES, R. (1985) *Islam*, London, Batsford.
TARANTINO, M. *Stories for the Life of Muhammad*, Islamic Foundation.

Shabbat — *Some Suggested Resources*

BROWN, A. (1988) *Religions*, London, Longman.
CHARING, D. (1983) *The Jewish World*, London, Macdonald.
CHARING, D. (1984) *Visiting a Synagogue*, London, Lutterworth.
COLE, W.O. (1981) *Five Religions in the Twentieth Century*, Amersham Hulton.
DAVIS, M. (1978) *I am a Jew*, London, Mowbray.
ILEA TEACHERS' CENTRE *The Shabbat Experience* (teachers' pack).
LAWTON, C. (1984) *I am a Jew*, London, Franklin Watts.
LAWTON, C. (1984) *Matza and Bitter Herbs*, London, Hamish Hamilton.
PAULAC, L. *Jewish Tales* Jewish Education Bureau.
SHAP WORKING PARTY (1977) *Calendar of Religious Festivals*, London, Commission for Racial Equality.
SHAP WORKING PARTY (1986) *Festivals in World Religions*, London, Longman.
SHERIDAN, S. (1987) *Stories from the Jewish World*, London, Macdonald.
TURNER, R. (1985) *Jewish Festivals*, Hove, Wayland.
WOOD, A. (1984) *Judaism*, London, Batsford.

Holi — *Some Suggested Resources*

AGGARWAL, A. (1984) *I am a Hindu*, London, Franklin Watts.
BAHREE, P. (1982) *The Hindu World*, London, Macdonald.
BAHREE, P. (1984) *Hinduism*, London, Batsford.

Eid-Milad-Un-Nabi
(Muhammad's Birthday)

STAGE 1	STAGE 2	STAGE 3	STAGE 4
	Possible aspects of Eid-Milad-Un-Nabi to be explored		
Preparing for birthdays Anticipating special days Looking after precious things Preparation for Eid-Milad-Un-Nabi at home	Muslim symbols — crescent and stars — prayer carpet — Qur'an Life in a Muslim home: — dress — food — prayer — ablutions Muslim stories and rhymes	5 Pillars of Islam: prayer, affirmation, fasting, almsgiving, pilgrimage Muslim worship Arabia — climate/geography Journey of Muhammad Dietary laws in Islam	Prophets in religion, for example, Muhammad, Jesus, Abraham Life and teaching of Muhammad Pilgrimage in religion Birth ceremonies in religion
	Celebrating Eid-Milad-Un-Nabi		
Dressing dolls in shalwar and kameez Using the senses to explore Eid-Milad-Un-Nabi: sight — colour and shape in Islam sound — call to prayer touch — prayer carpet smell — perfumes/spices	Dressing up in shalwar, kameez, sari Making birthday cards Tesselating shapes and patterns Using curves and loops in drawing	Making a model of a mosque Stories of Muhammad's early life Celebrating Eid-Milad-Un-Nabi at school Islamic writing and design	Visiting a mosque Design/calligraphy/Arabic writing/alphabet Greetings in Islamic culture
	Possible topics to be explored		
Birthdays Parties Parents/carers Babies Journeys	Family Teachers Water Special Books Gardens	Thanksgiving Qur'an Deserts Making decisions Poverty Birth	Pilgrimage Astronomy Orphans Charities Communities Spiritual leadership

Shabbat
(Sabbath)

	STAGE 1	STAGE 2	STAGE 3	STAGE 4
Possible aspects of Shabbat to be explored	'Special days' at home Getting ready for special days	Getting ready for Shabbat in a Jewish home Israel in pictures Story of Israelites in the wilderness	Celebration of Shabbat in Jewish communities Signs and symbols of Shabbat, for example, candles spice box challah Torah	Jewish worship Celebration of Shabbat in Israel Signs and symbols of Judaism Biblical references to Shabbat Dietary laws
Ways of celebrating Shabbat	Using the senses to explore Shabbat sight — candles touch — spice box taste — challah sound — music/song smell — spice box/hot challah	Traditional Shabbat foods Fruits and vegetables of Israel Shabbat music/song Creation stories	Laying a Shabbat table Poems and songs welcoming Shabbat Making cholent	Barmitzvah Shabbat Celebrating a Shabbat meal 'Hora' — Shabbat folk dances Visiting a synagogue
Possible Themes/Topics	Homes/families Clothes Candles/light Cleaning	Bread Wine Light/darkness Weddings/brides Special places Remembering	Synagogue Family Life Light and darkness in world religions New beginnings Promises Journeys	Sacred books and sacred writings Thanksgiving Peace Laws Prayer Behaviour/rules Communities

Holi

STAGE 1	STAGE 2	STAGE 3	STAGE 4
Preparations for the festival at home Pictures of Holi celebrations Traditional stories of India in picture books	Signs and symbols of Hinduism: Om/Aum Temple Clothes Bell India in pictures Myths and legends of Holi in picture books	Stories of Holi, for example, Krishna and Putana Prahlada Signs and symbols of Holi colour/fire/coconuts The Indian celebration of Holi	Legends of Hindu warriors Spring festivals in world religions Hindu worship and belief Holi as depicted in Indian music and art
Dressing dolls — saris and dhotis Movement to Indian music Celebrating Holi at home	Bonfire/Holi party Holi masks Mixing colours Making paper flowers and garlands Tie-dye and batik	Cooking Indian foods, for example, rice dishes Making swings and decorating with flowers Dramatization of stories of Krishna	Celebrating Holi in the community Hindu feasts and fasts Making traditional Holi dishes
Light Fireworks/bonfires Colours Flowers	Water Fire Fairs and circus Special foods Harvest	Jokes The seasons Beginnings India	Spices Fasting Festivals of light Fire in world religions

BENNETT, O. (1987) *Holi*, London, Hamish Hamilton.

BROWN, A. *et al.* (1988) *Religions*, London, Longman.

COLE, W.O. (1981) *Five Religions in the Twentieth Century*, London, Hulton.

COLE, W.O. (1983) *Religions in the Multifaith School*, Amersham, Hulton.

COVENTRY MINORITY SUPPORT GROUP *The Festival of Holi* (pupils' materials).

COVENTRY MINORITY SUPPORT GROUP *Holi* (teaching pack).

COVENTRY MINORITY SUPPORT GROUP *How a Hindu Prays.*

COVENTRY MINORITY SUPPORT GROUP *A Story for Holi.*

HEMANT KANITKAR, V.P. (1985) *Hinduism*, Hove, Wayland.

KILLINGLEY, D. (1984) *A Handbook of Hinduism for Teachers*, Newcastle, Grevatt and Grevatt.

OLDFIELD, K. (1987) *Hindu Gods and Goddesses*, London, CEM.

SHAP WORKING PARTY (1977) *Calendar of Religious Festivals*, London, Commission for Racial Equality.

SHAP WORKING PARTY (1986) *Festivals in World Religions*, London, Longman.

SHAP WORKING PARTY (1987) *Shap Handbook on World Religions in Education*, London, Commission for Racial Equality.

Easter — *Some Suggested Resources*

CAREY, D. *et al.* (1982) *Festivals, Family and Food*, Stroud, Hawthorn Press.

CHAPMAN, J. (1984) *Pancakes and Painted Eggs*, London, Hodder and Stoughton.

COLLINSON, C. and MILLER, C. (1985) *Celebrations*, London, Arnold.

KILLINGRAY, M. (1986) *I am an Anglican*, London, Franklin Watts.

THE LIVING FESTIVALS VIDEO SERIES Program 1 Section on Easter, CEM.

MAYLED, J. (1987) *Creation Stories*, Hove, Wayland.

PETTENUZZO, B. (1985) *I am a Roman Catholic*, London, Franklin Watts.

ROUSSON, M. (1985) *I am a Greek Orthodox*, London, Franklin Watts.

STORR, C. (1984) *The First Easter*, London, Methuen Children's.

Planning a School Curriculum for Religious Education for all Pupils of all Abilities

It is not the function of a County Agreed Syllabus to determine how a school should organize its curriculum. The implementation of the agreed syllabus is, however, the professional responsibility of teachers.

The variation in local education authority policy and practice is

Easter

	STAGE 1	STAGE 2	STAGE 3	STAGE 4
POSSIBLE aspects of easter to be explored	Symbols of springtime Mothering Sunday Preparation for Easter celebrations	Springtime customs at home and in the community Signs and symbols of Easter, for example, eggs, rabbits, Easter gardens, laurel, chickens, candles	Easter story with reference to Jesus' entry into Jerusalem Easter customs in religious communities History of Easter customs	Signs and symbols of Easter, particularly the cross Easter story as depicted through art, music, drama, poetry Ritual and customs in the community and worldwide
Ways of Celebrating Easter	Easter cards and spring decorations Seasonal cookery (eating) Carnival	Colours at Easter — Liturgical Stories about spring Springtime songs Easter decorations	Easter songs and music Easter decorations Traditional Easter foods (making) Stories of forgiveness and friendship, or good over evil and dramatization	Cooking simnel cakes, hot cross buns. Stories of those who have brought new life to others, for example, Helen Keller, Martin Luther King, Mary Seacole Movement and drama to convey hope, despair
Possible topics to be explored	Bulbs Baby animals Birds Mothers Eggs	Growth Flowers Birth/new life Trees Spring Friends	The cycle of the seasons Conservation Light and darkness Hope and joy Life Death	Hope, joy, triumph, metamorphosis. History of Easter foods Self sacrifice Fasting and feasting Courage

remarkable. Some LEAs are asking schools to produce a framework of policy for children with special educational needs. Even when this request is not being made, many teachers are eager to plan their own strategies. The suggested curriculum guidelines are not intended to be definitive or prescriptive — rather it is hoped that they will encourage schools to think about their own curriculum structures. There are sound reasons why individual schools should compile their own religious education curriculum which contain the aims, learning experiences, attitudes and skills outlined in the County Agreed Syllabus. These will include:

(i) all work should relate to the experience, religious and social background of the children, taking into account the local environment and the community;

(ii) aims set should build upon pupils' previous experience and prepare for future religious development without unnecessary repetition of topics;

(iii) the curriculum should allow for flexibility and change in its content, giving teachers autonomy to include current events and concerns whilst taking into account the diversity of religious belief and expertise amongst staff;

(iv) resources should be adequate and readily available;

(v) the approach to religious education should include both implicit and explicit aspects of the subject;

(vi) the scheme should show how objectives are being achieved throughout the school, allowing for religious education to be integrated into other areas of the curriculum;

(vii) the planning of the curriculum should be a corporate exercise involving all staff at each stage of its development.

First Steps in Planning a Curriculum

There are some fundamental questions which it is suggested that staff should attempt to answer before outlining curriculum content. These might include:

— What educational purpose does the school seek to attain?
— What educational experiences can be provided which will help attain these purposes?
— How can the educational experiences be effectively organized?
— How can it be determined whether the purposes are being attained?

Schools' Council Working Paper 70 suggests that the ability to recognize and to respond to stages in childrens' cognitive development is 'part of the teacher's essential armoury' in curriculum development. Four possible stages of religious development are outlined in the suggested objectives for religious education below. The stages are not, however, necessarily dependent on chronological age. They are best described as a 'framework' on which the subject or topic content of the curriculum will depend.

By the end of each stage of development it is hoped that pupils will have been given a range of experiences which will have contributed to:

Developmental objectives
Stage 1
— an awareness of self and wonder of being alive;
— the development of an interest in the natural world;
— an experience of feelings such as joy and empathy through celebration and story.

Stage 2
— an awareness of physical identity and individuality;
— an awareness of self in relation to other people;
— a capacity to form relationships;
— the development of healthy attitudes of self-worth and value;
— an exploration and perception of the beauty and pain of the natural world;
— a capacity to communicate experiences and emotions;
— a capacity to acknowledge personal response to emotions;
— an experience of celebration and ritual through story and ceremony.

Stage 3
— an understanding of self in relation to others and of the interdependence of humankind;
— an understanding of the diversity in ability and behaviour of other people, learning to value the contribution which each person makes;
— a capacity to enter sensitively into other people's experience through day to day situations and relationships;
— an awareness of the significance of celebration and ritual in the lives of other people;
— the capacity to reflect upon stories and literature from a variety of religious traditions.

Stage 4
— an understanding that relationships demand response and responsibility;
— the capacity to reflect on human experiences such as belonging, compassion, courage;
— an awareness of responsibility for the natural world

— the development of positive and fairminded attitudes towards a range of religious practices and beliefs;

— an understanding of human response to belief through the creative and expressive arts;

— an appreciation of the ways in which significant experiences in life are expressed through ritual and celebration.

Attitudes

For children to understand religion, it is important that they should be learning to express positive attitudes to life. These will include:

Attitudes to Learning — the desire to learn about themselves, their relationships and the quest of humankind for meaning and purpose.

Attitudes towards themselves — a feeling of personal value and worth, healthy self-esteem and integrity.

Attitudes towards others — including acceptance, appreciation, tolerance, sensitivity, fairmindedness.

Attitudes towards the physical and natural world — of respect, wonder, awe and responsibility.

Skills

Learning skills is extremely important for children with learning difficulties since many pupils will have to be taught those which their peers learn naturally. These skills may include:

Communication skills   such as listening, language, reading and writing

Investigatory skills   such as enquiry and discovery.

Expressive skills   such as those found in art, drama, music and movement.

Whilst teachers will wish to develop skills appropriate to their pupils' ability, it is possible to outline some of the capabilities which will make a large contribution to childrens' religious understanding. These will include:

— the ability to consider questions of human existence such as 'who am I?', 'why am I alive?', 'why did this happen to me?';

— the ability to understand and to interpret information in pictures and in books;

— the ability to acquire information through experience, observation and listening;

— the ability to enter imaginatively into another persons' experience and to appreciate their attitude to religion;

— the ability to develop the capacity for enjoyment at being alive;

— the ability to appreciate aspects of life which evoke wonder and awe and to communicate these experiences through drama, movement, music, art and writing;

— the ability to appreciate the purpose for and response of human-kind to festival, celebration, ritual and symbol.

Topics or learning experiences

Topics or learning experiences can be approached in various ways. Firstly the teacher can use actual situations. Secondly there is what can best be described as the 'contrived experience' such as telling a story or using a video which shows other peoples' experiences of life. A third way is through the expressive arts which mirror the life experiences common to us all.

Topics do not necessarily have to contain something explicitly religious for religious education to be taking place, but generally they will include the opportunity for aesthetic, spiritual and creative experiences, taking into account the childrens' ability, background and developing skills and attitudes.

It is helpful if notes are prepared on topics for non-specialist RE teachers who will be using the curriculum. These notes might contain:

— information;
— more precise objectives for teaching the topic;
— implications for the teacher of material included in the topic, including the use of artefacts, dietary rules, etc;
— possible teaching methods;
— suggested resources and bibliography.

Evaluation

Evaluation helps teachers to assess if their religious education is successful and appropriate to the pupils' needs and whether the aims, objectives, attitudes and skills are being fulfilled in a stimulating, relevant and interesting way.

Evaluation should be a continuous process which allows for adjustment in learning strategies if necessary. It is valuable in providing parents and colleagues with an account of what children are achieving and it can also give information regarding classroom organization, resources and teaching methods.

Effective evaluation requires a deep personal knowledge of children. It is extremely difficult to record evaluation on paper and objective evaluation will probably not be possible in such areas as values and attitudes unless progress is evaluated in terms of behaviour, for example, cooperation and responsibility.

One way of evaluating might be by looking at the learning experiences provided in the following three areas.

(i)   content of topics;

(ii)   teaching method, for example story, drama, discussion;

(iii)   classroom organization, including opportunities for pupil participation and integration, the forming of relationships and cooperation.

The aims of the school curriculum could also be questioned in the light of these areas. However we choose to evaluate, I believe we should evaluate each module we teach each time we teach it. In this way the curriculum will not remain static. It will grow and develop. The Warnock Report, the 1981 Education Act and the Education Reform Act 1988, were milestones and signposts which reviewed progress and pointed the way to future development. But the future quality of religious education remains the responsibility of the teacher.

References

DEPARTMENT OF EDUCATION AND SCIENCE (1977) *Curriculum 5–16*, London, HMSO.

DEPARTMENT OF EDUCATION AND SCIENCE (1978) *Report of the Enquiry into the Education of Handicapped Children and Young People* (The Warnock Report) London, HMSO.

DEPARTMENT OF EDUCATION AND SCIENCE (1981)'*Education Act*, London, HMSO.

DEPARTMENT OF EDUCATION AND SCIENCE (1988) *Education Reform Act*, London, HMSO.

SCHOOLS' COUNCIL WORKING PAPER NO. 70 (1981) *The Practical Curriculum*, London, Methuen Educational.

ROBINSON, E. (1977) *The Original Vision*, Oxford, RERU.

7   The Role of the RE Consultant

Elaine Bellchambers

I was given my first religious education consultant's post, along with several other areas of the curriculum, in 1977. It was a town school of approximately 450 children, many of whom came from London overspill families. An all-white school in an established estate area, it had a mix of new influx and old town families, where the parents had also attended the school. The headteacher was interested in religious education and as I had studied RE at college (called 'Divinity' in those days!) I was asked to do the job.

My first thoughts did not exactly lead me to panic, but I did wonder how I might teach the children all the academic facts I thought they should know about Christianity. Upon reflection I realized that all the higher education baggage I had acquired could, if I wasn't careful, be a hindrance. I needed to forget this for a while and look at the children, their needs and abilities. What was going to be relevant to them? What could they hope to make sense of? How might I get them to think, reflect and ask questions about some of the unique phenomena in life? I was also very aware of the emotive nature of the job which I had been given. Everybody has views and some personal experience which resulted in acceptance or dismissal. I was up against those who had dismissed religion and felt that the curriculum was sufficiently crowded without adding a subject that they personally had rejected. Then there was the believer who might disagree with my approach. The existing curriculum guidelines were bulky and dated, the sort which fills the teacher with dread, aims and objectives one after another but no practical hints on how to achieve them.

To gain more confidence in order to do the job I decided my first priority would be to improve my own skills as a teacher. I attended a broad variety of in-service courses in order to see how the educational drift was going. I looked into the skills approach to education and began to evaluate my classroom technique and slowly, by degrees, improved it. This process, humbling and painful to start with, proved in the long run to be more than worthwhile. I knew my weaknesses and could compensate, resulting in a sharpening of my general awareness and confidence.

For a year I muddled along, confused by the mass and variety of resource material. What should I buy? Sets of books or a staff resource book? Film strips or slides? Should I choose things that appealed to me and I would use, or more obvious material that colleagues would feel happier with? Needless to say, I compromised and took the middle way. I bought a mixture, justifying it by hoping that my use of less explicit material might inspire others to have a try.

By this time my head had become heavily involved in religious education curriculum matters and was putting a lot of energy into the subject. What with the pair of us, the rest of the staff felt very 'fed up' with what they considered to be a 'bandwagon' and the mention of anything vaguely religious resulted in bad feeling.

It was at this point I decided to do a further professional study course in religious education. I was feeling emotionally drained by the knocks and undercurrents of resistance and was beginning to doubt my own convictions as to why I thought RE to be of value. I needed support and some input into my own education. I approached the head and he agreed. The course was better than I had hoped for. Obviously there were areas I felt could have been improved but the balance between one's own study and classroom practice was excellent. I came away each Tuesday refreshed, more confident and much happier. The course lasted a year and involved four major pieces of work, two essays and two schemes of work. Successfully completed, with the diploma in my hand, I was ready to continue the battle.

After discussion with the head, the staff decided to embark on a school policy which was to be based on a topic grid. This policy allowed total integration of all subject areas. Each consultant chose topic themes which they felt best encapsulated the skills and content required. These then were pooled and after discussion the staff chose fifteen topic themes from all curriculum areas for each age range. Care was taken in trying to get a balance of disciplines.

For example:

Junior — Year Four

	AUTUMN		SPRING		SUMMER
(L)	Communication	(RE)	The church	(SC)	Study trip/environment
			Easter		Health education
(H)	Explorers	(L)	Make believe	(RE)	Another culture
	Autumn				
	Toys	(M)	Pattern/shape	(H/S)	Change
(RE)	Festivals	(SC)	Levers/pulleys		Water

We then set about trying this approach. We were able to choose from the topics within the terms. If a language topic took priority one term, then the next term the other disciplines took priority. I went through all the topic themes and looked for implicit and explicit areas of religious education within them and then gave these suggestions to staff. The grid was reviewed frequently in order to evaluate and check progression. It did a lot to defuse the perceived dominance of RE. Religious education was now considered an integral part of the curriculum topics and was thus made, for many, more relevant and slightly easier to handle.

In-service days on implicit and explicit religion followed. However I soon found that staff began to give me the answers they thought I wanted when questioned about the RE they were doing, but that they were not necessarily doing the job I felt they should be doing. I had to get into classrooms to find out the truth and support the teachers. But, as it is difficult for the head to release a member of staff on a regular basis without cover, my opportunities rarely materialized and I had to be content with colleagues' forecast books and what I heard or saw.

Assemblies began to feature regularly on my timetable. As the 'expert' I was the obvious choice to do the largest number of assemblies. This gave me the opportunity to explore possible types and forms of worship. Nevertheless, I learned to say no quickly!

One of the most difficult problems I found (and still do) is dealing with the religiously committed teacher whose aim is to make the children into believers. For the most part these are well-meaning people who want to do their best for the children. However, except in a voluntary-aided school, it is not the job of the school to nurture a faith. Rather its job is to help the child to step into the shoes of others and try to understand answers to questions raised by all societies.

A View of the Consultant's Role

The first and most important task of the consultant is to ensure that good primary practice takes place in this subject area. Religious education needs a sound basis upon which to build. Careful thought and planning needs to go into the programme, its processes and progression. From the outset the difference between teaching religious education and moral education needs to be stated. Many teachers feel that it is the responsibility of religious education to transmit moral values to children. It is quite true that religion is concerned about morality, but morality is found outside religion as well as within it. Each religion has an ethical dimension so morality is within religion. Equally a person can follow a moral code without it being within a religion. The consultant needs to be aware of the teachers who are doing moral education and not religious education and point them in the right direction. It is not good enough to say 'My religious education is the example I set and how we treat each other in class and in school'. RE is much more than that. Experience of, and reflection on, the world and its nature are deepened by learning about how people have interpreted natural phenomena often in religious terms. More explicitly religious material is then studied when the children investigate people and their life commitments. The child's imagination is an aid to this understanding of the explicit dimension of religion. It gives him/her an insight which makes possible a sensitive appreciation of what religion is about. As teachers we need to foster and develop this imagination. But religious education is set apart from the rest of the curriculum because it has a special status which may present problems.

The special status of RE as a part of the basic but not the National Curriculum is important. It ensures that RE has equal standing in relation to the core and foundation subjects within a school's curriculum, but is not subject to nationally prescribed attainment targets, programmes of study and assessment arrangements. However, a conference established by a local education authority under Schedule 5 of the 1944 Act to review a locally agreed syllabus may recommend the inclusion of attainment targets, programmes of study and assessment arrangements in locally determined forms in their proposal.

Because there are no nationally devised attainment or assessment criteria, it falls to the consultant to ensure that his/her area of responsibility does not become a Cinderella subject. It could become the case that if there is no form of assessment then the subject may be dealt with in a casual, superficial manner. The children may consider it of no real value and so dismiss it. The consultant therefore has to bring to the subject a spark, that certain something that lifts it out of the doldrums and shows it to be the exciting, fascinating and totally absorbing subject that it is.

Religious education can be a minefield. The average teacher often feels very insecure, knowing some aspects of Christianity, probably mystified by a great deal more and feeling bewildered as to how to decode and teach the children. They may or may not have a religious commitment, either way this should not affect their role, but probably does! How can I teach something I don't believe in? If the teacher does not hand on to the children a body of knowledge and some experience of religion then they are deprived of being able to make a sound decision about whether they wish to believe in later life. We have no right to hinder a child's development in this way.

Can I be sufficiently objective in my teaching considering my personal religious commitment? Yet all teachers know that too much forcing of ideas, theories and beliefs upon children kills their interest and that is the last thing the committed teacher wants.

Like other consultants within a school, the RE consultant needs some academic knowledge in order to have credibility with his/her colleagues. He/she needs to have confidence working in this area and helping others to understand the complex diversity within it. Therefore in-service education for the intending consultant is essential. The ideal teacher for a religious education consultant is an open-minded person, who is prepared to allow children, through all areas of the curriculum but especially language, literature, music, dance, drama and art, to experience and try to understand a variety of people's answers to questions about the meaning and purpose in life. As teachers we are involved in developing the whole child, not just filling them with facts. We need to explore religion(s) in order to promote understanding by attempting to stand in the shoes of religious believers.

The Job

What exactly does the consultant do? This depends to a certain degree on the needs and conditions prevalent within individual schools, but there are obvious areas that may be common to all.

Firstly the school staff, led by the head and consultant needs to discuss and work out schemes of work and progression. All LEAs have agreed syllabuses with aims and objectives for RE which must be referred to. Hampshire's two documents *Paths to Understanding* and *Following the Paths* are quick, easy to read and understand, with plenty of examples to guide the teacher. An ideal resource!

Careful handling of the sensitivities of colleagues needs to be considered: all have a right to air opinions and to be listened to. This is possibly one of the most difficult jobs for any consultant. There is no easy answer; understanding, tact, support and firmness are all brought into play.

Consultants need to gain the confidence and cooperation of their colleagues and should set them an example. Their classroom must reflect good primary practice, especially within RE. Display is important, it acts as a stimulus. Children look and chat about what they see, staff reflect upon display and its effect. Ideas are shared, other views considered, encouragement is given to those needing an initial impetus.

Colleagues working together in groups or as a complete staff on large topics allows for greater brainstorming, exchange of ideas and problems. Each teacher is then able to add his/her special strength to the overall project and ideas that are slightly adrift are more easily corrected. The cooperation of colleagues is vitally important. The consultant needs them to review mailings or test-use resources which can be done quite simply by saying to a member of staff, 'I'd value your opinion on this resource. Perhaps you'll look at it and see if you can use it. Please let me know how you get on.'

Building up Resources

Buying resources is important. Old fashioned or moth-eaten posters, tatty Bibles or books send out clear messages to the children. Religious education, like every other curriculum area, needs to have its share of capitation. The consultant may have to fight and justify his/her needs more than other subject areas but he/she must and it will repay dividends when he/she gets a good set of resources. There is a plethora of resources available and advice from local advisers will be probably necessary. The consultant may also find that local advisers will give him/her a little extra money for something they may have specifically recommended.

Visit teachers' centres and view materials available, talk to other RE consultants, call in the advisory teacher, then decide what will suit the situation. Good quality mailings with ideas and resources for given topic themes are very useful. I recommend the Primary Mailings of the Christian Education Movement. These magazines contain posters, topic booklets plus articles that keep you abreast of current thinking and accounts of work tried in the classroom.

Sets of slides are generally of more use than filmstrips, a couple of relevant slides can do wonders for a lesson and offered to a colleague is going to enhance professional reputation. Slides need not be specifically religious, those which reflect the world in its diversity, that allow the children to develop awareness and reflect upon what they see, all contribute to the implicit or spiritual religious development. So take the opportunity of doubling up with other areas of the curriculum.

A collection of religious artefacts, ie. a Christian box, brings into the classroom first-hand experience of 'silent teachers', the symbols within Christianity which play such an important part in its tradition. These artefacts offer the teacher an exciting and interesting way into an exploration. Such a box might include a family Bible, a cross, paschal candle, rosary, a prayer book an icon, priests' vestments, music, etc.

Naturally, as we live in a global village, I should hope the consultant to be in the process of collecting resources from other traditions, perhaps an Indian box or a Jewish box containing special clothing, sacred writings, pictures, statues and music. All have a place within these boxes. One word of warning here, take care with use of such artefacts, they can stimulate interest over many lessons. Don't reduce the visual experience and interest value by using all of them at once.

Collections of stories from the Bible, secular stories and a wide variety of stories from other cultures to be told at story time should be made. Choice of Bible is a matter of taste; the Good News Bible is easily understood while the King James Bible is best for its beauty of language.

Plenty of visual material in the form of posters is necessary. This acts both as a stimulus and a reminder. A good cross-section of materials from various religious traditions should be collected including such themes as Rites of Passage, Festivals, Christ in Art, Pilgrimage, Sacred Books, Sacred Places and the lives of major religious figures.

Music from a variety of cultures, including, of course, music that is purely reflective in nature (no cultural link necessarily) and of a more specific nature, i.e. The Exodus theme from the film, provides the teacher with a handle into lessons, allowing the child to be reflective and express feelings through dance and drama.

Keep a watchful eye on television programmes and radio broadcasts which may be useful and also remember the advisory staff and Teachers' Centre and possibly your nearest institution of higher education. These people are very happy to help where they can.

The Consultant's Development

A good teacher is a teacher who is still learning, who is still in contact with the processes the children are going through. It sharpens his/her own techniques, keeps him/her aware of the levels of concentration and the sorts of things the mind retains. Therefore I would expect a consultant to be regularly attending in-service courses. Such courses keep the consultant in touch with recent developments, give him/her the opportunity to meet colleagues with similar interests and to come into contact with a diversity of experience and views with all the challenges such situations present. They give him/her the opportunity in which to further his/her own knowledge, to assess his/her own situation and to return in order to tackle the difficulties in their various guises, ie. reorganization of resources or difficult colleagues.

Courses often bring together RE teachers from the locality, making the liaison and support process between schools easier. The swapping of ideas and resources and the coupling of schools for in-service may mean that advisers are happier to visit and do an INSET day as they are reaching a wider audience.

Whatever else courses do, it is essential to attend them if the teacher wishes to remain a professional. Education moves fast, professionals keep up. Having attended a course, staff meetings need to be arranged in order that dissemination can take place and all may benefit from current thinking.

The sharing of resource material and ideas within the school will lead the consultant into the role of INSET leader for the occasional day closure. These may take various forms but will possibly include: What is

RE? How do I teach it? A look at the school's policy; Evaluation of school's policy and amendments.

Input of a specific nature may also take place, i.e. assemblies, Bible stories, another culture. These may be led by the consultant, adviser/advisory teacher or a consultant from another school. Either way, time and situation must allow the staff the opportunity to discuss inputs and question if they so wish, plus the opportunity to review resources if available.

Assemblies strictly speaking are not the brief of the RE consultant, they are the headteacher's responsibility. Obviously the consultant's brains will be picked and doubtless 'family' assemblies and the larger ones will fall to his/her lot. What must be borne in mind is the Education Reform Act 1988 ruling on assemblies: (i) ... in the case of a county school the collective worship required in the school by section 6 of this Act shall be wholly or mainly of a broadly Christian character; (ii) ... collective worship is of a broadly Christian character if it reflects the broad traditions of Christian belief without being distinctive of any particular Christian denomination; (iii) ... collective worship, shall be such as may be appropriate having regard to any relevant considerations relating to the pupils concerned which fail to be taken into account in accordance with sub-section 5; (iv) those considerations are: (a) Any circumstances relating to the family backgrounds of the pupils concerned which are relevant for determining the character of the collective worship which is appropriate in their case; and (b) their ages and aptitudes.

I see the consultant's role with regard to assemblies to be in an advisory capacity, to check, for example, that the forms of daily worship are applicable to the children and not an opportunity for reminding children of the school rules. Hampshire's *Paths to Understanding* (p. 119) may be helpful for the consultant in formulating what an effective assembly is:

> It almost goes without saying that the nature and forms of worship should be closely related to the needs, experiences and capacities of pupils if the activity is to have any real meaning for them. The younger the pupils, the more necessary it will be — as in the teaching of a subject — to start from the concrete experience. Decisions as to how far it will be useful to move into the realms of abstraction will require sensitivity and experiment. Such decisions would no doubt be informed by, but not bound by, particular theories of intellectual development. The importance of imaginative and emotional elements in worship should also be fully recognised.
>
> Many traditional forms of worship, which incorporate difficult concepts and often start from formulated doctrines, will

therefore be inappropriate. The basic content will be, for example, experiencing and expressing wonder and delight in the natural world or reflecting on human experiences of birth, growth, love, suffering, death etc. Discovering adequate forms, which invite full participation, will be an exciting task. When content and form are right, experience, reflection and celebration will (as in any true worship) feed back into the lives of the pupils, affecting both the kind and quality of their experience.

Collective worship allows for many different responses to the stimulus. It is this we are after, not a corporate act.

Liaison

Liaison with the local secondary school helps the consultant to keep an overview of his/her subject area and the way it advances in secondary education. Contact with agencies related to the school's immediate environment helps the teacher to be aware of the problems and pressures faced by the community which may have some bearing on the attitudes and behaviour of the children. It also allows for a sharing of ideas, the children going out and doing something for the community and the community coming in to the school, resulting in a healthy respect and responsibility towards each other. Getting to know your school governors and taking them through your area of responsibility, its strong points and its weakness, helps both yourself and them. Most governors are very keen to find out about and understand education and are in need of opportunities to learn. Handled carefully the governors will be grateful for the time and effort put in by the teacher for their benefit and will support him/her in her task. This is vital if one considers the powers governors now have.

Good communication with the community outside the school extends the teacher's resources and often the most unlikely people have experience the teacher can draw upon. For example, how do you explain to children what monsoon rain is like? You can show them a film, but it is even better to get somebody in who can add that human dimension, how it feels, the smells, the effect on the storm drains.

But of course, not all adults feel able to talk to children. They often find it a very threatening situation. The teacher can take it easier by arranging small groups or by getting the children to ask questions. Then there is the other extreme, the person who is out to sell a particular idea or belief. This is not tolerated in county schools, so if the teacher is thinking of inviting somebody in, who may be in the slightest way contentious, then a telephone call to the adviser is essential. Explain why this visitor is important to your scheme of things and how (hopefully) the children will benefit educationally. Remember, the visitor is a resource to increase learning, not a diversion.

Organizing resources within a school is a personal matter dependent upon availability of space and access. Generally speaking I like to keep collections of artefacts of one faith together along with posters and books, housed in stackable plastic boxes and well-labelled. Film strips, ideally cut up and made into slides, and then kept in see-through plastic slide holders, again clearly labelled are a very important resource.

A separate section of a shelf should be kept for staff resource books. These are sometimes kept separately in the staff room, but often if a teacher is in the resource room pottering about he/she will pick up interesting books and begin to browse. Make sure the RE ones are in a prominent position and eye catching. My personal preference was to keep the resources within one area and not diversified too much. If it's RE I'm looking for I'd rather go straight to it.

Getting Started

If this is a new job at a new school, then allow yourself time in order to settle down and get to know your colleagues. Look at the resources the school already has, make decisions about accessibility and whether the resources are sufficiently used. Talk to staff about what has gone on before. Find out what they feel they need, You need to get an overview. These are little tasks that can be done with the minimum of fuss and yet are essential to start the teacher off on a sound footing.

Your classroom must reflect good primary practice with a well-balanced curriculum. Demonstrate your overall professionalism by keeping up-to-date in all areas of the curriculum. Display in the classroom immediately tells the visitor, professional or otherwise a lot about the teacher and the standard of work being achieved. As the RE consultant your classroom is the example that colleagues will look to for inspiration and understanding. Don't miss the opportunity! It is important not to be apologetic: religious education is exciting and very relevant to children's experience. It is also part of a child's educational entitlement as defined in the Education Reform Act.

Spread yourself, don't limit display such as these to your room only. There is always somewhere in a school for displays to be mounted. Organize exhibitions of newly-acquired resources in the staffroom. Displays might include sacred books, religious symbols, religious paintings, clothing, ideas on celebration, belonging ... Invite comment both from staff and children in order to evaluate the effectiveness of your display. Talk with colleagues as to the topic work they are doing and perhaps you might be able to make an input in their work by providing them with display material or by offering to exchange expertise for a couple of lessons. This working together and pooling of skills really does pay off. Relationships of trust and interdependence are forged, each understands the others problems and opportunities of varying strategies for tackling these difficulties may arise. When members of staff work together, individual teachers begin to feel they belong and are of value. In this way, the ethos of the school is enhanced and children are quick to pick this up. Teachers cooperating happily and effectively is a good example to set children.

Get to know your primary adviser with special responsibility for RE. Involve them in some of the projects you undertake. Remember that they are advisory and rarely in my experience criticize teachers who honestly seek their help and are trying to do the job. So don't be put off because you may feel inadequate. At some point in their career that adviser probably also felt inadequate and perhaps sometimes still does! Your county may have a primary advisory teacher. He/she will in all probability be doing the job on a part-time basis and teaching the rest of the week, so his/her feet will be firmly on the ground as to what will or will not work in the classroom; why not call him/her in and pick his/her brains? There is no point in suffering unnecessarily, the people are here to support you, so use them.

It is important also to decide in which areas of religious education you intend to develop an expertise. I, for example, decided to select two main religions that I found particularly interesting and to make them my own special subject areas. I chose Christianity because I live in a society that has Christianity as the principal religion. My other choice was Hinduism, my interest prompted by its apparent contrast with Christianity. With the Christian religion my main area, together with one other religion, the children in my care are going to have both experience, and build up an understanding, of their own traditions and those of another, rather than doing a 'Cook's Tour' of world religions which can be a confusing experience.

Multicultural Education

This area of multicultural education should not really be the preserve of religious education. There is the argument that good music teaching and curriculum will include music from other cultures and that a study of literature of history should also include investigation into another culture's literature and history. But in my experience, in practice, it more often falls to the lot of the RE specialist to develop the idea of seeing how others live. This is perhaps inevitable as so many cultures are so undergirded by religious belief and practice that it is difficult, if not impossible, to separate religion from culture. This is certainly why RE is often a driving force in a school's multicultural work.

We are not expecting, and certainly don't want, the children in our care to become indoctrinated or nurtured into a particular faith (unless it is a voluntary-aided school) and I doubt if looking at why a Hindu child goes through a particular puja at a shrine to Shiva is going to effect a change in belief. It may, however, explain to children that the Hindu is not worshipping an idol but that the image is a signpost, a window into God, an idea that they have in common and can respect.

The argument is greater than this and here is not the place to discuss it. Better that this is done as a school staff, but the RE consultant would be expected to be totally committed to its teaching. Christians are taught to love one another. A difficult, nigh on impossible task, yet with a little more knowledge and understanding we stand more chance in achieving this goal. How then can we not teach about another culture? Christian faith tells that we must try and love our neighbours. Let us first try to come to some sort of understanding.

The role of the consultant when dealing with work of a multicultural nature is that of an overseer. Such work has four major approach problems before a teacher even starts to teach and I am indebted to Bronwen Lewis, formerly of the Southampton World Studies Centre, for the categorization of these problems. The consultant needs to be on the lookout for these problems. Let us take India as an example. First there is the tourist's eye view of the country. Everything is quaint, curious and charming with the emphasis put upon the exotic or snake charmers and elephants. Second, there is the 'packet of tea' approach. This implies that people overseas exist to grow our tea/sugar or cotton, to provide us with exotic holidays. Natives are always seen as happy and smiling, singing in the sunshine and waiting on tourists. We are the happy tea drinkers snug arount the fire at home.

Then comes the 'pathological view', that the truth being a long way removed from the glossy images which photographs and films may promote. In fact everything is desperate, people are dying from starvation or flooding and suffering hurricanes or earthquakes. Lastly there is the 'pat on the head'. They've been rather behind, what with mud huts, large families and poor diets. But, if they follow our example they will be all right. Cars and automated industry are considered by the Western world to make a country 'developed'.

The consultant must watch for these types of approaches and point out to the member of staff if the approach becomes too one-sided. Balance is essential, discuss the variety within the country, just as there are vast differences within our own. We will be failing in our task if we create or endorse stereotypes. Our job is to promote understanding and empathy.

You will in all probability meet resistance and although your 'expertise' will win during staff meetings, the reality may well be the paying of lip-service to the idea. Very little can be done, possibly the only feasible answer is to ensure that the children in your class do meet another culture. In time some form of attainment targets and assessment of religious education will arrive, having been set up and put into motion by your county's Standing Advisory Council for Religious Education and these targets and assessment will expect the child to have some knowledge of another faith and its culture.

Evaluation

Apart from working a topic approach and developing a flow chart and perhaps noting which stories were read when, there appears to be very little, if any form of record keeping. So a problem appears when the teacher attempts to evaluate his/her work. I think evaluation needs to be considered alongside the objectives of the agreed syllabus. These objectives will in all probability deal with such basic concerns as, the children gaining knowledge, developing skills of expression, investigation, reflection, that they should deepen their understanding of life, be open minded, sensitive towards others and so on.

Particular sorts of work within RE can be evaluated quite easily, for example, symbolic representations, people in the Bible, knowledge of the Bible, facts about the life of Jesus, Palestine in the time of Jesus. However, the personal and spiritual side that relates to deeper insights and attitudes developing within the child cannot be measured. At this point the teacher needs to fall back on his/her own judgment and ask him/herself whether the work the children are involved in is realistic and relevant, bearing in mind their experience and backgrounds. Are there genuine opportunities for open-ended discussion and work which allows for making value judgments? What possibilities are there for the children to express themselves through creative writing, art and craft, music, dance and drama which allow for religious influence? He/she might also consider just how much demand there is for resources, old and new. This does give an indicator as to whether religious education in the school is on the move.

References

DES (1989) *Circular No. 3/89 'The Education Reform Act'*, London, HMSO
HAMPSHIRE EDUCATION AUTHORITY (1980) *Paths to Understanding*, Winchester, Hampshire Education Authority.
HAMPSHIRE EDUCATION AUTHORITY (1986) *Following the Paths*, Winchester, Hampshire Education Authority.

8   Developing RE in Topic-based Approaches to Learning

Dennis Bates

A third year student teacher specializing in RE was somewhat dismayed to find, when she visited the village primary school in which she was to undertake her teaching practice, that the topic prescribed by the school for her class of top juniors was 'spiders'. The college required that she integrate RE into a topic approach in her practice and since 'spiders' formed part of a carefully planned programme, the school wasn't inclined to accede to the student's request that a topic more suitable for RE should be chosen. Changing schools proved impossible so a tearful student was faced with the task of 'getting RE into spiders'. The work had to incorporate a multicultural dimension and so the student chose the story of Muhammad and the spider as the starting point for the RE aspect of the topic. Since the children had never encountered any religion other than Christianity in their school work, the student felt that some introduction to Islam was essential in order to give the story a context. The result was that 'spiders' became the means whereby the children of a small Humberside village learnt about Islam.

The topic was well planned, covering a variety of areas of the curriculum (science, language, art and RE) and involving a range of learning experiences. A knowledgeable and sensitive Muslim research fellow from the college visited the school, talked to the children about Islam and answered their prepared and spontaneous questions. There was a strong emphasis on child centred learning methods — individual research, group discussion and planning — and the written and art work on Islam and the other areas covered by the topic was of a very high standard. The whole experience was educationally excellent; but was this an example of good integrated topic practice involving RE? Was there really a natural connection between 'spiders' and Islam? Did the children's work on Islam contribute to their understanding of spiders? Or did the topic became a peg on which to hang RE?

It is, of course, arguable that means of giving the topic an RE dimension other than explicit subject content were open to the student. Some would contend that a better course would have been to have avoided religious subject content and to have focused instead on the intricacy and beauty of spiders' webs, illustrated through slides or (better still) seen one morning in the school grounds with the dew still on them; or the fascinating life history of the spider and the number and diminutive size of newly hatched spiders. Many agreed syllabuses of RE (including that of Humberside) have objectives for the early and middle years which involve 'in depth' exploration of the natural world in order to evoke the experiences of awe and wonder and a sense of order and design which for some suggest the existence and activity of God.[1] A problem with such 'implicit' approaches is that not everyone would see them as having anything necessarily to do with RE at all.

This brief case study raises some of the problems which may be involved in integrating RE into a topic approach to learning, and indicates some of the ways in which current agreed syllabuses suggest that RE may be approached through it. In what follows, these and other issues will be considered in the light of an analysis of the development of topic approaches to learning both in general and with specific reference to RE; and guidelines for good topic practice in RE in the era of the National Curriculum will be suggested.

Topic Approaches to Learning in Primary Schools

The recent practice of topic approaches to learning in primary schools has its origins in the strongly child-centred phase of curriculum development in primary education of the late fifties and sixties inspired largely by the work of Piaget and given official recognition by the Plowden Report (1967). This advocated enquiry rather than didactic approaches to learning in primary schools — 'Finding out' has proved to be better for children than 'being told' (*ibid.*, p. 460), and suggested teaching by (among other methods) project, 'centre of interest' or topic. Such methods are designed:

> ... to make good use of the interest and curiosity of children, to minimize the notion of subject matter being rigidly compartmental, and to allow the teacher to adopt a consultative, guiding, stimulating role rather than a purely didactic one. (*ibid.*, p. 198)

Plowden envisages much of the curriculum being organized around topics although it warns against the danger of artificiality if too much is linked to one topic; better to have a number of topics going at once.

It is clear that Plowden viewed topic primarily as a child centred learning method involving exploratory, experiential, activity based approaches in which teachers assisted children to be the agents of their own learning. It is also clear that Plowden intended it to become the dominant approach of primary schools to the organization of the curriculum. During the sixties and seventies, topic approaches to learning in primary schools became popular although they rarely became the universal mode of curriculum organization or the focus of 'whole school' planning. Rather, a *laissez-faire* attitude prevailed in which individual teachers tended to pursue topics chosen by them or their class.

In schools in which, according to recent research projects, at least 14.8 per cent (Galton, Simon and Croll, 1980, p. 192) and as much as 75 per cent (Eggleston and Kerry, 1985, p. 82) of time was spent on topic or project work, this led to a range of problems and, during the late seventies and eighties, topic approaches came under criticism from HMI as well as more partisan sources. Nigel Stewart, in his concise and helpful survey (Stewart, 1988 , esp. pp. 2–5), points out how topic practice was faulted for its lack of coherent structuring, its piecemeal approach to knowledge, its repetitiveness and lack of progression.

However, measures were already being taken to resolve these problems. A major contributor to this process during the seventies was the Schools Council *Place, Time and Society* project, the concern of which was history, geography and social science 8–13 (Blyth *et al.*, 1976). This advocated a topic approach to work in these subjects in the middle years centred around the development of four common substantive concepts (communication, power, values and beliefs, conflict/consensus) and three common methodological concepts (cause and consequence, similarity and difference, continuity and change) but also on a recognition of the distinctive contributions of the subject disciplines. The keynote was not integration but the use of subjects as resources in interrelation with each other; and there was a flexible view of the balance of subject contributions to each topic, determined by the demands of the topic.

This reaffirmation of the important role of the subject disciplines in providing the cognitive building blocks of topic and the importance of careful, coherent planning, lent momentum to the process of reorientation of topic away from the child to the curriculum. Topic was becoming less a child-centred learning method and more a way of organizing subject content. Behind these developments lay the influence of Jerome Bruner's ideas and especially his emphasis on the importance of structuring learning around the fundamental ideas of the subject disciplines and their associated skills and attitudes (Bruner, 1960, pp. 17ff.). Bruner's notion of concept building through a 'spiral curriculum' in which key concepts are revisited at increasing levels of complexity over the child's school experience came into prominence in several influential studies (especially Gunning, Gunning and Wilson, 1981). It is this writer's view that a Brunerian developmental approach has much to offer RE for the future.

Writing during the mid-eighties, Eggleston and Kerry found schools adopting various strategies for ensuring balance and structure in topic, notably selecting a range of topics, each based on a major subject area, to be studied over a period; or choosing broad topics, each susceptible of contributions from various subject areas, planned typically be means of a flow chart. A few schools were even starting from a concepts, skills and activities analysis and selecting content accordingly (*ibid.*, p. 87). Humberside LEA promoted such an approach in its primary schools from the mid-eighties (Stewart, 1986).

Topic and the National Curriculum

Although the role of subjects is central to the National Curriculum, its supportive documents make it quite clear that the methods by which schools deliver it are for them to decide; topic or thematic approaches are clearly cited among these. Indeed, in *Science For Ages 5 to 16* (1988), the science curriculum is defined in terms of themes and Humberside LEA has formed five topic 'umbrellas' from these:

Materials
Energy, forces and movement
People and how they live
Plants and animals
Earth, atmosphere and spaces

— with a range of recommended topics under each 'umbrella' — as the basis for the greater part of the curriculum in its primary schools. Such an approach usefully focuses schools' attention on a previously neglected area in primary education but runs the risk of providing too subject related a base for the adequate treatment of the broad curriculum. Certainly, it is very difficult to include an adequate RE element in the schema as it now is. However, as the foundation subjects issue their own attainment targets, the base from which topics are selected is likely to be enlarged. Unless LEAs issue guidelines showing how their existing agreed syllabuses may contribute to this process or, better still, develop new agreed syllabuses on National Curriculum lines, RE is likely to be seriously handicapped.

Far from jeopardizing the place of topic approaches, the National Curriculum could provide exactly the right incentive for schools to overcome the deficiencies of earlier practice and give integrated topic work the rigour and structure which it has often lacked. Topic is now going to have to be geared to the attainment targets of National Curriculum subjects and careful selection of topics and whole school planning are now no longer optional but essential. For some however, this undermines key aspects of topic practice, above all the freedom of teachers and children to negotiate topics which are centred in children's concerns and 'actively involves them in ... planning, executing, presenting and evaluating' their work (Tann, 1988, p. 4). It is true that the demands of the National Curriculum leave little room for such spontaneous activities but it is very important that many of the *learning methods* characteristic of child-centred topic practice — individual and group investigation, co-operative learning, learning from first hand experience — should figure prominently in the new situation.

The Development of Topic Approaches to RE

The development of topic[2] work in RE has passed through three phases which have to some extent reflected the broader developments outlined above as well as important changes within the subject itself. It is now entering a fourth phases as the attainment targets of the various subjects in the National Curriculum come to dominate curriculum planning and RE begins to adapt itself to the new situation (REC, 1989; AREAI, 1989; Westhill, 1989; Copley and Priestley, 1990; Jackson and Starkings, 1990).

The Goldman Phase

During the sixties child-centred topic practice was related to an RE curriculum still dominated by the Bible and concerned to nurture children into a non-denominatioinal form of Christianity. Harold Loukes, the Quaker educationist, pioneered experiential approaches to RE for secondary school pupils (Loukes, 1961), introduced the phrase 'readiness for religion' (Loukes, 1963) and suggested experiental approaches for primary schools (Loukes, 1965); but it was Ronald Goldman who had greatest impact on primary school RE. On the basis of his research into the development of children's religious thinking (Goldman, 1964), Goldman and a group of teachers produced an influential book and RE materials for primary schools utilizing a topic approach (Goldman, 1965a and 1965b). The Piagetian developmental schema on which Goldman's suggestions were based, has dominated approaches to primary RE ever since.

This schema rejected direct subject study as unsuitable for infants and lower juniors who were still at the intuitive stage or in the early phase of concrete operational thinking; children only became 'ready' for such direct study in the top junior/early secondary years; and the formal consideration of religious concepts and doctrines was only suitable for children of mental age 13+ who were entering the stage of formal operational thinking. In the infant and junior years, an experimental approach was adopted which attempted to relate the subject matter of RE (then, the Bible) to the children's experience. Carefully selected Biblical material had to be introduced in the context of 'life themes' which aimed to 'relate religion to life by emphasising the total unity of experience' (Goldman, 1965a, p. 110). 'Life themes' were of two main types — general primary topics such as 'homes', 'pets', 'people who help us', and topics drawn from the imagery of Biblical language, for example 'bread', 'light', 'shepherds and sheep'. Only in the final year of primary education were subject themes recommended — 'What is the Bible?' and 'Jesus'. However, for both Loukes and Goldman, it was not just the Biblical material which provided the religious dimension in thematic work. Both were influenced by the 'new' or 'secular' theology of the early sixties which saw ordinary experience — explored in depth — as a source of religious knowledge and insight. However, Goldman never followed this thinking through fully in his curriculum suggestions. It was in phase 2 that it was applied in a thoroughgoing way to thematic work in primary school RE.

A Neo-Goldmanian Phase

During the seventies Goldman's ideas were developed and adapted to a situation in which the world's major religions became the content of the subject and the development of 'understanding' of religion, not nurture into Christianity, became the aim. The seminal Lancaster Schools Council Working Paper 36 (1971) not only advocated this change in the character of RE, but identified and commended as complementary the two types of approach to RE which underly the thinking of Loukes and Goldman in the sixties — experiential ('implicit') and subject orientated ('explicit'). These became the bipolar organizing principle which has dominated curriculum development in RE to the present time. The study of 'explicit' religion was almost universally geared to Ninian Smart's six (now seven[3]) dimensional analysis of religion. This vastly expanded awareness of the range of religious subject content usable in school education and provided it with a structure which could readily be adapted to developmental criteria.[4]

Despite the radical change in phase 2 from Christian nurture based on Biblical study to the empathetic study of the great religions of the world, Christian 'secular theology' became central to 'implicit' thematic approaches to RE in primary schools. The all too frequent artificiality of Goldman's incorporation of Biblical material into his life themes was noted by Grimmitt (1973) among others. Grimmitt and Holm (1975) both argued that since, according to secular theology, ordinary experience explored in depth was a source of religious insight, there was no need to incorporate explicit religious material into a theme for it to contribute to religious education. Following the logic of this argument they developed 'depth' and 'human experience' themes respectively. These included no explicit religious content; their role was to provide an experiential basis for explicit religion either concurrently in parallel explicit or 'dimensional' themes (Grimmitt) or consecutively at a later stage (Holm).

Objectives and programmes of study reflecting this type of thinking were embodied in the primary and middle years sections of most agreed syllabuses of the late seventies, notably the influential Hampshire syllabus (1978). Whilst sharing the same assumptions in some measure, two Schools Council publications of the late seventies (1977a and 1977b) provided a clearer conceptual structure for RE which, together with HMI's analysis of the curriculum in terms of eight (later, nine) 'areas of experience' and reintroduction of the concept of the 'spiritual' (DES 1977), augured the next phase of development.

A Structural Phase

During the eighties the conceptual structure of religion and the skills and attitudes required for and fostered by, its study and understanding have become a major focus of concern. A new generation of agreed syllabuses, for example Cambridgeshire (1982), Berkshire (1982) and Durham (1982a and b) embodied these structural concerns more overtly than phase 2 syllabuses. Responding to the criticism that much implicit topic work — in effect 'depth' themes — seemed to have little to do with RE, the ILEA agreed syllabus of 1984 related its implicit objectives more closely to explicit content. Hampshire County Council issued guidelines for topic work which also stressed tighter planning and structuring using a skills and activities framework (Hampshire, 1986).

The language of depth theology receded although its assumptions still survived and phase 2 thinking continued in agreed syllabuses in association with the new terminology (see, for example, Oldham, 1989; Rotherham, 1989; Surrey, 1987; Salford, 1987). The relation of religion to the 'spiritual' and ethical areas of experience and PSE became the major focus of debate. Grimmitt argued that humankind's spiritual 'capacity', 'awareness' or 'competence' (Grimmitt, 1987, pp. 126–7) underlay personal, moral and religious development; the language of spirituality replaces the language of depth theology in Grimmitt's thinking but the results, in terms of curriculum development, are phase 2 ideas in fresh terminological clothes. His suggestions are aimed at secondary schools but the logic of his arguments applies also to primary schools. The development of children's 'spiritual' awareness through practical classroom exercises has recently been argued to be central to primary school RE (Hammond and Hay *et al.*, 1990).

Piagetian developmentalism and Goldman's application of this to RE came under growing criticism. The adequacy of Goldman's research methodology, its theological assumptions and the inferences drawn from it for curriculum development in RE, were queried (Slee, 1986 and 1987), and in both RE and moral education (Bottery, 1990) Piagetian limitations on children's ability to grasp abstract ideas was called into serious question. Coupled with the increasing influence of Bruner's notion of a spiral curriculum centred in the development of key concepts, renewed confidence was lent to the possibilities of more direct subject study with young children (Watson, 1987, chapter 12). This emphasis is also embodied in the Westhill project handbook which provides a useful concepts, skills and attitudes analysis of RE (Westhill, 1986, chapter 2), and in the project's materials on Christianity, Islam and most recently (1990) Judaism in which the first books start with 7-year-olds. Although the project's rationale for its thematic materials owes much to the theology of phase 2, its 'life themes' are not 'depth' themes; carefully organized illustrative subject content is incorporated into them.

How May RE Contribute to an Integrated Topic?

Over the three identified phases, clear patterns of practice have emerged in integrated topic work in RE. Two broad answers (a and b) to the sub-title question may be identified with a third (c) occupying a slightly different category:

(a) By incorporating developmentally appropriate 'explicit' subject content from the Bible (phase 1) or world religions (phases 2 and 3). In phase 3, the emphasis is often on developing the concepts which underlie the knowledge.

(b) By exploring children's experience of (in particular) the natural world, self and relationships in depth with a view to (i) highlighting the experiences on which religious concepts and beliefs are allegedly based; (ii) developing key skills and attitudes necessary for the study and understanding of religion; and (iii) raising the 'ultimate' questions to which religions provide answers.

(c) By exploring key religious images drawn from life, for example 'light', 'water', 'fire', 'wheel', with a view to introducing the symbolic nature of much religious language and deepening children's understanding of its meaning.

(a) and (c) are relatively uncontroversial although developmental strictures on the selection and treatment of RE subject content for topic have had unfortunate effects as will be argued below; and some feel that religious images are best dealt with in context, that is, when directly considering explicit religious subject content. However, (b) the 'implicit' approach, has led to problems and confusions and requires more detailed attention. Although much of the following section is rather critical in character, it is this writer's view that it is important that the inadequacies of the theory and practice of implicit RE are fully recognized so that a sounder basis may be laid for the future.

Implicit RE and Topic

The so called 'implicit' or indirect (Goldman, 1965a, p. 88) approach originally arose in the context of secondary RE as a teaching method which attempted to breathe new life and relevance into the rather arid, factual Biblical RE of the late fifties and early sixties. Harold Loukes developed what came to be known as the 'social problem' approach for 14–15-year-olds; this started by exploring subjects of relevance to adolescents — relationships, money, authority — and then examined what the Bible and Christian teaching had to say about them (Loukes, 1961). However, in its application to primary RE by Loukes, Goldman, Grimmitt and Holm, the implicit approach became more than a pedagogical method. Through its association with secular theology,[5] it became the means of making a large part of the primary curriculum legitimate subject matter for RE. Thus, any aspect of experience, if explored in sufficient depth, could potentially disclose religious meaning or insights and could be embraced within RE; in particular, the study of the natural world, humans and relationships (Loukes, 1965, p. 102). In this sense, Loukes argued, 'all education is religious and all subjects are the servants of religious education' (*ibid.*, p. 147). It was on this basis that the vacuum of subject content created by Piagetian developmentalism in the early years was filled.

Depth Themes

Grimmitt's 'depth themes' (1973) and Holm's 'human experience themes' (1975) exemplified this approach in its purest form and Grimmitt's work proved particularly influential during the seventies and early eighties. According to Grimmitt, 'depth' themes provide the child with an opportunity to examine his ordinary experiences more closely 'and discern new dimensions within them' (Grimmitt, 1973, p. 54). More particularly, they aimed to 'practise the skill of reflecting on his own experiences at depth, develop insight into himself and his feelings ... other people and their feelings, [and] insight into what constitutes a distinctly human relationship between self and others' (*ibid.*, p. 159). Depth themes could embrace virtually any topic — homes, pets, food, clothes, holidays, colours, shapes — and were purely secular — that is, devoid of religious subject content. However, they were intended by Grimmitt to relate to such content in parallel 'dimensional' themes (based upon Smart's six-dimensional analysis of religion).

Grimmitt devised a schema on three types of implicit, or in his terms 'existential' themes which would run in parallel and interact with, three categories of explicit or 'dimensional' theme at varying stages across the age range of compulsory schooling.[6] Depth themes, which covered the total age span provided the foundation for the whole structure. Since religious concepts and doctrines (allegedly) originally arose from reflection on experience, the child's 'in depth' reflection on common experience should lead him to discover them for himself; or at least to raise the ultimate or 'frontier' questions about life's meaning and purpose which 'are central to religion or religious thinking' *(ibid.,* p. 57). As will be seen below, the recent Westhill project thematic materials (Westhill, 1989) adopt this rationale.

However, it was conceded that the child might need some help in this process, and Grimmitt saw it as the teacher's task to spot links which would enable the child to forge 'conceptual bridges' between the experience derived from depth themes and religious concepts. However, it was his hope that bringing religious concepts 'within the ambit' *(ibid.,* p. 54) of the depth theme — by means of dimensional themes — would be enough to enable the child to spot the link for him/herself. Thus, a 'depth theme' on awe and wonder which focused on the natural world could be linked to a 'dimensional' theme on the religious experience of awe and wonder in the lives of great religious leaders such as Jesus or Muhammad *(ibid.,* pp. 54 and 95); and a depth theme on 'friendship' could provide an experiential basis for religious concepts such as discipleship, forgiveness, self-sacrifice and salvation *(ibid.,* p. 58). Grimmitt's complex schema assumed an extraordinarily high level of existential concern and seriousness in primary school children who were cast in the mold of earnest 1960s radical believers questing for (religious) meaning in the depths of secular experience. Their teachers also were credited with considerable theological sophistication.

Hampshire RE

This thinking was translated into curriculum programmes in many agreed syllabuses of the late seventies and early eighties, most influentially that of Hampshire (1978). This has the following objectives for children of 4–8 (an illustrative selection of topics suggested by the syllabus is given after each objective):

    (a)   to grow in awareness of themselves, and to develop a positive attitude to their own emotions, life and learning (me — who am I? my body, my senses, growing, belonging);

(b) to grow in awareness of others, and to develop relationships in a secure and tolerant setting (families and friends — caring, sharing, helping, listening and belonging; customs);

(c) to develop their interest in and their ability to reflect upon, the world around them (spring — different forms of new life; awakening; spring customs);

(d) to clarify and enlarge their ideas about religion (festivals, places of worship, stories from the religions).

The first three objectives clearly embody the 'implicit'/existential approach and the fourth, the explicit/dimensional. The implicit themes are effectively depth themes and the explicit themes reflect the ritual and mythological dimensions of religion in Smart's terms. The interrelation of the two approaches is emphasized by the syllabus when it points out that the material for objective (d) is 'likely to be interwoven with the material for objectives (a) to (c)' (*ibid.*, p. 16). However, according to the rationale for depth themes, this needn't happen for the topic to contribute to RE. The first Hampshire handbook *Paths to Understanding* (1980) gives a good example of this ambivalence.

Two Infant Schools and the Topic 'Myself'

Two infant schools' interpretations of the agreed syllabus's aims and objectives are included; both choose the theme 'myself' but their treatment of the RE element is very different. The town school feels it necessary to include explicit content in the form of hymns and Bible stories to illustrate the various topics within the theme; for example, in the topic 'senses', the hymn 'God always listens' and the gospel story of blind Bartimaeus (*ibid.*, p. 19). Despite the nominal link, these sit very uneasily in the programme and undoubtedly have the flavour of the token RE element. This school was evidently traditional in its selection of illustrative subject content. Other content, focusing upon initiation/ welcoming ceremonies or naming in world religions might have been more successful. By contrast, the village school includes no explicit religious content in its treatment of the same theme (*ibid.*, pp. 6–9) or in its treatment of the theme 'sharing and caring' (pp. 14–17); however, it does so in its theme 'autumn and winter' in the form of religious festivals (pp. 10–13) which cohere naturally and make a useful contribution to the theme. In an editorial note (p. 5), the village school's purely implicit approach to the themes 'myself' and 'sharing and caring' is justified as RE because its concern is said to be with 'the prerequisites of religious understanding'. However, these 'prerequisites' seem indistinguishable from the prerequisites of general education and personal development.[7]

Schemes such as that of Hampshire tend to assume that the link between the implicit and explicit objectives will be obvious to teachers and that the understanding of religious experience embodied in them is as evident and uncontroversial as the kind of empirical experience under-lying maths and science. Alan Brine's evaluation of the implementation of the middle years section of the Hamsphire agreed syllabus did not confirm this (Brine, 1984). Many teachers did not understand the relation between implicit and explicit RE or how implicit RE contributed to the process of understanding religion (*ibid.*, pp. 76–9). To those, like Grim-mitt and Holm, immersed in the secular theology of the sixties, such 'in depth' exploration of experience led naturally to the discernment of religious concepts and perspectives. This was because, for them, the whole of experience was pregnant with religious meaning. As John Sealey (1985) points out, the implicit approach is 'a religious believer's way of seeing the world' (p. 53).

To those — both teachers and children — who did not share or understand this view, depth and human experience themes seemed to be more evidently associated with environmental studies, moral education or social studies. This whole phase of curriculum development in RE was an exercise in applied secular theology which, it was expected, would be easily understood, readily embraced and effectively implemented by teachers. These expectations were not fulfilled and it was arguably never appropriate for curriculum materials to be based upon such subjective and controversial foundations. It is simply a fact that for many, perhaps most, teachers and children, the in-depth analysis of common experience does not lead to the discovery of explicit religious ideas or concepts, neither does it assist in any very specific way with their understanding.

This is not to deny that the contemplation of nature may have pro-found aesthetic, and spiritual significance; but for many, that 'spiritual' significance does not necessarily relate to the concepts and beliefs of the great world religions. Definitions of the spiritual tend to be orientated either towards a metaphysical notion of humankind's quest for meaning, value and identity (DES, 1980; Grimmitt, 1987), or towards an exper-iential view which more often than not is strongly religious in character (Hay, 1982; Hammond and Hay *et al.*, 1990). But many who would not wish to call themselves religious are moved with awe and wonder by much of what they see and hear of the natural world but would not see this as implying anything beyond itself. Similarly, deep insights into self and relationships may have crucial influence on moral and philosophical understanding; but need say nothing about religion.

The interpretation of experience is dependent upon the framework of ideas which is brought to its interpretation. To interpret experience religiously requires religious language and concepts and these have to be learned, as do the manner and contexts of their use. The argument being presented here does not deny the importance of children realizing the centrality of affective experience to religion. It simply contends that religious experience can only be learned about from religious people and from contact with religion in its various aspects or dimensions. Both children and teachers with religious backgrounds and/or commitments may be able to assist this process but it is unrealistic and inappropriate for religious experience to be manufactured or concocted in the classroom. The experience provided by implicit topics such as those of Hampshire is so general as to be susceptible of numerous interpretations and applications, few of which are easily seen as religious by either teachers or children.

In effect, the implicit approach embraces spirituality, morality and the hidden curriculum under the umbrella of religious education. However, as HMI curriculum documents make clear, the whole curriculum contributes to the spiritual area of experience. Religious education makes its own important and distinctive contribution but is not synonymous with it. Implicit RE in primary schools is the child of the marriage of depth theology and developmental psychology. It has provided subject matter for RE at a time when RE's own proper subject matter was declared largely unsuitable for young children. But the subject matter it has provided and the purview it has claimed greatly exceed the proper boundaries of RE. It is high time for RE to withdraw to its proper boundaries. It is not its job to cater for the total moral and spiritual development of children; however, it has an important contribution to make to that development and at a time when depth theology is nearly forgotten and Piagetian developmentalism and the 'mischievous half truth' of readiness (Bruner, 1974, p. 473) are seriously questioned, the subject's educational profile, in the primary school in particular, cries out for revision. Such a revision should distinguish much more clearly than is the case at present between RE and personal, social and moral education (see Lang, 1988).

The Development of Skills and Attitudes

However, the drafters of the Hampshire agreed syllabus see its implicit objectives as being concerned not only with the exploration of experience relevant and helpful to religious understanding but with the development of key skills and attitudes; indeed it sees this as RE's 'fundamental task' in the first school (*ibid.*, p. 12). Grimmitt also saw his depth themes as developing the skill of reflection on experience. This concern with the development of skills and attitudes reflected general curriculum trends expressed in DES publications of the late seventies (DES, 1977 and 1980). Both the Schools Council's *Groundplan for the Study of Religion* (1977a) and its primary RE project publication *Discovering an Approach* (1977b) were concerned to provide RE with a more precise structure by means of a concepts, skills and attitudes analysis, and Hampshire reflects something of the latter publication's influence. This suggested a structure of four interrelating strands for RE in the primary school:

The exploration of experience
The development of capacities
The development of attitudes
The exploration of religion

The implicit/explicit schema is retained but skills (capacities) and attitudes are separated out as specific concerns of primary school RE.

Several phase 3 agreed syllabuses, notably those of Cambridgeshire, Durham and Berkshire, identify and list skills and attitudes important to RE. Those of Berkshire are:

Skills	**Attitudes**
Enquiry	Curiosity
Expression	Open-mindedness
Empathy	Critical mind
Interpretation	Tolerance
Reasoning	Self-confidence
Meditation	Consideration
	Appreciation
	Commitment

The syllabus points out (Berkshire, 1982, p. 9) that much general topic work in primary schools which has no religious subject content can help to foster these skills and attitudes and thus help to achieve the aims and objectives of RE.

However, even those skills and attitudes which are particularly important for RE — empathy, reflection, respect and consideration for others — are also important for other subjects, and their development should be central to schools' 'hidden curriculum'. The incorporation into RE of themes having no religious subject content but aiming to develop such skills and attitudes must be questioned. This does not mean that it should not be recognized that such skills and attitudes are relevant to the RE process wherever they are developed; but it does preclude the content and context of such work where it makes no reference to religion from being counted as RE. RE should be concerned with showing how such skills and attitudes can be developed through the study of religion — visiting, for example a church or mosque, interviewing religious people, observing a religious rite or ceremony.

Ultimate Questions

The Westhill project thematic materials,[8] published in autumn 1990, follow phase 2 thinking in selecting 'ultimate questions' as their major rationale. The project handbook (Westhill, 1986) adopts the implicit/explicit schema although with new terminology — 'shared human experience' and 'traditional belief systems'.[9] By 'shared human experience' is meant experience which is common to all or most human beings but which is also 'significant'; that is, experiences which 'have prompted and continue to prompt puzzling or ultimate questions about life (*ibid.*, p. 16). 'Ultimate questions' are defined in a more recent Westhill publication as 'questions to which people respond by saying what they believe, questions to which there are no final answers but answers of faith' (Westhill, 1989, p. 7). The project identifies seven areas raising such 'ultimate questions': authority, meaning value, purpose, identity, origins and destiny. Examples of 'ultimate questions arising from these areas, some of which surely do not fulfil the requirements of the above definition, are:

Why should I do as you say?
Is there a God?
What is truth?
What is most important to me?
Why don't we care?
What is life for?
Who am I?
When does life start?
Why are we different?

The 'life themes' approach aims to explore 'an aspect of shared human experience in order to develop an understanding of that experience and the ultimate questions it raises' (*ibid.*, p. 41). In the project's materials, the following life themes are developed, each being broken down into four topics:

The natural world
Relationships
Rules and issues
Stages of life
Celebrations
Lifestyles

The topics within each theme are each illustrated by five pictures, three on general experience and two on religious illustrations/answers. Thus the topic on 'fruits of the earth' (which is one of the topics deriving from the theme 'The natural world') has pictures on harvest, coal mining and fishing together with pictures of a harvest festival in a church and the Jewish festival of Sukkot. These are accompanied by notes giving suggestions for work and further background information for teachers. Illustrations of how the various topics and pictures could contribute to fulfilling attainment targets in science and language are also given. The quality of the materials is very good and they give teachers many good ideas.

The danger with the 'ultimate questions' rationale is that most of the questions are so broad and susceptible of answers at so many levels and from so many disciplinary and religio-philosophical standpoints that focusing on orthodox religious answers or illustrations may have the appearance of apologetic contrivance. Good teaching will always encourage children to ask questions, but not only are many of the questions listed above of an inappropriate nature and level for primary school children, they are manifestly intended to provide openings for religious answers. Already formulated religious 'answers' seem to be going in search of questions which enable them to show their relevance to human life. The whole approach is firmly rooted in apologetic secular theology with its concern to show (allegedly sceptical, secularized 1960s person) the relevance of religious answers to many of the questions raised by an in-depth exploration of 'secular' experience. It is quite possible to establish meaningful and natural connections between religion and common experience without resorting to this dated theological device with its confessional associations. However, the Westhill thematic materials offer many good things to teachers and children despite their rationale!

It is this writer's view that the continued use of the implicit/explicit framework for the subject in the new world of the National Curriculum is an unwise policy and that it is a pity that the Westhill team (Westhill, 1989) and the FARE project (Copley and Priestley, 1990)[10] chose to continue to employ it in their suggestions for attainment targets in RE. The Westhill team identify three profile components':

A   Knowledge and understanding of religious belief and practice.
B   Awareness of life experiences and the questions they raise.
C   Exploring and responding.

C, which has just one attainment target, is concerned with the development of skills, attitudes and 'personal responses'. (The last mentioned includes semi-devotional activities and has clear nurturing overtones.) The team acknowledges the problems associated with implicit approaches, especially the danger that 'you can do it without any reference to religion' (*ibid.*, p. 7). However, it feels that the approach makes the subject accessible and relevant to children and young people and opens up possibilities for cross curricular work.

Although many good and educationally acceptable ideas emerge from both the life themes materials and the 1989 handbook, it is this writer's view that the theoretical paraphernalia of the implicit/explicit rationale with its outdated and inappropriate theological assumptions should be jettisoned or 'retired' in David Attfield's gentler phrase! (Attfield, 1984, p. 10). Rather than form a distinct 'implicit' approach or profile component as in B above, suggestions should simply be given as to how the attainment targets and statements of profile components such as A and C can be approached through integrated topic work. Good teachers will always be looking for ways of making subject matter interesting to children and this will sometimes involve starting from something familiar to them and relating the subject to that. But let implicit RE remain as it began — simply a teaching method.

Good Practice in Topic Work in RE

Integrated topic work can offer a means whereby RE can make a meaningful contribution to children's education and be part of the main-stream of the educational process in the era of the National Curriculum. However, the publication of the attainment targets of the foundation subjects will inevitably see an increasing emphasis on topics drawn from these subjects as well as the core subjects. RE will be able to contribute more naturally to topics deriving from more history, geography and language attainment targets than most others; but the danger will be that RE's ambivalent basic curriculum status will see it dancing wholly to other subjects' tunes, if it dances at all! It is this writer's view that, where a topic approach to curriculum planning and implementation is adopted, RE coordinators will need to ensure that some subject-based RE topics are included in topic programmes in order to ensure that RE receives coherent and structured rather than piecemeal and marginal treatment.

Good topic practice in RE is practice in which both the best traditions of topic and RE are respected. Respecting the best topic practice will involve the careful selection, planning and structuring of topics on a whole school basis; the use of varied teaching methods, particularly those actively involving the child in his/her own learning and utilizing, where possible, first hand experience; and the provision of adequate resource material. Respecting RE will involve ensuring that the following preconditions are fulfilled:

(i) It should be included as part of a whole school approach to curriculum planning and not left to individual teachers to deal with as and when they can.

(ii) Some of the themes and topics chosen should be suitable for the natural inclusion of significant aspects of RE and consideration should be given to including religious topics also to ensure that (iii) may reasonably be fulfilled.

(iii)   There should be pattern and coherence in the total experience of RE which the programme provides (that is, that it should relate to the aims and objectives or attainment targets of an agreed syllabus or a school RE syllabus)

In order to ensure that these preconditions are fulfilled, the appointment of RE coordinators for schools is vital.[11]

A Checklist of Key Questions to Ask

It will be helpful for teachers to ask the following questions when planning the RE contribution to an integrated topic:

(a)   What are my aims and objectives for the topic as a whole and the RE element in particular?

(b)   What significant knowledge, concepts, skills and attitudes important in the RE process does this topic naturally allow?

(c)   Does the RE content of the topic make the children think as well as add to their knowledge?

(d)   Does the RE content really enhance the children's understanding of the topic?

(e)   What range of learning experience is being provided for the children in the topic as a whole and in the RE aspects in particular?

(f)   What provision has been made for the first-hand experience in the topic as a whole and the RE aspects in particular?

(g)   How does the RE content of this topic contribute to the total programme of RE for the class?

(h)   Is there an adequate range and variety of resources to satisfy the children's learning needs?

Commentary on Selected Key Questions

Significant Knowledge

It will be clear by now that the understanding of religion which underlies this chapter is defined by the concepts, beliefs, practices, customs and traditions of the major world religions. It will also be clear that by religious education is meant first of all the process of coming to a knowledge and understanding of these religions and in particular

Christianity and the principal religions practised in Britain (Education Reform Act, 1988, para. 8.).

In this process, the use of religious language and the exploration of the meaning of key religious concepts should figure from earliest times, as Brenda Watson argues (1987) (p. 159). Such language and concepts will already be familiar even to infants through school worship; classroom work should give children the opportunity to explore the meaning of these terms in an open, discursive educational context. Piagetian developmentalism has resulted in a serious neglect of the use and exploration of religious language and ideas with infants and lower juniors and the application of Bruner's spiral curriculum approach to its development in RE is long overdue.

It is the subject content of religion and the concepts which underlie it which form the 'core of RE', not the implicit/existential quest for meaning (Grimmitt, 1973, p. 51); and knowledge of this subject content is necessary for teachers to do their jobs in RE. Luckily, there are now a great many clearly and concisely written books which will assist non-specialists (see 'selected resources' under references at the end of the chapter) and lots of sensible advice to guide them (David Day's contribution of the *Shap Handbook on World Religions in Education* (edited by Brown, 1987) is a good example).

This greater subject focus will not mean a narrow academic study divorced from children's experience, provided that methods such as those listed below are used; neither will it mean indoctrination if children are encouraged to evaluate and discuss religious language and ideas, including the frank recognition of alternative ideas and perspectives. Many children come from homes in which religious belief and/or practice does not figure and some come from anti-religious homes. It is not the purpose of RE to nurture children into a religious view of life; an adequate education in this area must take secularism and agnosticism seriously and not patronizingly. Every child's story should count and all can be put to good educational use by sensitive and caring teachers.

Good RE practice will involve:

— exploring the meaning and use of religious language in life, story and ceremony;
— utilizing local religious buildings — churches, mosques, synagogues etc. as educational resources;
— meeting and talking with representatives of religions in the community;
— encouraging the children to share their personal knowledge and experience of religion;
— becoming aware of typical and important religious activities — worship, prayer, festivals etc;
— discussing religious concepts, beliefs and behaviour openly;

— discovering how religious beliefs affect people's lives, behaviour and attitudes;
— exploring the influence of religions on culture and society — starting with the local community.

All of these activities are well within the capacity of primary school children and will involve the development of important transferable skills and attitudes as well as the acquisition of knowledge and understanding.

A simple test to ensure that question (b) is satisfied is by asking the following supplementary question:

Does the RE content of the topic involve the children in the use of distinctive religious language and concepts?

If it does not, then it will not contribute significantly to the children's religious education although it may support the RE. process through, for example, the development of key skills and attitudes. But beware, RE coordinators, of too many topics in which the RE contribution is given solely in terms of skills and attitudes!

Making the Children Think

It is all too easy for RE to become multifact religious education (Grimmitt, 1987, p. 137). Good topic practice stresses the importance of children's active involvement in the learning process and the development of their thinking (Schools Councils, 1972; SCDC, 1985; Stewart, 1986; Wilson, 1984; Antonouris and Wilson, 1989). A greater focus on carefully organized investigative activities along the lines indicated above, and on group work in topic practice in RE, would enhance this aspect greatly. A large part of understanding religion is understanding people who are religious and how they think and behave; and children can derive more of the feel and ethos of religions from visits to religious buildings, especially when worship is taking place, than from books or videos however well written or produced.

It is far more educative for children to meet, listen to, question and talk with religious people than to have doubtful 'religious' experiences contrived for them in the classroom or to derive all their information from secondary sources. It is also far more educative for them to work together on carefully prepared resources in well organized group work and to discuss and report back on this than to sit and listen and then write. Rather than try to direct children's attention to 'ultimate' questions, encouragement should be given to them to formulate their own questions and, as often as possible, to find their own answers. However, there is a central role for teacher formulated questioning also. Wilson emphasizes the importance of carefully structured questioning designed to classify, interpret, extrapolate from and evaluate information (Antonouris and Wilson, 1989, pp. 15–16) and his work on developing and assessing children's thinking by means of a 'concept ladder' has value for RE (Wilson, 1984).

Good RE Topic Practice in Practice

The same student whose experience of 'spiders' is described and discussed at the beginning of this chapter had a more fortunate situation on her final teaching practice. In this, she found herself in a junior school on the outskirts of a well-known seaside resort. Serial visits in the term preceding her practice allowed her to develop a good relationship with the class of top juniors with which she had been placed. After some discussion with the head, the class teacher and the college tutor, the topic 'caring' was selected. The student felt that this gave her plenty of scope for good work in both RE and moral education. She found the Westhill project handbook (Westhill, 1986, p. 40) helpful but, like all good teachers, developed her own ideas. The key idea which she tried to develop through the theme was that of motivation to caring — why people go out of their way to care for others, often in face of hardship and danger to themselves. The key concepts were those of 'vocation', 'call', 'duty' and 'service'.

She selected case studies which illustrated varying kinds of motivation to caring: (i) from Indian religion (Hinduism) and culture — Gandhi's work for the outcastes; (ii) from Christianity — Mother Theresa and her work in Calcutta; and (iii) from a voluntary institution with strong local roots — the lifeboat service. She was anxious to avoid a common fault of much RE practice — a tendency towards preaching and, in this case, the suggestion that all caring must be religiously motivated. The case study of the local lifeboat station was intended to illustrate that not all caring was necessarily religiously inspired. Individual lifeboatmen had varying motivations, but prominent among them was a sense of tradition, service and duty. The theme attempted to show how religions provided inspiration for caring whilst indicating also that not all caring was religiously inspired.

The topic was planned to last about eight weeks and covered a large part of the broad curriculum — *history* (of India, the Raj, Indian politics and nationalist movements, the life of Gandhi; of the lifeboat service nationally and locally); *geography* (village and town life, the Indian economy, poverty and wealth); *social studies* (the caste system, traditional social customs, dress, food); RE (Hindu and Christian concepts and beliefs — notably ahimsa (non–injury/violence) as a religious and political principle, the religious duty to love one's neighbour, the religious understanding of vocation as the call of God, the expression of these beliefs and values in the lives of Gandhi and Mother Theresa); *moral education* (the concepts of justice, duty, responsibility). In addition, the children saw something of the art and heard some of the music of India; and undertook plenty of creative work in *art, handicraft, language and drama* (see below).

The class was used to formal class teaching but the student organized the children into groups and involved them in as much *group research, discussion and activity* as proved practicable. She amassed an impressive array of *resources*, including video material on Gandhi and numerous *artefacts and pictures as well as books and stories* on all aspects of the theme. An *assembly* was organized on the story of the blind men and the elephant which involved the children in dressing up in Indian dress, helping to make a model elephant and of course narrating and acting the story in front of the school. There was *a visit* to the local lifeboat station, *interviews* with the coxwain and crew on the basis of both *prepared and spontaneous questions*, an inspection of the lifeboat, and stories of rescues and personalities off the east coast. These activities were of course designed to develop key skills and attitudes which were duly listed and evaluated by the student.

A few readers will by now be smiling knowingly and reflecting on their own superhuman efforts to achieve a high grade on final TP. This example is not intended to illustrate normal practice but to underline the key ingredients of good — but not perfect — practice. The student's summative evaluation found that the children still found difficulty in understanding why people should, in a well known Yorshire phrase, 'do owt for nowt'; but that they had shown significant advances on the pre-practice evaluation in their knowledge and understanding of the key ideas of Hinduism and Christianity. They had found the case study of Mother Theresa particularly warming and admired the courage and determination of Mahatma Gandhi and the lifeboatmen. The student felt that she had perhaps included too much material and expected too much of a rather moderate class with more than its share of socially and educationally 'difficult' children; and there was probably truth in these reflections. But the classroom displays and the children's enthusiasm, hard work and sheer enjoyment of the experience said quite enough about the success of the topic.

This chapter has been more concerned with principles than with detailed, worked through examples of practice. It is hoped, however, that teachers will find the criteria it cites helpful in assessing topic suggestions in curriculum materials such as those listed at the end of the chapter, and in planning their own topic work in RE in all phases. However, the new situation in which all schools and teachers find themselves under the National Curriculum poses fresh challenges to RE and we are only in the early stages of attempting to meet those challenges. It is also hoped that this chapter has given some helpful pointers to assist this process.

Notes

1 Thus, Harold Loukes, argues:

> A lesson on spiders, an argument about Charles I, a study of the climate of Peru, the story of Oedipus: these are all as 'religious' as the story of Abraham if they are treated personally and set the hearers off into the depth ...' (Loukes, 1965, p. 164)

2 In RE the term 'theme' has generally been preferred to 'topic' (Goldman, 1965a; Grimmitt, 1973; Holm, 1975). John Hull argues that 'theme' connotes something broader than 'topic' (Hull, 1984, p. 125); thus, 'change', 'communication' and 'difference' might be thought of as themes whereas 'hands', 'babies' and 'pets' might more appropriately be designated topics. The first Hampshire RE handbook (Hampshire, 1980) tends to favour this view, often using 'topic' of the constituent elements of 'themes' ('... to illustrate how these themes may be broken down into topics ...' p. 48). This usage is also adopted by the recent Westhill project, which, like Goldman, designates themes 'life themes'. (Westhill, 1986 and 1990). However, the later Hampshire handbook (Hampshire, 1986) prefers 'topic', with 'sub-theme' being used for the elements making up the topic. There is clearly no uniform pattern, and, in Hull's (1984) definition.

> A theme is a unit of work organised around a topic which is known to the child from first hand experience. (p. 125)

the two terms could easily be interchanged. Kerry and Eggleston (1988) have the following:

> Topic work includes all those areas of the curriculum (other than basic reading and number skills) which are explored in a thematic way. (p. 18)

3 The seven dimensions which 'help to characterize religions as they exist in the world' are now the 'Practical and Ritual', the 'Experiential and Emotional', the 'Narrative or Mythic', the 'Doctrinal and Philosophical', the 'Ethical and Legal', the 'Social and Institutional' and the 'Material'. This additional seventh dimension is said by Smart to be 'the incarnation of the "Social and Institutional" dimension in material form' (*The World's Religions*, 1989, p. 21). The original six dimensions were the Ritual, the Experiential, the Mythological, the Doctrinal, the Ethical and the Social (*The Religious Experience of Mankind*, 1969).

4 In RE programmes for primary schools during the seventies and eighties, explicit subject content was almost universally selected from the ritual, experiential and mythological dimensions. Such material, dealing with the colourful externals, affective experiences and stories of religions, was deemed suitable for children at the intuitive and concrete operational stages of development. Doctrinal, ethical and social material was considered appropriate for secondary RE. Among recent writers, Derek Bastide uses

Smart's dimensions in his introduction to RE in primary schools (Bastide, 1987, pp. 26–34) and most recently, Mary Hayward has used Smart's seven-dimensional analysis in framing attainment targets for RE (Jackson and Starkings, 1990, chapter 2). It is the argument of this chapter that more emphasis should be given in primary RE to developing religious concepts and language. A rather wooden interpretation of Piagetian stage theory has often resulted in the material drawn from these dimensions being used in a purely illustrative and factual way which avoids cognitive challenge and the exploration of language. The full exploitation of the use of story can do much to rectify this but it is possible to make language and concepts an important focus when using any religious material.

5 The 'New Theology' of the early 1960s, also frequently called 'secular' theology was popularized by Bishop John Robinson's book *Honest to God* (1963). This drew upon the thinking of three leading radical theologians (Bultmann, Bonhoeffer and Tillich) and suggested a retranslation of Christian belief into the language and thought of the twentieth century. Tillich's attempt to utilize the language of depth psychology in this process was particularly influential in RE, as Grimmitt's *What Can I Do in RE?* illustrates (see especially chapters 2, 4 and 5). Mixed, the case of Loukes, with his Quaker natural theology which had a somewhat Wordsworthian flavour to it, and the ideas of the German theologian Rudolph Otto, the major assumptions of this theology as they were applied to RE may be summarized as follows:

(i) that the concepts and beliefs of religions originally derived from reflection on human experience;

(ii) that reflection in depth on common experience today may lead to the discovery or rediscovery of religious concepts and beliefs.

More specifically, it was held:

(iii) that religions arose as ways of answering the 'ultimate' questions (about the meaning of life, death, suffering etc.) that life experiences raise;

(iv) that certain types of experience (for example, awe and wonder) were particularly important in generating religious concepts and beliefs (this idea owes much to Rudolph Otto's important study *The Idea of the Holy* (ET, 1923);

(v) that (therefore) if children and young people explore their experience in depth, are made aware of the ultimate questions which life experiences raise, and experience awe and wonder, they will encounter the experiential basis of religion and will thus be able to understand, and relate to, the concepts and doctrines of explicit religion when they are introduced to them.

This whole process of thought is highly questionable. Even if religion arose in the way suggested, the vast cultural changes which have ensued since the origins of religion mean that modern humans may not so easily arrive at religious concepts and beliefs or find religious answers to life's questions as persuasive as primitive humans. Moreover, it is simply a fact that for the great majority of people, religious beliefs and concepts are learned in childhood and related to experience. They do not derive from experience. Religious awe and wonder (Otto's 'sense of the numinous') results from bringing the concept of God or the supernatural *to* experience. It is qualitatively quite different from naturalistic awe and wonder. The notion that the experience of awe and wonder at the beauty of nature will somehow generate the idea of God, or provide an experiential basis for it in children's minds is simplistic and romantic. It reflects the adult experience of believers with a mature grasp of religious concepts; it in no way reflects how they derived those concepts in the first place. Religious education in schools should begin, as this chapter argues, with the introduction and exploration of religion in the cultural and social environment of the child and should have special regard for religious concepts and language. It should not be the job of teachers to concoct an experiential basis of such concepts and language; this should develop with the child's growing awareness of their use in a variety of contexts. Language and experience belong together.

6   Grimmitt's three 'existential' types of theme are 'depth themes' (from age 5), 'symbol and language themes' (from age 9) and 'situation themes' (from age 11). These run in parallel with three 'dimensional' types of theme based on Experiential, Mythological and Ritual material (from age 5), Social and Ethical material (from age 11), and Doctrinal material (from age 14).

7   Implicit RE is said to consist of the 'sum of the child's experiences' from which he/she is able to develop 'those basic sensitivities without which no person can develop fully and without which the religious quest cannot even be begun' (Hampshire, 1980, p. 2). These sensitivities and attitudes are said to include 'wonder in the face of the mysteries of existence and growth; reverence for life; development of moral discernment' (*ibid.*). However, these are described as 'basic building blocks for an understanding of any subject and which should be developed by the total school curriculum' (*ibid.*). It is one thing for RE to be said to draw on general educational and personal skills, attitudes and experiences; it is another for them all to be embraced within RE.

8   I am indebted to John Rudge and Geoff Teece for kindly allowing me to see extracts from these materials before they were published.

9   A third aspect is added to the RE process by the Westhill project — 'Individual Patterns of Belief'. This is the contribution of personal knowledge, experience and insight which children and teachers bring to their classroom work. However, it is clear that it is the other two approaches which constitute the main framework for RE since they form the basis for the project's curriculum materials. It is, nonetheless, helpful for this important aspect of the educational process to be highlighted in this way.

10 The FARE project interim report (Copley and Priestley, 1990) identifies two profile components for RE — (A) Reflection on meaning; and (B) Knowledge and understanding of religious belief, practice and language. (A), which is clearly the implicit approach has three attainment targets ((i) Awareness of mystery; (ii) Questions of meaning; (iii) Values and commitments). (B), the explicit approach, also has three attainment targets ((iv) Religious belief; (v) Religious practice, (vi) Religious language).

11 The crucial importance of the appointment of RE coordinators in primary, first and middle schools to ensure continuity and progression in topic/ thematic work in RE is stressed by HMI in a recent report (DES, 1989, paragraph 39, p. 9).

References

ANTONOURIS, G. and WILSON, J. (1989) *Equal Opportunities in Schools: New Dimensions in Topic Work*, London, Nichols Publishing/Cassells.

AREAI (1989) *Religious Education for Ages 5 to 16/18*, Association of Religious Education Advisers and Inspectors (may be obtained from St Martin's College, Lancaster).

ATTFIELD, D. (1976) 'Conceptual research in religious education', *Learning for Living*, **15**, 3, spring.

ATTFIELD, D. (1984) 'Implicit religions', *British Journal of Religious Education*, **7**, 1, autumn.

BASTIDE, D. (1987) *Religious Education 5–12*, Lewes, Falmer Press.

BENNETT, N. and DESFORGES, C. (1985) *Recent Advances in Classroom Research*, Edinburgh, Scottish Academic Press.

BERKSHIRE COUNTY COUNCIL (1982) *Religious Heritage and Personal Quest*, Reading, Berkshire County Council.

BERKSHIRE COUNTY COUNCIL (1990) *Religious Heritage and Personal Quest Principles into Practice*, Reading, Berkshire County Council.

BLYTH, W.A.L. *et al.* (1976) *Place, Time and Society 8–13*, London, Collins.

BOTTERY, M. (1990) *The Morality of the School*, London, Cassell.

BRINE, A. (1984) *The Agreed Syllabus for Religious Education in the Middle Years*, London, Schools Council.

BRUNER, J. (1960) *The Process of Education*, Cambridge, MA, Harvard University Press.

BRUNER, J. (1974) *Beyond the Information Given*, London, Allen and Unwin.

CAMBRIDGESHIRE COUNTY COUNCIL (1982) *Religious Education 4–16*, Agreed Syllabus of Religious Education, Cambridge, Cambridgeshire County Council.

COPLEY, T. and PRIESTLEY, J. (1990) *A FARE Deal for RE: The FARE Project: An Interim Report*, Exeter, University of Exeter School of Education.

COX, E. and CAIRNS, J. (1989) *Reforming Religious Education*, London, Kogan Page.

DES (1977) *Curriculum 11–16*, London, HMSO.

DES (1980) *A View of the Curriculum*, London, HMSO.

DES (1988) *Science for Ages 5 to 16*, London, HMSO.

DES (1989) *Agreed Syllabuses and Religious Education*: The Influence of the Agreed Syllabus on Teaching and Learning in Religious Education in three Local Education Authorities, London, HMSO.

DURHAM COUNTY COUNCIL (1982a) *Growing in Understanding*, Durham, Durham County Council.

DURHAM COUNTY COUNCIL (1982b) *Aids to Growing in Understanding*, Durham, Durham County Council.

EGGLESTON, J. and KERRY, T. (1985) 'Integrated studies' in BENNETT, N. and

DESFORGES, C. (Eds) *Recent Advances in Classroom Research*, Edinburgh, Scottish Academic Press.

GALTON, M., SIMON, B. and CROLL, C. (1980) *Inside the Primary Classroom*, London, Routledge and Kegan Paul.

GOLDMAN, R. (1964) *Religious Thinking from Childhood to Adolescence*, London, Routlege and Kegan Paul.

GOLDMAN, R. (1965a) *Readiness for Religion*, London, Routledge and Kegan Paul.

GOLDMAN, R. (Ed.) (1965b) The 'Readiness for Religion' booklets (Rupert Hart Davis) written by various people including P. and F. CLIFF, R. DINGWALL, M. HUGHES.

GRIMMITT, M. (1973) *What Can I Do in RE?*, Great Wakering, Mayhew McCrimmon.

GRIMMITT, M. (1987) *Religious Education and Human Development*, Great Wakering, McCrimmon.

GUNNING, S., GUNNING, D. and WILSON, J. (1981) *Topic Teaching in the Primary School*, London, Croom Helm.

HAMMOND, J., HAY, D. *et al.* (1990) *New Methods in RE Teaching: An Experiential Approach*, Harlow, Oliver and Boyd.

HAMPSHIRE COUNTY COUNCIL (1978) *Religious Education in Hampshire Schools*, Winchester, Hampshire County Council.

HAMPSHIRE COUNTY COUNCIL (1980) *Paths to Understanding*, London, Macmillan Education.

HAMPSHIRE COUNTY COUNCIL (1986) *Following the Paths*, London, Macmillan Education.

HAY, D. (1982) *Exploring Inner Space*, London, Penguin.

HOLM, J. (1975) *Teaching Religion in School*, Oxford, Oxford University Press.

HULL, J.M. (1984) *Studies in Religion and Education*, Lewes Falmer Press.

HUMBERSIDE COUNTY COUNCIL (1981) *Agreed Syllabus of Religious Education*, Hull, Humberside County Council.

ILEA (1984) *Religious Education for Our Children*, London, ILEA.

JACKSON, R. and STARKINGS, D. (Eds) (1990) *The Junior RE Handbook*, Cheltenham, Stanley Thornes.

KERRY, T. and EGGLESTON, J. (1988) *Topic Work in the Primary School*, London, Routledge.

LANG, P. (Ed.) (1988) *Thinking about Personal and Social Education in the Primary School*, Oxford, Blackwell.

LEALMAN, B. (Ed.) (1980) *The Total Curriculum in Relation to RE*, London, CEM.

LOUKES, H. (1961) *Teenage Religion*, London, SCM Press.

LOUKES, H. (1963) *Readiness for Religion*, London, Friends Home Service Committee.

LOUKES, H. (1965) *New Ground in Christian Education*, London, SCM Press.

MANCHESTER CITY COUNCIL (1985) *Multifaith Manchester: Agreed Syllabus for Religious Education*, Manchester, Manchester City Council.

MUMFORD, C. (1979) *Young Children and Religion*, London, Edward Arnold.

OLDHAM METROPOLITAN BOROUGH COUNCIL (1989) *Religious Education: Agreed Syllabus*, Oldham, Metropolitan Borough Council.

OLDHAM METROPOLITAN BOROUGH COUNCIL (1990) *A Book of Curriculum Plans and Resources to Accompany the Agreed Syllabus*, Oldham, Metropolitan Borough Council.

PLOWDEN REPORT (1967) *Children and their Primary Schools*, London, HMSO.

RELIGIOUS EDUCATION COUNCIL (1989) *Handbook for Agreed Syllabus Conferences SACREs and Schools*, Lancaster, REC (may be obtained from St Martin's College, Lancaster).

ROTHERHAM METROPOLITAN BOROUGH COUNCIL (1989) *Building Together: The Agreed Syllabus for Religious Education*, Rotherham, Metropolitan Borough Council.

SCDC (1985) *Developing Pupils' Thinking Through Topic Work*, Harlow, Longmans.

SALFORD, CITY OF (1987) *Religious Education Planning and Practice*, City of Salford Education Department.

SCHOOLS COUNCIL (1971) *Religious Education in Secondary Schools*, London, Evans Methuen.

SCHOOLS COUNCIL (1972) *With Objectives in Mind: Science 5–13*, London, MacDonald.

SCHOOLS COUNCIL (1977a) *A Groundplan for the Study of Religion*, London, Schools Council.

SCHOOLS COUNCIL (1977b) *Discovering an Approach*, London, Macmillan Educational.

SEALEY, J. (1985) *Religious Education: Philosophical Perspectives*, London Allen and Unwin.

SIMON, B. and WILLCOCKS, J. (1981) *Research and Practice in the Primary Classroom*, London, Routledge and Kegan Paul.

SLEE , N. (1986) 'Goldman yet again: An overview and critique of his contribution to research', *British Journal of Religious Education*, **8**, 2, spring.

SLEE, N. (1987) 'The development of religious thinking: some linguistic considerations', *British Journal of Religious Education*, 9, 2, spring.

SMART, N. (1969) *The Religious Experience of Mankind*, London, Collins.

SMART, N. (1989) *The World's Religions*, Cambridge, Cambridge University Press.

STEWART, N. (1986) *Developing Children's Thinking Through Topic Work*, Hull, Humberside Polytechnic.

STEWART, N. (1988) *Integration or Disintegration? Developing a Policy for Topic Work in the Primary School*, Hull, Humberside Polytechnic.

SURREY COUNTY COUNCIL (1987) *The Agreed Syllabus for Religious Education in Surrey*, Croydon, Surrey County Council.

TANN, S. (1988) *Developing Topic Work in the Primary School*, Lewes, Falmer Press.

TEECE, G. (1990) 'Attainment and early years RE', *Child Education*, November.

TICKNER, M. and WEBSTER, D. (Eds) (1982) *Religious Education and the Imagination*, Hull, University of Hull.

WATSON, B. (1987) *Education and Belief*, Oxford, Blackwell.

WESTHILL (1986) *How Do I Teach RE?*, London, Mary Glasgow.

WESTHILL (1989) *Attainment in RE*, Regional RE Centre (Midlands), Westhill College.

WESTHILL (1990) *Life Themes in the Early Years*, Cheltenham, Stanley Thornes.

WILSON, J. (1984) 'Concept ladders in primary school topic work', *Trent Papers in Education*, **84**, 2, Trent Polytechnic.

Selected Recommended Resources and Guides to Good Practice

BASTIDE, D. (1987) *Religious Education 5–12* (Falmer Press) — An very readable guide to the theory and practice of primary RE, including an introduction to thematic teaching more sympathetic to implicit approaches than this chapter; and a concise, informative guide to the key aspects of the major world religions.

BERKSHIRE COUNTY COUNCIL (1990) *Religious Heritage and Personal Quest: Principles into Practice* (Berkshire County Council) — Contains many useful examples of themes deriving from the Berkshire Agreed Syllabus's seven-dimensional analysis of RE (based upon Smart's six-dimensional analysis of religion) and providing a skills and attitudes analysis of each one. Is not strong in its treatment of 'Concepts and beliefs' and still retains much phase 2 thinking and practice in its 'implicit' suggestions.

BROWN, A. (Ed.) (1987) *The Shap Handbook on World Religions in Education* (Commission for Racial Equality) — An excellent authoritative guide to resources for teaching world religions and also containing many helpful, brief, practical essays on good classroom practice and current issues.

Christian Education Movement 'Exploring a Theme' series includes many booklets, each devoted to exploring a specific theme; these include myself, places of worship, journeys, food, communities, stones, harvest, fire, spring festivals, water, festivals of light, barriers, special books, gifts and gift bringers, symbols, questions, and leaders. A very helpful series but some of the above criticisms of implicit RE apply on occasions.

COLE, W.O. (1984) *Six Religions in the Twentieth Century* (Hulton) — A very informative, clearly written introduction to the six major world religions — Buddhism, Christianity Hinduism, Islam, Judaism and Sikhism.

HAMPSHIRE COUNTY COUNCIL (1986) *Following the Paths* (Macmillan) — Contains a useful introductory essay on topic planning and six suggested themes (change, food, an approach to India, memories and remembering, belonging, difference) covering the whole primary age range worked through in detail.

JACKSON, R. and STARKINGS, D. (Eds) (1990) *The Junior RE Handbook* (Stanley Thornes) — Contains brief, practical essays on most aspects of primary RE.

RANKIN, J., BROWN, A. and HAYWARD, M. (1989) *Religious Education Topics for the Primary School* (Longmans) — Gives examples of subject based topics in three age groups — 5–7, 7–9, and 9–11 — to be followed during 1991 by a companion book (same authors and publisher) *RE Topics Across the Curriculum*. Very sound and practical.

WEBB, J. (1990) *Multi-Faith Topics in the Primary School* (Cassell) — Includes brief but clear introductions to Christianity, Hinduism, Islam and Judaism and seven topics worked out in detail.

WESTHILL (1986) *How Do I Teach RE?* (Mary Glasgow) — Contains sensible and practical advice on planning integrated topic work (pp. 39–49) although its two specified approaches to RE ('systems' and 'life themes') are too prescriptive in their structure.

WESTHILL (1989) *Attainment in RE* (Regional RE Centre (Midlands) Westhill College) — Gives some useful examples of themes, based on attainment statements for the two primary key stages — food and home and families for key stage 1; and beginnings, and special place for key stage 2. All of these are worked through in detail with example content, questions to raise, teaching and learning activities and assessment suggestions.

WESTHILL (1990) *Life Themes in the Early Years* (Stanley Thornes) — See text of chapter for commentary. Despite old fashioned rationale, these materials are of excellent quality and offer a great deal to children and teachers.

9   The Use of Artefacts in the Classroom

Vida Barnett

'But It's Only a Candle . . .'

The infants pushed their way through the school doors, carefully carrying cardbox tubes from the inside of toilet rolls and rolls of paper towels. On the hall table they saw the three candles used in the previous day's assembly, candles used in Christian naming ceremonies. They chattered among themselves, remembering the visitors, the singing, the discussions which followed in the classroom. John, Hyam, Shavinda, Khadija began to sing: 'This little light of mine, I'm going to let it shine . . .' A member of staff had brought her new baby to visit them. Sweets had been passed round so that everyone could join in the celebration. She shared her hopes for the baby's future — that she would be happy and healthy and help people. What values did the children think were important? Young Ben thought that the baby should grow up, make a lot of money and buy ice-creams whenever she wanted to, but Karen said she hoped the baby would learn how to make people happy. Other suggestions included the securing of a job, a big house, lots of clothes, a place in the local football team (!), popularity. Why?

The baby's grandfather shared his memories of the baby's naming ceremony. She was called Louise. He had been given a candle to put in her bedroom, to be lit on each birthday. The minister asked him to help her bring light, warmth, freedom from fear to the people she met — helping, teaching, giving, warning.

Umar described what happened when *his* baby sister was brought home from hospital. Their parents wanted her to grow up to follow God, who is 'Light', to follow the example of Muhammad, (p.b.u.h.), also described as a light. Bahadur told how Guru Nanak's father wanted him to be wealthy, but Nanak wanted to be a light and teach people — that was more important to him than having lots of money and power.

The headteacher showed them a statue of Mary, Joseph and baby Jesus. What hopes and fears had they for their son? Might he become a good carpenter, a rabbi? What did Jesus think important when he grew up? Why do Christians sometimes call him 'The Light of the World?'

The infants decorated pieces of paper with pictures of a naming ceremony, or of a young child being a 'light'. They fastened them to the cardboard tubes and mounted them on a wall display with appropriate sentences. In another classroom, posters of light-giving situations were designed, songs and poems composed. One group imagined they *were* candles and described *their* feelings during the ceremony. Fonts were designed and decorated with narrative and symbolic patterns, as were naming cards. Others discussed posters from OXFAM, Christian Aid, Justice and Peace, the Salvation Army. Imaginary stories were written to illustrate the posters. A Muslim boy wrote of what he thought Muhammad's family would have wished for him, a Jewish girl of Moses' parents. How had they become 'lights'? Older children collected examples of other ceremonies when lights were used, and why — Advent, Christmas, Easter, funerals, marriages, private prayers, the Jewish Sabbath, Hanukah, Diwali: of different naming ceremonies, discussing words and symbols, discovering *relevant* points of discussion for *everyone*. A huge circle covered one wall, half yellow, half grey. A boy and girl stood in the centre. The yellow half showed them bringing light, the grey bringing darkness. Eleven-year-olds discussed areas of darkness in their world — pain, lies, bullying, hunger, homelessness, persecution, illiteracy, unemployment, war. They prepared a liturgy in word and song for assembly, throwing out challenges to *everyone* to think and act! Their teacher led a simple discussion on why we *should* be 'lights', speaking briefly of the Jewish and Muslim creation stories which stress that the world is a gift and we should be good stewards, good regents.

So much work developing from three inexpensive candles — work which was interesting, creative, relevant for all, helping growth! Everyone had contributed to an understanding of Christian values, and vice versa.

Across the town, in other classrooms, three candles were displayed, ceremonies briefly discussed, accounts written up and drawn — and soon forgotten.

What and Why?

A religious artefact is a handmade or machine-made object. It is used as part of ritual worship (for example, a chalice), as a support to worship, as a focus for reflection and meditation (for example, an icon, a plaque of words from the Qur'ān), as decoration which creates or bears witness to a worshipful environment (garlands). Many act as channels of communication between worshippers and the Unseen, or their inner-self. Some speak of deep commitment, witnessing to others (capels, turbans, jewellery). They express praise, sorrow, gratitude, obedience, remembrance.

Early humans crossed the time barrier into the civilized world as they began to ask questions of their environment. What, who made the noise of running water, of rustling leaves? What, who ordered the seasons, created them and killed them? Could they contact these unseen beings, control them? Speech, drama, art, music, crafts, mathematics, architecture all developed as they sought to answer these questions. As the Unseen was given form, the numbers of hymns, stories, rituals, artefacts increased. The symbolic nature of artefacts often helped the worshipper to articulate what he/she could not capture in words. How could the peoples of the Indus speak of the power which created rivers and mountains, brought success and failure, seemed kindly and cruel; how could they articulate their hopes that they could seek help and guidance? Brahman was too great to be conceived — but they could describe an aspect, a quality. They captured these in the symbolic statues of the Hindu pantheon, each statue speaking of Brahman in a different, relevant, helpful way — as Brahma (Creator), Vishnu (Protector), Shiva (Lord of Change, as in death), Krishna (who cares for creation), Saraswati (who helps humans be creative).

The concrete brought the unknowable into the material world, acted as a secure peg on which to hang hopes, fears, joys, sorrows. Within the context of story and action artefacts helped humans focus and reflect upon important questions — Who am I? Why should I? Why suffering? Why death?

These universal questions have not changed. Children and teachers alike still ask them. Artefacts can help us focus on these questions in the classroom, help children develop and grow towards meaningful decision-making as they begin to take control of their lives.

Please Let Me Speak

The artefact which is merely described and copied remains an empty vessel, relevant only for others, soon forgotten. When filled with facts, symbolism, discussions, stories, creative writing and craftsmanship it nourishes, promotes growth, and bubbles away singing a song to encourage user *and* spectator to think, decide, act.

Muslim prayer beads remain dumb if the children are merely told that they usually consist of ninety-nine beads in three equal sections separated by a different (imam) bead, or of thirty-three beads which are 'told' three times. They may be used for the repetition of three short prayers, or of the Excellent Names of God. Even if the prayers are copied, names learnt, they remain irrelevant, except to Muslim children. There is no dialogue, the beads are dumb. A comparison with the Christian rosary may provide a small sound but little coherence.

How different if the children analyze the three prayers, decide which they think most important, discuss why Muslims want to repeat it, imagine how belief in it might affect behaviour, wonder if they should also choose to act in a similar way — and why? How different if they choose two or three excellent names, discuss why Muslims believe them, imagine what actions should follow belief. Why do some people think prayer is important? Are there any stories of Muhammad (p.b.u.h.) and prayer? He said: 'Prayer is a refreshing stream into which you dip five times a day' Why? Posters, stories, poems can reflect appropriate conduct and lead to discussions of *everyone's* conduct and values. Children can make up their own excellent names and prayers — or if there is no religious belief, prayers for others to say or statements of personal intent.

The Importance of Touch

(a) Something actually handled in the classroom can bring the reality of religious experience closer than videos, slides and films, especially if linked with both a portrait — picture of a worshipper using the artefact and with a story. The laying of the Sabbath table, the lighting of candles, breaking of bread and pouring of wine gives incentive to become involved in the experience of another, not to accept it, of course, but to learn from it as the individual's thoughts are sharpened and expanded. The partial re-enactment can be linked to appropriate themes within the curriculum, the emphasis altered to expand work being done — on creation, responsibility for others, light, food, family. Candle-sticks and Kiddush cups can be designed to reflect thinking within the individual's *own* lifestyle. We are *not* teaching Judaism, and therefore we may alter the parameters of learning or alter the emphasis; the Jewish child must remember the words and actions used on the Sabbath together with the underlying concepts. The non-Jewish child will wish to concentrate more on remembering the underlying teaching rather than the actual words. The Jewish child may concentrate on the journey of the Exodus to Sinai where the Covenant was given, including the command to 'keep the Sabbath'. Perhaps the non-Jewish child will first wish to explore stewardship, thinking of food projects in Africa, harmful aerosol sprays, playground bullies, although at some point, an exploration of the Sinai experience can be very thought provoking. Thus, the Jewish people do not become strange or peculiar, engaged in 'odd' rituals, but people concerned with mutual challenges and decision-making, prompting everyone to think a little harder.

(b) Multi-faith RE is sometimes accused of creating confusion, a result of learning about rather than learning with or learning from worshippers. Information focused upon that which can be handled however is usually clearly remembered. A GCSE student once wrote of the Ka'aba as being a golden temple on an island in the River Ganges! Had the student handled a prayer mat depicting Makkah, a compass, two pieces of white towelling for ihram, had she discussed prayer, pilgrimage, places visited, experiences shared, perhaps the confusion would not have arisen, especially if research had been entered into when designing prayer mats. The feelings of importance, enjoyment, commitment to which the artefacts bear witness would have clarified memories of knowledge gained.

(c)   Films and videos are not always accessible, the object in situ in the place of worship not always clearly perceived or remembered because of lack of time. Artefacts are immediately available in the classroom and require no equipment.

(d)   It is important to try and arrange for visitors to share experiences in the classroom, but they do not always know how to hold the children's interest. If given two or three artefacts and asked to explain how they use them, what they mean to them, communication can soon be established. 'Is your puja plate like this one? What do you say when you use it? Is the statue before which it is laid real? Why is it important to you? Why do you pray?'

I Made That

No faith is offended by the making of artefacts. Judaism positively encourages it. Its craft books point the way for activities in all faiths. Mass cloning, straight copying is not always helpful however. As with the candles, the choice of symbol, quotation etc not only to inform but to reflect opinion is very important. A model takht may be simply presented but an accompanying poem to show how it stresses the importance of Guru Granth Sahib, the swords symbolizing the fight for freedom and justice, prasad emphasizing brotherhood will lead to relevance and impact. A mezuzah might show a Torah scroll, but for the non-Jewish pupil it might show a helpful deed within the home, or a Muslim child might write the name of Muhammad who shows Muslims, by example, how to keep their laws. (It will, of course, not show a picture of Muhammad who must never be portrayed.) Posters, songs, stories may again accompany the model and duty to God, love of God need not be the only point of reference in a situation of non-belief. Equally the children can design the model for people of faith. There need be no question of hypocrisy, lack of integrity, denial of commitment.

It should be remembered that all artefacts are precious to the committed. Whilst important to use the junk box and be creative, care should be taken and sometimes new materials used. A badly cut piece of paper rolled round two iced lolly sticks may cause confusion if used with a story of Jews willing to die rather than desecrate a scroll! The teacher may have prepared a more elaborate model, older children may help — or scrub the sticks, don't use a damaged piece of paper, very carefully write a few words of scripture (The Lord is my shepherd) and take care. The making should not be to fill in the last ten minutes of a lesson. When completed, place in a carefully decorated 'Ark' or box. Take them to the synagogue on a visit to show the rabbi when he shows you *his* scrolls — and sing your songs for him when you ask him to read a psalm to you.

I'm Worried

Concerns regarding integrity in respect of one's own beliefs have been addressed earlier in the chapter. In learning from each other we enrich and deepen our own personal quest, we do not endanger it. Sharing is a recognition of the exploration of common questions and the use and making of artefacts is part of the sharing process. They speak to us and by altering the emphasis we have a dialogue, not an affirmation of simple commitment.

How far can we act out situations in the classroom using artefacts? For some teachers this will be seen as drama, no different from participating in plays and films. All actors in Jewish families in 'Fiddler on the Roof' do not have to be Jewish.

Perhaps this is too simplistic, however, for in the classroom we are asking children to consider the importance of commitment, challenging them to develop parameters for belief and action. Perhaps there is much we *can* share but each teacher will, after much thought, decide on their own line of demarcation. To keep a Qur'ān covered and in a high place with nothing on top of it, to wash all hands before touching it are marks of respect to and for others, just as we would cover our heads in a Hindu temple and refrain from smoking and playing transistor radios in a church. Only those who acknowledge that Muhammad (p.b.u.h.) was a man of God and that the book contains words of God — though not as direct revelation without human interpretation — would follow the custom of putting the book three times to lips and forehead before reading. Children should be asked to show respect, but not such commitment.

As those who are always making classroom decisions, teachers will not always use the same lines of demarcation. When using a Muslim prayer mat, some will ask children to perform the prayer positions to help internalize the symbolism or enter into the feelings of a Muslim.

Others will describe, show pictures of prayer but not encourage performance, feeling that this implies a special relationship of commitment with the Prophet who showed people how to pray.

A re-enactment of part of a Passover meal, laying the table, joining in a song, shouting out the names of the plagues, spilling a drop of wine to show that one can never fully rejoice when people suffer, innocent or guilty, because such suffering causes God suffering in Jewish eyes, may all help children understand the intense feelings of Jewish participants. To stop and make clear that 'Now, a Jewish family would say "*We* were slaves in Egypt"' ensures that the children realize they are sharing a commitment to justice and freedom, but not to Judaism.

Children may handle a chalice and packets of communion wafers, talk about and watch the service, share biscuits and orange juice at the close, reversing the New Testament practice of a common meal, sharing friendship and brotherhood, preceding the sharing of bread and wine by the committed. Most teachers would hesitate to ask children to bless bread and wine and give it to the rest of the class as in an Anglican or Roman Catholic Eucharist.

In different ways we will use the best educational practices of participation without 'endangering' children's own stances and beliefs. Finally, we can all join in congratulatory parties — 'Let us help Ranjit and Shabara celebrate Diwali — Jonathan and Katy celebrate Christmas' joining in *carefully* selected activities.

What If I Make a Mistake?

Great care will always be taken to handle artefacts without causing offence, but the teacher should not become so strangled by her fears that he/she does not use them at all. I once made a foolish, thoughtless and serious mistake. I understood a Turkish shopkeeper's mime regarding a 'carpet' to mean that the muezzin slept on it in the mosque after giving an early summer call to prayer. It was in fact a cover for a funeral bier and had embroidered on it words from the Qur'ān. How could I have suggested that such words would be placed on the floor, how could I have failed to see the discrepancy! Justifiably humiliated, I faced my Muslim colleagues. 'Don't worry. What the children will remember is your presentation of Islam as thoughtful, caring, important, having something to say to *them* — not the unbalanced picture of the news media.' Of course, I didn't make the mistake again!

The following points may help. People do not always follow the same practices but by choosing those which cause no one offence, we can feel 'secure', even if such practices are not followed by everyone.

Vida Barnett

In Christianity

When speaking of the Eucharist/The Last Supper use an ordinary loaf or *sealed* packets of wafers.

In Islam

Use damp paper towels or a bowl of water before handling a Qur'ān. Always quote from it when opening it. 'In the name of God, the Merciful, the Mercygiving' or 'God is Light' are appropriate. When designing artefacts, never depict the Prophet (p.b.u.h.), God, or ask Muslim children to depict people — though they may do so if their family accepts educational validity. If a Christian song is used in assembly, have the Qur'ān brought in after the singing and/or removed before it. Never put plaques, etc. with words of the Qur'ān on the floor of a dirty surface. Do not destroy an old Qur'ān or plaques etc. Give it to Muslim organization or contact.

In Judaism

Small imitation scrolls which may be used in the Simchat Torah procession can be handled with respect, but tell the children not to attempt to touch the handwritten scrolls in the synagogue. Use empty mezuza cases, or place your own written 'scroll' within them. Keep tefillin in a box and only display, not handle, especially if you are a woman. Keep prayer books, copies of marriage or funeral services etc. in a clean place and do not destroy them. If they cannot be used any longer, take them to a member of the Jewish community. It is preferable to use 'new' artefacts for Passover, as for many they become unacceptable if used on any other occasions.

In Hinduism, Sikhism, Buddhism

Do not touch the sacred texts in places of worship or the shrine figures in the Hindu temple. Never touch Sikh objects in the presence of tobacco or alcohol.

Prepare children for the fact that members of the faith may handle objects more casually. Make sure they understand the difference between symbolism and superstition. Jews may fast for twenty-five hours if a scroll is dropped in the synagogue as a mark of sorrow; the floor may be washed in a special way if the consecrated communion wine is spilt — but not because worshippers are afraid that otherwise they will be struck by lightening!

Also, decisions may have to be made on educational grounds in respect of the wishes of very orthodox members of a faith. Some Muslims do not agree with a non-Muslim ever handling a Qur'ān, for example. Most teachers would accept the validity of handling it with care.

Artefacts by Adoption

Within the classroom there may be an argument for artefacts by adoption. Muslims sometimes speak of *three* books of Revelation — the created world itself, the lives of the prophets, the scripture all bear witness to God, are all gifts of God. Before using artefacts connected with ritual, some teachers might like to use the children's known world to raise those universal questions which artefacts also raise. The wonder with which we explore our world, both in terms of the immensity of space and the use of the microscope, prompts questions of origin and of our treatment of all facets of creation. The growth of babies within the womb, and their potential, — physical, intellectual, creative and emotional are part of the debate. Read about the birth of a baby kangaroo in Gerald Durrell's *Two in a Bush*. Thus the questions arise from immediate experience and can be developed in learning experiences.

We Can't Afford Them

School budgets make cost a challenge. Islamic, Sikh and Hindu artefacts are often inexpensive, as are some Jewish and Christian objects. Only the individual can decide whether to buy one beautiful, costly artefact to emphasize the importance of religion, or to buy a number of inexpensive ones.

'Home-made' can be a good 'second best', especially if much time and care is spent by the teacher on her contribution. Jewish children design their own channukiah, Christian children their own jewellery. Sometimes members of communities will make contributions.

I once shared a Sabbath day with a friend. The havdalah ceremony was marked by the use of a lovely silver kiddush cup, but the equally beautiful spice box was left on the shelf. A jam jar containing two nutmegs and covered with wax paper was used — so that we would all remember that it was the *symbolism* that was important.

Artefact 'boxes' can sometimes be borrowed from teachers' centres. A group of schools might combine, each providing a box which could be borrowed by others. These could relate to individual faiths, to an aspect of a faith — festivals, or to a theme — naming ceremonies/light. A course might be planned to discuss, research and produce work cards of both a factual, discussive and creative nature.

Vida Barnett

Basic Collections

(a) *Christianity*

Candles	Crib
Crosses and crucifixes	Advent ring
Rosary	Advent calendars (CAFOD etc.)
Jewellery	Tambourine
Small statues	Home/community Festival cards
Icons	Personal stations of the cross
Incense	Hassock
Stole	Confirmation gifts
Chalice (a pottery goblet?)	Patten

(b) *Hinduism*

Puja tray	Incense holder
Small statues	Garlands
Diwali lamp	Jewellery
Festival cards	Ganges water

(c) *Islam*

Qur'ān stand	Small Qur'ān and cover
Prayer beads	Prayer mat
Compass	Calligraphy plaques
Jewellery	Festival cards

(d) *Sikhism*

Kara	Turban
Kanga	Turban length
Kirpan	Jewellery
Copy of Japji	

(e) *Judaism*

Prayer shawl	Capel
Mezuzah	Small model Torah scroll
'Sabbath' candlesticks	Kiddush cup (wine glass)
Passover plate	Packet of matzos
Small yad	Small shofar
Jewellery	Festival cards
Mourning candle	Havdalah candle
Channukiah	Haggadah

(f) *Buddhism*

Statues of the Buddha

Where Can I Buy Them?

Cathedral shops and Christian religious bookshops
Synagogue shops
The Jewish Bookshop, Woburn House, Woburn Place, London, WC1H
  0EP.

The Jewish Educational Bureau, 8 Westcombe Avenue, Leeds, LS8 2BS.
Mosque shops
Paigham-E-Islam, 423 Stratford Road, Birmingham, 11.
The Islamic Cultural Centre, Regent's Park Mosque, 146 Park Road, London, NW8.
Gohil Indian Arts and Crafts, 381, Stratford Road, Birmingham, 11.
Articles of Faith, Bury Business Centre, Kay Street, Bury BL9 6BU.

Accompanying Resources

Pictorial Charts Educational Trust, 27 Kirchen Road, London, W13 00D.
Slide Centre Ltd, 143 Chatham Road, London, SW11.
Philip and Tacey (materials and ideas for Festival craftwork), Northway, Andover, Hampshire, SP10 5BA.

GINSBERG, M. (1983) *The Tattooed Torah*, New York Union of American Hebrew Congregations.
GOLDIN, B.D. (1988) *Just Enough is Plenty*, London, Heinemann.
GOTTLEIB, Y. (1982) *The Gift of Challah*, Aura Publishing.
ILEA RELIGIOUS EDUCATION TEACHERS' CENTRE (19) *Needles and Nails — Introducing Religious Symbols*, London, ILEA.
SALOP, B. (1957) *The Kiddush Cup Who Hated Wine*, London Jonathan David.
TAUBER and ABRAHAMS (1979) *Integrating Arts and Crafts in the Jewish School*, Behrman.
WINTERS, C.-A. (1981) *Cheng Ho's Voyage or Uncle Ma King's Gold Leaf Qur'an*, American Trust Publications.

Note

A series of short packs by the writer will shortly be available. There is an introductory pack and one for Christian, Jewish, Muslim, Hindu and Sikh artefacts. Each contains detailed suggestions based on flexible work-cards for four artefacts, which can be adapted for individual classrooms. These point to short facts, more detailed facts, discussion starters and creative work. Each card is accompanied by 'work tags' to help with the answers and by lists of resources — addresses, stories, books etc.
They will be available from:

The Shap Advisory and Information Office,
81 St Mary's Road,
Huyton,
Liverpool, L36 5SR

or from: Sacred Trinity Centre, address above, which will also supply the artefacts.

One Will Suffice

A small Sefer Torah Scroll stood on the desk throughout the term. Why was so much care taken when writing it? What did its decorations mean? Why was it kept in the ark? Why do people feel they need a scripture? Does God talk to us? How? Why is the scroll processed in the synagogue? Why held up? Why do people touch it with their prayer shawl or prayer book? Why should people accept laws and not act as they wish? Why are the Commandments important? What is significant about the phrase regarding rest on the Sabbath — 'and Thy manservant and maidservant'? What of Simchat Torah? Why do Jews *dance* with the Torah? Why are the last *and* first chapters read? Why at the boy's Brit Milah does the father pray that he learns to love the Torah? What does the boy say when he becomes Bar Mitzvah, Son of the Law? What happens when it can no longer be used? Why will Jews suffer and die rather than desecrate the Torah? Is anything worth dying for? What do we think most important?

Questions, research, arguments, creative work, some relating to Jewish beliefs, some to the children's beliefs, occupied every moment of the RE lessons. Fifty-seven important questions were raised by one artefact. The teacher had worked *with* the children to find answers, to clarify and change opinions. All had become more thoughtful, more able to take charge of their lives in a very confusing world.

10   The Place of Story in RE

Carole King

It was the week before Easter; thirty absorbed year 3 children were gathered around the teacher in the story corner, as she read the concluding pages of *The Velveteen Rabbit*. As she closed the book to signal its ending, there was a visible, almost tangible feeling of release from tension — the story was over, the spell was broken.

Then:

'How could that happen?'
'Toy rabbits can't cry. There are no fairies.'
'It's a silly ending.'

Suddenly Matthew spoke:

'Of course it's not true, like it says in the story.
But it is true really. It's about heaven.
What happens when you die.'

The teacher said nothing, waiting for an appropriate response. Puzzlement gave way to pondering and she knew from the children's comments that Matthew's words were being attended to. A lively and intense discussion about death and Heaven followed, linked to the central thread of the story, that it was the boy's love for his toy rabbit that had made it *real*, whole, perfect.

'What is REAL?' asked the Rabbit one day, when they were lying side by side near the nursery fender, before Nana came to tidy the room. 'Does it mean having things that buzz inside you and a stick-out handle?'
    'Real isn't how you are made', said the Skin Horse. 'It's a thing that happens to you. When a child loves you for a long,

long time, not just to play with, but REALLY loves you, then
you become Real.'

'Does it hurt?' asked the Rabbit.

'Sometimes', said the Skin Horse, for he was always truth-
ful. 'When you are Real you don't mind being hurt.'[1]

In a year 4 class, *Charlotte's Web* was nearing its end, both teacher and
pupils moved to tears by the concluding pages. In the third year, *The
Lion, the Witch and the Wardrobe* had stimulated much lively, sensitive
discussion, with art, drama and written work around the themes of
friendship, betrayal, sacrifice, death and resurrection: themes which were
integral to both *The Velveteen Rabbit* and *Charlotte's Web* and to the story
the year 6 children had shared, *Goodnight Mr. Tom*. It was the sharing of
stories like these throughout their school life that had provided the fourth
years with experiences which would help them as they read together St
Mark's narrative of the death and resurrection of Jesus. For they were
story experiences which would enable them to begin their tentative
explorations into the nature of the God whom Christians call Father and
whom they worship, through the study of the story of what befell his son
and why.

The stories mentioned here had been chosen with care, appropriate
to the ages and interests of the pupils and with *Charlotte's Web* and
Goodnight Mr. Tom, matched to the class topic work on farming and the
Second World War respectively. The teachers recognized that story is
important in a number of ways:

> it provides an enjoyable focus for class activity;

> it helps pupils to enlarge their own experiences of life — of what
> happens and why. It increases understanding of what it means to be
> human;

> it helps pupils to recognize that others have shared their experiences
> and feelings — they are not alone;

> it provides a safe distancing framework for dealing with things that
> worry or frighten them.

And it is true, story can and does do all these things and many more.
Matthew's comment at the beginning of the chapter shows us that, and
also that story can be one of the ways we come to understand and make
sense of things which puzzle us. We learn through story in a way we
never learn through the other discourses of school.

The narrative/story is always a more powerful force than other
discourses. With story, it is not a question, as with other discourse, of
proving that it is all absolutely true, but of realizing, as did Matthew with
The Velveteen Rabbit, that it contains truth.

Story is holistic, uniting both the cognitive and affective. When we are involved in a story both intellect and emotions are engaged, and we struggle to make sense of what we read, to relate it to our own experience, and to discover, in so doing, more about our common humanity, and ourselves as individuals. Emily, Cathy and Eve demonstrate this in the following excerpt from a discussion on Judy Blume's novel *It's Not the End of the World*.

Cathy:	*It's Not the End*, good?
Eve:	Well, her parents get divorced.
Emily:	I think it's good —
	Say some of our parents are divorced.
Cathy and Eve:	Yeh.
Cathy:	She sort of ...
Emily:	It sort of helps you, doesn't it?
Cathy:	It helps you as it acts as though in real life sort of.
Emily:	It makes you ... There's you thinking like you're the only one —
Cathy:	It's real life.
Emily:	And no one knows how you feel but when you read the book you can understand that other people feel the same way as you.

Eve's parents are divorced and she has obviously found comfort in identifying with the character and realizing she is not alone. She searches for meaning in her own life through the events and characters in the story she had read and shared. The sharing is important as it allows her to articulate her thinking. It also enables her friends to appreciate something of Eve's feelings through their own involvement with the story's heroine.

As teachers, we do not generally talk about why we use story. We feel, perhaps intuitively, that it is right to do so, at least for younger children and we know that older pupils should be encouraged in their private reading. But as our pupils grow, so the time for shared story may be squeezed out of the timetable and story then loses its sense of importance and becomes a time filler, which may then be only one step from seeing it as a time waster.

For in our Western world, science rather than religion has come to be the way through which we explain the world and how it works. We have adopted a reductionist, rather than holistic, view of the universe, and this is reflected in the school curriculum, in its emphasis on separate discourses of knowledge and sets of skills. And of course, science does not use the story to convey its findings, to teach about truth. Thus teachers can be forgiven for believing that story is fine for small children, but as they grow older they must learn 'to put away childish things'.

Harold Rosen makes a strong plea that stories are not just for children, to be discarded as they become more able to use more abstract forms of discourse, but should be valued as an important, even vital element in our lives. He quotes Barbara Hardy:

> My argument is that narrative, like lyric or dance, is not to be regarded as an aesthetic invention used by artists to control, manipulate, and order experience, but as a primary act of mind transferred to art from life ... What concerns me here are the qualities which fictional narrative shares with that inner and outer story-telling that plays a major role in our sleeping and waking lives. For we dream in narrative, remember, anticipate, hope, despair, believe, doubt, plan, revise, criticize, construct, gossip, learn, hate and love by narrative. In order really to live, we make up stories about ourselves and others, about the personal as well as the social past and future.[2]

The last sentence is a powerful and continuing argument for valuing story in our own classrooms. For if we are to have life abundantly, we need not only our own inner and outer story telling, we need to hear and read the stories which others write and tell, otherwise we cannot grow in understanding.

Children themselves demonstrate an innate capacity for story, as if some inborn instinct does indeed tell them that story is a way of making meaning, of understanding. They tell us this with their persistent 'Tell me a story'. They show us that not only does story involve them emotionally and cognitively, but often physically as well. Very often when listening to a story, their bodies are still, yet not relaxed; very often it seems that every part of their being is engaged with the story.

Good teachers recognize and feed this need for story. They know also that a lively fidgety class can, paradoxically, be calmed by the heightened tension that can be achieved by listening to a well chosen story. Nor is this behaviour confined to children. The preacher can always be sure of concentrated attention for his anecdotal illustrations, less so for his interpretation.

What Kind of Story for Religious Education?

The answer to this question must be all kinds, but not all stories, for not all stories are written in the way that will enable children to be fully engaged. We do not expect that the kind of light reading we pick up at station and airport kiosks will generally provide much inner satisfaction. As adults we should be aware that the stories which make most demands on our abilities as readers, are most likely to prove of greater interest and value in our lives. So too for our pupils, and they will need our help and support if they are to become hearers, readers and writers of stories which challenge and enrich their experience.

The stories we need to use should already be in our class and school libraries: stories of different genres and cultures from *Sleeping Beauty* (once adapted for an infant Easter assembly!) to *The Turbulent Term of Tyke Tiler* and the Anansi stories. We do not need story that is explicitly religious, for that is read to confirm and strengthen an existing belief, but story which will help children to have a religious perspective on life, to be 'religiate' in the same way that they are numerate and literate. For this we need to provide story experience which will nurture their innate capacity for awe and wonder, which is where it all begins. As Edward Robinson says:

> To wonder at something means, for the moment at least, to feel small in its presence. A capacity for wonder is the first condition for the experience of the transcendent.[3]

Many people have difficulty in grasping what is meant by the transcendent. At its simplest it is the kind of feeling we may have when we see a beautiful sunset: the kind of experience that makes us stop and wonder at creation and our place within it: it may also lead us to feeling a profound sense of being at one with the world.

Wondering leads to questions about identity, purpose, worth and relationships, questions which are the concern of all religions and which allow us to perceive that there is a mystery at the heart of life. Religious education should be concerned with this mystery and with suggesting that the religious perspective may be one way of coming to terms with it.

The best children's writers deal in their work with the search for meaning to this mystery. Their stories give opportunities both to raise questions and to explore answers. They challenge children to see anew and make it possible for them to grow in understanding, as Matthew and Eve have demonstrated.

Very often too, their stories will introduce religious themes and symbols: they will be stories about quest and pilgrimage, light and darkness, loss and retrieval, sacrifice, love and suffering. Reading them and identifying with the characters and their adventures helps children to recognize the relevance of these themes to their own lives, and prepares them for story which is explicitly religious.

Story in Use

Sometimes we need only to offer the story and let the children take from it what they will, but often they will need to talk about it in small groups so that they can explore together and learn from each other. They need to talk about what concerns or puzzles them personally, not only what the teacher thinks is important. Taping such group talk should convince teachers of its value, for our pupils are often far more perceptive and sensitive than we realize.

Older children can be encouraged to keep reading journals in which they jot down their own comments and responses to the story and the questions it poses, as a simple way of recording and encouraging their own thinking, and as a basis for future work. The following are useful suggestions for getting started:

> Ask questions about the characters and events.
> Predict what will happen.
> Comment on the way the characters change and why.
> Comment on the unexpected.
> Relate your own experiences to what happens.
> Record the way your feelings change towards the characters.

Fantasy, myth and legend are rightly suggested for use in religious education: stories concerned with an epic struggle between good and evil like *The Iron Man* by Ted Hughes or the work of Lloyd Alexander. However the six stories referred to here are less obviously concerned with good and evil and for that reason, they are worth introducing as examples of how stories which have no apparent relevance for religious education can be used.

Gorilla by Anthony Browne (1983), published by Julia MacRae (infant+)

This picture book appeals to all ages. It tells of Hannah, who lives alone with a father who has no time for her. She desperately wants a gorilla for her birthday, but is dismayed by the toy one her father gives her on her birthday eve, and flings it away. While she sleeps, it changes into a real, huge, gentle gorilla who takes her on a night adventure to the zoo where the sad caged primates mirror Hannah's own imprisonment in loneliness. Next day all is changed as both text and illustration reveal, for they have moved from the darkness of loneliness and alienation, to the brightness of love and reconciliation.

It is a challenging book, and as children try and make sense of it, they come to see that not everything can be explained. There is indeed a mystery, reflected in the symbolism in the illustrations, a feature which even very young children recognize. Hannah's world has changed, but how and why?

Not so Fast Songolo by Niki Daly (1987), published by Puffin (1987), (infant)

Shepherd and his granny leave their African village for a day in the big city and the story depicts in words and pictures the warm relationship between grandmother and grandson. Shepherd (nicknamed Songolo by his grandmother) is able to help his elderly grandmother cope with the bustle of city life; young and old both have important roles to play. It is a story about love and care and personal worth, and has a universal appeal.

Chris and the Dragon by Fay Sampson published by Puffin (8–10 years)

This is a humorous story and like *Not So Fast Songolo* is about friendship and worth. Children who never get chosen for anything special at school will identify with Chris and his problems both in school and out. Asking them whether or not they would like Chris as a friend provokes much lively and perceptive discussion about friends, differences, loyalty and class trouble makers: about the way people behave and the need to respect and value individuals.

Shine by Jill Paton Walsh (1981), published by Macdonald (8 years+)

The earth is destroyed but a group escapes to colonize another planet. The story is sparsely written but exciting as it describes their journey through space and the first months on the planet. It raises many questions about what people need for survival:

    water and food;
    shelter and warmth;
    light;
    rules for community life;
    technology;
    care for the environment;
    story.

The colonists appear to have no religious beliefs or practice, nor any sacred books. Children can be encouraged to explore the implications of this lack of recognized religion for the life of the community, and in so doing to consider its relevance or not to their own lives.

Goodnight Mr. Tom by Michelle Magorian (1981), published by Puffin (9 years+)

Willie is evacuated from London and the harsh care of his 'religious' mother to Little Wierwold where he is billeted on old Tom, a morose and unfriendly widower. The relationship which develops between these two is the salvation of each. It is a story about the redeeming power of love, a story which deals with almost every aspect of life ranging from child abuse to coming to terms with death. Though sensitively written, it is full of action and excitement and because it is difficult to predict, it stimulates much wonder.

The Secret Garden by Frances Hodgson Burnett (1951), published by Puffin (Juniors)

Like Willie, Mary, the main character in this story, finds herself forced to live in new surroundings, with people she does not know. There are many similarities with *Goodnight Mr. Tom* and Mary, like Willie, comes to love and be loved, and in so doing brings healing to her own and others' lives.

Towards the end, Mary, Colin, Dickon and even old Ben Weatherstaff feel wonder in the power of the natural world around them to regenerate, in the power newly given in their own lives to be living and whole. They are indeed like Adam and Eve in Paradise before the Fall.

So full of joy are they, as the story nears its climatic close that they seek to express it and give thanks for this magic. Ben Weatherstaff suggests they sing the Doxology. Dickon sings it first and Colin speaks:

> 'It is a very nice song', he said. 'I like it. Perhaps it means just what I mean when I want to shout that I am thankful to the Magic.' He stopped and thought in a puzzled way. 'Perhaps they are both the same thing. How can we know the exact names of everything? Sing it again, Dickon. Let us try, Mary. I want to sing it, too. It's my song. How does it begin? "Praise God from whom all blessings flow"?' And they sang it again, and Mary and Colin lifted their voices as musically as they could, and Dickon's swelled quite loud and beautiful — and at the second line Ben Weatherstaff raspingly cleared his throat, and at the third he joined in with such vigour that it seemed almost savage, and when the 'Amen' came to an end, Mary observed that the very same thing had happened to him which had happened when he found out that Colin was not a cripple — his chin was twitching and he was staring and winking, and his leathery old cheeks were wet.
>
> 'I never seed no sense in th' Doxology afore', he said hoarsely, 'but I may change my mind i' time'.

Children and adults can understand this joy and sense for themselves the magic and the power of which Mary and Colin speak and which they celebrate in song. Though set in almost another century, it speaks to us today of the things which are important in our individual and collective lives. It contains, like the other stories mentioned, truths about the human condition, about human hopes and desires, realization of which can lead towards this sense of the transcendent so vital in our religious education, if it is not merely to become yet another body of knowledge. For to teach religious education without some recognition of this element, is like teaching children to read individual words and never allowing the joy of becoming real readers caught up in the mystery of creation.

Telling and Writing Stories

Though receiving and responding to story is a vital part of the use of story in religious education, it is not the whole. Pupils need the chance to make, tell and write their own stories. James Moffett tells us:

> Whereas adults differentiate their thoughts into specialized kinds of discourse such as narrative, generalisation and theory, children must for a long time make narrative do for all. They utter themselves almost entirely through stories — real or invented — and they apprehend what others say through story.[4]

Recent research by Carol Fox[5] has shown how young children do indeed make 'narrative do for all'. Like the best kinds of children's fiction, the content of children's oral stories deals with the enormous themes of life, with birth, death and their accompanying emotions, and with the forces of good and evil. Story is clearly used as a way of discovering what it means to be human. Through retelling known stories and making up stories of their own, children are able to explore events, issues and questions which puzzle them and as they do so, to grow in understanding.

Nursery and infant teachers who have always read and shared stories with their pupils should capitalize on the knowledge that story telling is important and ensure that both time and opportunity are given for individual children to tell their own stories. Betty Rosen goes further, using oral story telling with secondary pupils. Writing about her account of her work Harold Rosen says:

> 'We should militantly assert that the students in this book are meaning makers, even when — perhaps especially when — they are retelling. They rework the stories they have heard to make new meanings, to shift their view of the world or to amplify it. At the same time they are constructing their own social selves, as Wayne Booth suggests:
>
> 'Who I am is best shown by the stories I can tell and who I am to become is best determined by the stories I can learn to tell'.[6]

Listening to, and reading children's stories is not just about monitoring and assessing their language development, it is also about recognizing the ideas the child struggles to understand through his/her storying, ideas that he/she sorts out as he tells or writes. Kate (3 years 10 months) demonstrates this in the following story told to her student nursery teacher just before Easter.

> Once upon a time there was a prince and he loved a princess but he was very very sad because she had died. But then the prince found her and she hadn't died. So they got married and lived happily ever after.

She had not heard the Easter story in school but she had heard a great many fairy stories and they had prepared for Easter with work on new life and growth in nature.

Towards the end of the autumn term, as part of their topic work, a year two class was read to each day from a selection of stories linked to the theme of midwinter festivals, ranging from *The Puffin Book of Christmas Stories* to Raymond Briggs' *Father Christmas*. Legend and myth were included as well as the gospel accounts of the birth of Jesus from *The Good News Bible*.

The pupils also brought similar books from home to read and share together. The stories were read and enjoyed with very little discussion, for the teacher allowed the stories themselves to speak to the children in whatever way was appropriate.

They especially enjoyed reading together from the Bible and many excitedly discovered the same stories in their own Bible story books at home or brought in family Bibles, allowing them to focus briefly on the Bible as a special kind of book. They also watched second year assemblies on Diwali and Hanukah where the stories at the centre of these celebrations were vividly dramatized as part of their topic 'Festivals of Light'.

When they wrote their own stories for this midwinter topic, their writing showed on the one hand all the excitement of Christmas itself, with Father Christmas, presents and all the expected features, but very often there was also another more reflective element. This is shown in the following stories.

Christmas Story

Once upon a time there was a little cat named Tabitha. She lived in a little bungalow. The man who owned Tabitha had a little barn where he kept an ox and a donkey. One day everyone was busy packing up their belongings of which they didn't have much. There were some people called Mary and Joseph. Joseph had to go to Bethlehem to be counted by the Romans and Mary was expecting a baby. Mary rode on the donkey and Joseph led the way. They stopped at a lot of inns but they were all full. Now came the time to see if the house where Tabitha lived had any space. Her owner said, 'Sorry the house is full but you can stay in my barn if you want'. So Joseph said, 'Yes please'. And they stayed in the barn. In the night Mary had her baby. She wrapped it in strips of cloth and put it in the manger. Then Tabitha came out of the house and into the barn and saw the baby. 'This baby is called Jesus. He is a special baby. He is God's son in a very special way.' Then Tabitha jumped onto Mary's lap and started purring. They stayed in the barn for a few days and Tabitha came to visit them every morning. A few days later they went home and Tabitha was sad. — Kirsty (7 years 4 months)

Has Kirsty used her beloved cat to put herself into this retelling of the traditional narrative? Certainly the cat's actions show us that the baby is special just as the angels and star show the shepherds and wisemen (and readers!) in the gospel accounts.

The Magic Present

Once upon a time on Christmas Eve, Darren and Carly were really excited because tomorrow was Christmas Day! They could not wait till Father Christmas came.

On Christmas Day everyone gathered around the Christmas tree, every present was wrapped up except one. It was a little guitar that was the only thing unwrapped.

It was most peculiar indeed. In the afternoon everybody was having a meal. The guitar stood up and played a tune. The tune was *The Raindrop*. As soon as he heard them coming back he fell to the floor. It was silent. Everybody wondered what the noise was. The guitar was not in the place they put it. Everybody wandered over and said, 'Play us a tune.' The guitar was shy. But he stood up and played a tune. *The Raindrop*! they shouted. Every day before Darren and Carly went to school they asked for the guitar to play a tune because that made them happy for the rest of the day. — David (7 years 6 months)

David, shy and sensitive, has given us the story of a special gift with magical powers: a gift which brings delight every day.

The Girl Who Left at Christmas

One day there was a girl called Rachel. She has two brothers. She was my best friend. But she lives in Yorkshire now, sometimes she comes to see me. I remember when she came to sleep.

In the morning she giggled happily. And the day after that it snowed.

We made a big snowman and we giggled happily.

The day after that it snowed again.

We giggled every five seconds. I was happy until she left but I remember her still.

I am sad but when I go to the school we used to go to I feel sad. But I know she has gone somewhere it is much better and a better school. Laura (7 years 10 months)

Christmas reminds Laura of a best friend and the good times they shared. It shows her accepting the pain of loss.

The Speaking Decorations

One Christmas Eve a boy called John was putting up the streamers. He said to himself, 'There we go. It's up!' Then a very funny thing happened. The streamer said, 'Good to be out of that attic.' 'I beg your pardon', said John. 'I said, "Good to be out of the attic."' This time John said, 'Are you a speaking decoration?' 'Not just me', said the streamer. 'All my friends — the bell, the star on the top of the Christmas tree and the angel on the mantelpiece. I am the boss so you should talk to me.'

'Okay', said John, 'tell me about the attic then'. 'Well the attic is cold in the night and there is no light.' 'Then tomorrow you will get some light because it is Christmas.'

'What is Christmas?' said the streamer. 'Well it's when you celebrate Jesus' birthday and you get a present.' 'I see', said the streamer. 'Can you bring me a ribbon?' 'Okay', said John. Next morning it was Christmas. John felt in his stocking. He found a ribbon and he said to himself, 'I will give this to the streamer.' So he went downstairs and ran across the hallway and got a chair and stood on it.

He hung it on the streamer.

When his mum's friends came round they all said, 'What a nice ribbon.' — Mark (7 years 7 months)

Here Mark shows us that he has grasped something of the theme of moving from darkness into light, which is at the heart of all the midwinter festivals whether pagan or not. He shows us also that he recognizes his own role in this annual but eternal drama, by giving a present, which is his own, for another's happiness. These are simple stories, simply written and firmly rooted in the everyday experiences of the four writers, yet they show us that they are concerned with more than just everyday things. They show us, as they seek to express something of the wonder and mystery which lies at the heart of the season with its emphasis on darkness and light, birth and gifts that they are concerned with the transcendent itself. And that is what we and they need if religious education is to be of worth.

Story in Assembly

If the act of worship is to be of value, it must provide pupils with something worth thinking about. Music, art, dance and drama can be used as a focus for thought, so also, can story. Because story operates on many different levels at once, one story can be told many times to the same children. Each time they hear it, it will speak differently to them. Once this is appreciated, it releases the teacher from the burden of always having to find new and appropriate stories to tell and read. Indeed, repeating stories is seen as crucial if our pupils are to grow in understanding of them. We are not surprised when they choose to reread favourite books. Why then, should we feel the need for constant novelty in assembly?

Yet where story is used in assembly, it is best done by teachers themselves. Nothing is more certain to negate children's interest in, and involvement with, the story if it is poorly read by a nervous pupil. The story must be well rehearsed: it needs to be performed, not merely read straight from the text with little or no prior acquaintance: it needs to be heard and valued as a gift, given to those assembled. Too often we ask children to read in assembly for their sakes, rather than asking adults to read for everyone.

Teachers need also to have the courage to tell publicly their own stories, for if we, as teachers recognize that we have made sense of our lives through storying, as we invite our pupils to do, then we owe it to them to share some of these sotries. Most of us are too dependent on assembly books, thereby ignoring our own individual resources.

On the Friday before Remembrance Sunday, one junior school head used sometimes to tell *his* story. Bringing in a heavy duty flying jacket, of the kind worn by air crew in the Second World War, he would tell the school about his first flight as a navigator. It was a cold night and he had not yet been issued with his own flying jacket. Seeing his plight, one of the most experienced and respected pilots offered to lend him his own jacket. He accepted this generous offer and wore it with pride. Next day he returned it, arranging to buy its owner a drink, as thanks, later in the week. But before that could happen the pilot was shot down and killed.

However many times it was heard, the power of the story and the sincerity of the teller never failed to hold the school in thrall. The jacket, left lying all day on the hall piano became, in time, a symbol for older pupils: a way of understanding something about sacrifice, pain and loss, and of why Remembrance Sunday was special for at least one person.

Jewish children who are present from infancy at family Passover celebrations hear anew each year the story of the Exodus. It is a central part of that celebration, ritually enacted through the sharing of certain foods, the saying of certain words. They grow in understanding of the story and its significance in their own lives, partly through their developing maturity, and partly through hearing it so often in a meaningful context. It is for them a living story.

Though for most of us it is not our job as teachers to nurture our pupils in any particular faith, they are entitled to hear and become familiar with stories which are part of the collective knowledge of large numbers of people. They are entitled to the chance to realize that to the people who know and believe them, these stories are powerful ways of understanding some of the most puzzling aspects of life itself. Assembly provides both the time and place for the sharing of these special stories.

Reading from the Bible can have a ritual element. Hearing the same stories read each year enables the listener to deepen his/her understanding. It matters not that the 6-year-old hardly comprehends the Nativity story as told by Matthew. What does matter is that he/she should have the chance to hear it again and again so that it becomes so familiar to him/her that it becomes part of his total experience of Christmas, the great midwinter festival, and that he/she will come to realize it in new ways and to make it his/her own.

He/she will be helped in this by all the other stories he/she has heard, read, told and written throughout his/her school life. He/she will know how to think and talk about story to make sense of it. He/she will know, albeit subconsciously, something of the potential of story for making, shaping and illuminating his/her own thinking. Of course, with maturity, he/she may reject the story as having nothing to say to him/her, but at least he/she will have made that decision from knowledge, not ignorance. He/she will have had the chance to know the story. For it is surely in the stories of the lives of the great religious leaders that their followers find understanding of what their faith is all about. The doctrine of incarnation which John describes so powerfully in the opening words of his gospel, is incomprehensible to many of us without the narratives describing the actual birth of Christ from the gospels of Matthew and Luke.

Similarly, it is the story of the passion and death of Jesus that leads us to understand the doctrine of atonement and redemption. This is why C.S. Lewis's The Chronicles of Narnia, each dealing with a major doctrine of Christian theology, provide pupils with such a ready way in to understanding them. Easter is real to third year juniors once they have both suffered and celebrated with Aslan and the children in *The Lion, the Witch and the Wardrobe*.

The following assembly ideas have been successfully used at a large junior school (not a church school). In each, the Bible story is placed in the right context, as being at the heart of the act of worship. Thus the story is special because it is linked to special events and celebrations, and the events and celebrations themselves are special because of the story. The use of symbols linked to the stories helps children to begin to understand something of the power of symbol for making meaning as well as reinforcing the liturgical nature of these assemblies.

Advent and Christmas[7]

Aims:	to enable staff and pupils to think about the theme of light versus darkness which is at the heart of all midwinter festivals;
	to enable staff and pupils to think about the significance of this festival for Christians;
	to give staff and pupils the chance to experience awe and wonder.
Resources:	an advent candle ring. This can be simply two identical pieces of wood, fitted across each other with holes drilled at each end and one in the middle where they cross. Four red candles are needed, one for each end, plus a white one in the middle;
	a taper and matches for lighting;
	several different versions of the Bible, for example, Good News Bible, Lion Children's Bible;
	five pairs of children;
	as many adult readers as possible plus time to prepare and rehearse them;
	a darkened hall (if possible);
	music to accompany the reading where appropriate.
Time:	There are four Sundays in Advent. Depending on when Advent starts and term ends, it should be possible to fit in four Advent assemblies. Ideally, one for each of the last four weeks of term is best, if not, keep them as separate as possible. The fifth, Christmas assembly, can be on the last day of term.

Advent 1

Adult:	Explains meaning of Advent and the candle ring.
Child 1:	Lights the first candle.
Child 2:	'We have the Advent candle ring to remind us of the Coming of Christ, the Light of the World'.

Reading

Two adults:	John, chapter 1, verses 1–5. (percussion accompaniment.)
Story:	A powerful story is needed here which centres on darkness versus light: a child terrified of the dark at night but reassured by a light: a blind person cured: dark represented by pain, suffering, or loneliness but overcome by hope, love and friendship.

Prayer/Hymn

Advent 2

Adult:	Reminds pupils about the Advent ring (all the candles should be unlit).
Children 1 and 2:	Repeat the words and lighting of the first candle as in Advent 1.
Child 3:	Lights the second candle.
Child 4:	'We light this candle to help us think of God's greatest promise first told by the prophets.'
Adult:	'A prophet is someone who sees what people are doing wrong, tells them what they should do and the rewards this will bring in their lives.'

Reading
Adult: Isaiah, chapter 40 verses 3–5 ⎫   one or both, with trumpet
        Isaiah, chapter 61 verses 1–3 ⎭   fanfare if possible.
Adult: Asks what the readings say and introduces another story to show how Jesus did change everything.

Reading
Adults: Luke, chapter 19 verses 1–9 'Jesus and Zacchaeus'

Prayer/Hymn

Advent 3

Adult:	Reminds the pupils of the significance of the candles for Advent.
Children 1,2,3,4:	Repeat the words and light the candles as for Advent 1 and 2.
Child 5:	Lights the third candle.
Child 6:	'We light this candle to remind us of John the Baptist who passed on God's message: "Get ready for your King."'

Reading
Adult: The story of the birth of John (Lion Children's Bible).
Adult: 'When he grew up, John left his home and went out into the desert where he began to preach and baptize people to prepare them for the coming of Jesus, their saviour.'
Adult: Mark, chapter 1 verses 1–3.
Adult: Mark, chapter 1 verses 4–8.

Prayer/Hymn

Advent 4

Adult:	Reminds the pupils of the significance of the candles for Advent.
Children 1,2,3,4,5,6:	Repeat the words and light the candles as for Advent 1, 2 and 3.
Child 7:	Lights the fourth candle.
Child 8:	'We light this candle to remind us of mother Mary who told God she would obey.'

Reading
Adult: Luke, chapter 1 verses 26–38.

Prayer/Carol

Christmas Assembly

(*All the red candles are lit before the assembly begins.*)
Adult: Reminds the pupils of the significance of the Advent candles and asks when the white candle should be lit. (Properly on Christmas Day.)

Reading
Adult: Luke, chapter 2 verses 1–7.
Child: Lights the white candle at the words, 'She gave birth ...'

Reading
Adults: (As for Advent 1) John, chapter 1 verses 1–5

Prayer/Carol

The repeated lighting of the candles and the power of the stories hold spellbound both staff and pupils; they are caught up in the liturgy of worship. Yes, of course some explanation is given and much work on related themes will be continuing in class alongside these assemblies. Yet it is the story that works upon the heart and mind of those who listen, not the other discourses. The lighting of the candles prepares them for something special; there is a hushed expectancy as it is done and they listen intently to the stories which follow.

This format can be adopted for use with younger pupils using simple stories linked to a theme such as myths and legends about Christmas evergreens. It can also be used as a focus for stories about other festivals of light, Diwali and Hanukah.

Easter

Aims: to enable staff and pupils to think about the theme of sadness versus joy and to feel the contrasting moods of Good Friday and Easter Sunday;

to enable staff and pupils to think about the significance of the festival for Christians;

to give staff and pupils the chance to experience awe and wonder.

Key resources (additional suggestions are made later):

a large wooden cross;

an Easter garden: traditionally this is a model of the tomb of Jesus made of stones and set in a moss garden decorated with spring flowers;

readers, Bibles and music as for Advent assemblies plus dance if possible.

Easter Assembly 1

The narrative of the last days, death and resurrection of Jesus can be serialized over several days at the end of spring term. It can be divided in a number of ways with a symbol provided as a focus for each reading as is here suggested. Readings from other gospels can also be used if preferred.

Day	Reading	Symbol
Monday	The triumphal entry into Jerusalem Mark, chapter 11 verses 1–11	Palm crosses from a local church or paper made palm crosses.
	The visit to the Temple Mark, chapter 11 verses 15–19	An overturned table and spilt money.
Tuesday	The last supper Mark, chapter 14 verses 12–26	Bread and wine
	The arrest in Gethsemane Mark, chapter 14 verses 27–51	A money bag
Wednesday	Peter's betrayal and the trial Mark, chapter 14 verses 53–72	A whip or a picture of a cockerel
Thursday	The crucifixion and death Mark, chapter 15 verses 1–39	A large cross
Friday	The Resurrection John, chapter 20 verses 1–18	An Easter garden

The symbol suggested for each reading should be introduced at the appropriate moment and left in view throughout the week until the last assembly. If individual classes can prepare a picture frieze of the narrative which can be added to each day; this too is a useful reinforcement. Simple silhouette representations of the twelve traditional stations of the cross can also be made and displayed for the reading of the crucifixion. Children working on these or on the frieze will be led naturally to look more carefully at the story and come to know it more fully.

The readings can be shared by groups of adults and pupils; however, the account of the trial and crucifixion lends itself admirably to choral speech, a neglected art form in most schools. Even 7-year-olds can cope with both the vocabulary and rhythms of the narrative. Some of it can be read together, other parts are best broken up into phrases and sentences which are shared by individuals or pairs of readers. As it nears its climax, it's a good idea to mark this so that as each child speaks for the last time, he/she turns his back on the listeners and, when the centurion's final words are spoken, they all kneel to reveal a large plain wooden cross, a focus for silent thought and prayer. Choral speech must be done well and therefore takes much rehearsing, yet it is worth it for the participants do, indeed, come to know this story by heart, and though much of its meaning may escape them at 7 years, it may be that at 17 or 70 its significance becomes real for them: it makes sense for them.

Easter Assembly 2

The narrative can also be presented in two contrasting assemblies: the first one should be the Good Friday one, when the account of the crucifixion is read with the cross in position and if possible, in a darkened hall. At one school the pupils discarded their bright red jumpers for that assembly as a mark of solemnity and staff also elected to dress in sombre colours. Thus the whole atmosphere with music and dance reinforced the idea of Good Friday as a time of pain, loss and darkness which made doubly meaningful the second assembly when the resurrection story was told and celebrated.

For this the hall was filled with flowers and displays of painted eggs with the Easter garden taking pride of place. The story was dramatized and was followed by a sharing of stories about spring festivities, most of which predate the Christian one, all of which celebrate new life. The assembly concluded with a parade of Easter bonnets!

Whitsuntide (Pentecost)

Whit Assembly

Aims:	to enable staff and pupils to recognize that this festival marks the beginning of the Christian church;
	to enable staff and pupils to appreciate something of the symbolic meaning of the power of the Holy Spirit;
	to give staff and pupils the chance to experience awe and wonder.
Resources:	red and white decorations (traditional Whit colours);
	a large cake iced in red and white and with twenty candles;
	readers, Bibles and music.

Part 1
Hymn

Adult:	Reminds the pupils that the disciples were frightened after Jesus had gone from them on Ascension Day, but that he had told them he would send his power to them.
Reading:	Acts, chapter 2 verses 1–12 (Good News Bible or Lion Children's Bible)
	Several readers or the narrative can be dramatized.
Adult:	A brief explanation that the Holy Spirit empowered the disciples to go out and preach the word of God and that its coming marked the beginning of the Christian church. Ever since that day men and women in every age have felt the power of the Holy Spirit and have tried to live their lives according to the way of Jesus and help others to do the same.

Part 2
(To follow directly or be spread over a period of days, in which case, Part 1 should end with the singing of 'Happy Birthday' and the lighting of the cake candles.)

Forty children are needed for this, two for each century since the beginning of Christianity. Each child finds (with help) the name of a notable Christian of that time and some brief information about his/her life. The children stand in a long line. Each holds up a large piece of card on which is printed the name and date of his/her subject; on the back may be written details about the subject. Very quickly, beginning with St Peter, the children call out their information so that the cumulative effect of twenty centuries of Christian life and witness may be felt. Every effort should be made to include Christians from other countries so that Christianity is recognized as a world faith, ending with living Christians like Archbishop Tutu and Mother Theresa. It is harder to find names and details about female Christians, but worth doing if the pupils are not to see Christianity as an essentially male preserve!

Adult: Concludes by reminding the children that this great chain of witness all began on the first Whit Sunday.

The row of children then link hands to represent the linking power of the Holy Spirit and sing 'Happy Birthday' to the church while the cake is carried in, candles alight to symbolize the tongues of fire.

A variation on this theme is to let off hydrogen balloons, symbols of the word of God going forth into the world. Subsequent assemblies can be used for telling, in more detail, the stories of some of the Christian men and women briefly mentioned here and for recognizing that ordinary people living in the local community are part of this great chain of Christian witness. Inviting local Christians, including parents, staff, governors and pupils themselves to tell their own stories is one way of enabling children to see that Christianity, like other great world faiths, does not belong to history.

Ultimately it all comes back to story. As teachers of primary pupils, we can never be sure of the way that story works within our pupils, yet if we ask ourselves about the stories we have heard, told, read or written, stories that have remained with us and have influenced the way we see the world, have helped us to make meaning, then we should realize that story is one of the most valuable assets we have in the classroom. For a story is like a seed sown, whose shoot if nurtured can provide grafting ground for the deeper understanding of those questions which lie at the heart of our existence.

Notes

1   WILLIAMS, M. (1983) *The Velveteen Rabbit*, London, Heinemann.
2   ROSEN, H. *Stories and Meanings*, London, NATE.
3   ROBINSON, E. (1986) 'The religious experience of life', *Review No. 16 East Sussex RE publication*, September.
4   MOFFETT, J. (1983) *Towards a Universe of Discourse*, London, Heinemann.
5   FOX, C. (1989) 'Divine dialogues' in ANDREWS, R. (Ed.) *Narrative and Argument*, Oxford, Oxford University Press and FOX, C. (1989) 'Children thinking through story', *English in Education*, Spring.
6   ROSEN, B. (1988) *And None of it was Nonsense*, London, Mary Glasgow.
7   Assemblies adapted from ideas in 'Share the word' (1976) London Church Information Office.

11 Drama as a Teaching Strategy in Primary RE

Kate Fleming

> Drama teaches us to think, to examine and to explore, to test by
> hypotheses and discover truth. Thus it is the basis of science as
> well as art. But also because it relates us dramatically to know-
> ledge, providing us with a significant and realisable relationship
> to content.[1]

The value of drama as a teaching strategy has long been established,
practice in school, however, is spasmodic and extremely variable in
quality. The history of it, also, is chequered, pioneers emerging with
fashionable ideas and methods, no praise, no blame, no proscenium arch,
everybody being everything, then suddenly these fade away, and another
set of strategies and doctrines appears to mystify us once again. Nevertheless the basic facts are steadfast, and if we believe Bruner's claim that
human beings possess a natural ability to explore their world, then drama
as a means to learning cannot be ignored. By setting up drama situations
in a wide variety of ways, teachers can provide children with the opportunity to explore their world in structured and safe conditions. This is not
the sole right and privilege of the drama teacher and the venue does not
have to be the hall. Children do not always need to be leaping about like
maniacs, expressing themselves and getting rid of their inhibitions; they
can be quiet, reflective, unexpressive and inhibited. All primary teachers
have this strategy at their disposal, irrespective of their own ability, and
each classroom holds the potential to create learning situations from
drama activities.

In a curriculum area like religious education, which has as its pivot
human experience, the use of drama as a teaching strategy should be both
obvious and effective. It can provide direct experience corresponding to
that of life, and through this children can come towards an understanding
of concepts, they can examine issues, solve problems, pose and answer
questions and develop a relationship to content. The experiential nature

of the activity reveals a need to discover and tease out meanings, which with a more academic strategy can be left untouched and veiled in mystery. This, of course, is dangerous ground. It is high risk teaching, making the teacher vulnerable, and encouraging children to question, to probe, to disagree, to search and not simply to be the passive recipients of doctrines and well-established, deeply entrenched ideology.

There could, therefore, be a subversive quality lurking there, which might appear incongruous to the cognoscenti of religious education. The parable of 'The Good Samaritan' offers some interesting insights into this incongruity. This familiar fable, illustrating doctrine and duty, must have been recounted at some stage in primary classrooms throughout the ages in every Christian and many non-Christian countries. The aims underlying the telling of this story using a drama strategy, could vary considerably from those underlying a more academic strategy. Whereas the latter aims to impart the sequence of the narrative and clarify a duty, the former can extend the aims to making the learning memorable, extracting significant elements, and exploring these abstract elements in a concrete form, offering an opportunity for the exploration of feelings and responses to the situations that emerge. It is the difference between reading the manual and driving the car.

> Children rarely forget what they have created, but unlike a paint-
> ing a drama cannot be thrown away or lost, it is a part of them
> and a part of you.[2]

The preparation and structure for a drama activity based on 'The Good Samaritan' has to be detailed and disciplined though this may be contrary to common belief both in and out of the profession. A delicate balance has to be achieved between creating a framework from which to work, and constructing a cage from which there is no escape. It is not a time when children do what they like, nor a session where the teacher plunges in head first. In order to implement the aims, therefore, it is necessary to work out a series of strategies, because the simple straight-forward enactment of the parable will not suffice. Acting out the narra-tive encourages preoccupation with who is going to be the mule and other complexities of casting, plot and scenario. It can be agony for the insecure and sensitive, create problems within group relationships and fuel feelings of elitism: the chosen few! The emphasis is on teasing out the meaning and creating an atmosphere which is rigourous, intellectually, emotionally, socially and spiritually. If, during this process, exciting dramatic sequences develop which could be shared, then this is an added bonus.

The parable needs to be broken down into areas of exploration on which to focus, the journey, for example, the brutal and cowardly attack, the idea of commitment, and the importance of caring and trust. The drama, therefore, could be divided into four sessions each with its own focus. The journey made by the traveller could be set in an environment different from one known to the children, as it would have been in the story, making it easier and safer to draw analogies to situations within their experience and relevant to their lives. It could be barren, hot, dusty and arid, the road carved out through jagged rock formations in which could lurk all kinds of danger. The initial response could come from handling pieces of rock and looking at slides of geological structures. Discussion about the qualities inherent in the inanimate matter could lead to exploration of body shape, giving form to ideas, and creating an environment through which the traveller could move. Presuming that the road from Jerusalem to Jericho was fraught with danger, and that was known to the man, children can work out ways of intensifying the atmosphere. What is threatening and intimidating, which sound or movements create fear, and what kind of tricks can imagination play. The children can take on the role of the traveller, moving through the rock shapes to experience, within the safety of the drama, how it might feel. The attack can pose horrific problems for teachers, especially the in-experienced, as it is a wonderful excuse for fighting with rulers and legalized anarchy. The traveller did after all encounter,

> ... thieves, which stripped him of his raiment, and wounded
> him and departed, leaving him half dead.[3]

It is necessary here to use a different strategy. What means can one devise to guide children away from recalcitrant behaviour and channel their energies to encourage them to think seriously about this part of the story. A useful link can be forged between the inanimate nature of the rock formation and the animation of the thieves. At what point does the traveller realize that the rocks are simply camouflage for the dust covered attackers, and why and how the rocks transform. The change might be imperceptible, the actual transition frightenly slow or horrifyingly fast, only the final realization that eyes are focused on the traveller can move the teaching naturally into the next part of the story.

The question of what makes the attack unfair and cowardly can promote interesting discussion and insight into the whole idea of power and overpowering, developing into imaginative situations which explore the feelings, problems and dynamics associated with one against the group, the outsider, the power of the group, and handling situations against the odds.

Drama, in conventional terms, may be an inappropriate strategy to use at this stage, and it might be advisable to choose another mode in which to work. The children might find concentration easier using still photograph techniques with a camera available to capture outstanding moments, all this is heavily dependent on discussion and problem solving.

The teacher, to develop this, might question the children specifically: if we move this person here how does this affect the overall effect of the photograph; if we change the body position or the facial expression of the attacker in this group will that affect the overall image that we are creating and other people are reading. What is each person in the group photograph thinking, feeling, anticipating and how does he/she relate to other members of the group. Alternatively, another art form could focus the exploration in more depth; slow motion movement developing into dance might prove a better vehicle for the translation of this concept into a communicable form, or a combination of percussion instruments used to heighten the tension and elevate the experience. It is, after all, the quality of the experience which affects concept formation and comprehension, the greater the experience, the more abstract, and thus valuable, a concept becomes.

The commitment of the Samaritan to the wounded man is both poignant and significant, its relevance to the children's world, however, needs unravelling. In order to tease out ideas and develop drama that has depth and substance it is sometimes necessary to start the exploration at quite a simple, even superficial level. In this case the opening activity can have a game-like quality, by placing some kind of symbol on the floor, a piece of clothing, a bundle, something amorphous, hard to identify, and inviting the children to walk past the symbol with as many different motivations as possible; too busy, too embarrassed, too frightened, too preoccupied, too late, and so on. The initial question is about commitment. Once this has been thoroughly explored, discussed and reflected upon, then children have the opportunity to enter into some kind of commitment which is dependent on the motivation giving their drama purpose. It is important that each individual child is left to decide if he/she is going to make that commitment and to what degree. This can bring out many different reactions and layers of behaviour, from total commitment to interested observer, to cautious concern from afar, to complete disregard. From observing each others' facial and bodily expression children can imagine the thoughts, private fears and anxieties that such a situation can generate, thus throwing a different light on the people in the story who, '. . . passed by on the other side'. Life, they discover, is not simply black and white, and human behaviour is intensely complex and multifaced.

The final section of this exploration has its focus on caring and trust, and the aim is two-fold. Children, some exceptionally so, need practice in looking after people, treating them gently, sensitively, and developing bonds of mutual trust. This is what the Samaritan did to the wounded traveller, in a situation which was dangerous, and it entailed giving up time and money to his commitment. This work has to start slowly with the children working on their own, handling material, imaginary or real, in different ways, so that they can consciously experience the sensations and formulate their accompanying thoughts. The starting point for this activity might come from a visual art session with clay. To this the drama can be added, a human sculpture, one wounded and one committed to help, so that the all-important moment of commitment is now, through the drama, under close scrutiny, blocked off from the real world, suspended in time, in which all the complications of the situation can be examined, changed, shared and absorbed. The other aspect of this activity that should come out in the all-important post-drama discussion is whether it is sensible to move people who are lying down and injured, how wise is it for primary school children to commit themselves to bodies in the street. The whole question of what one would do in similar real life situations is then discussed. These four workshops could be used as part of a religious education project, the first as a starting point with the fourth as a culmination. If, as mentioned earlier, the work has produced group or pair work which was dramatically interesting in visual or atmospheric terms then this could be developed into a presentation to be shared with others on a large or small scale, incorporating personal writing, music and dance generated by the wide ranging nature of the project.

The genesis of drama is in play, therefore it creates areas of learning which are natural, absorbing and consequently memorable. Instead of simply talking about, albeit talking is vital in the process, the potential is there to think from within. By experiencing from the inside children are able to discover the implications of a role which could lead to a change in understanding. In religious education opportunities for children to do this seem to be rare, and quite often this is because it is handled too carefully and roped off like some sacred artefact. Drama can be used to build bridges between curriculum areas and, as in life, religious education can emerge from highly unlikely sources. A weighing activity seems firmly planted in the maths and science domain, and indeed this is where it can start, but it is possible that in a parallel study, through drama, the idea of equilibrium, harmony, equality, or just proportion of weight or power can be extended to encompass life situations which reflect the human struggle of balance and imbalance. To look again, in a different context, at scales and weights as a metaphor for life can provide opportunities for children to think from within. The idea is rich in language potential, inviting discussion stimulated by the weighing process, and states of harmony and inequality. For example which side is disadvantaged, that which is weighed down, or that which is high and free; is that which is without weight advantaged, or stranded, helpless and without hope; what could the weights represent: guns, money, votes, people, land, faith, conviction. An appropriate strategy with which to develop this starts with simple pair work. The children explore, through movement and problem solving, and transfer the emphasis from low to high with the concentration on the moment of transition, equilibrium, when neither is high nor low. This can then be structured, the low position, for example one of weakness, and the high one of power, thus in the sequence the weak becomes powerful and the powerful becomes weak, with a transition which could be called conflict, negotiation, bargaining or persuasion. In concrete terms the children can interpret this in many ways, bully and bullied, master and slave, hunter and hunted, and this, when shared, can promote lengthy and in-depth discussion about issues which are of enormous importance in their lives. It can also provide a solid foundation for looking at specific Bible stories in religious education. Universal themes of good and evil, people coming from positions of weakness to win in impossible situations can easily be oversimplified and the learning value be virtually non-existent. David and Goliath, in the short term, is the story of the shepherd boy who kills the giant, but if the starting point were a set of scales, and the opportunity constructed to explore the whole idea of power, immeasurable intrinsic learning can take place, and this cannot be assessed. The need to stretch children's thinking into ideas which are abstract and beyond what they know, dramatically increasing the individual's ability to cope with life, has to be central to all teaching. Through this idea of transference world problems such as starvation, persecution, political and religious tensions can be interpreted and given a form, thus making them more manageable. Life and death featured in the work of a class of 9–10-year-olds, showing insight and an understanding of the mystery of infinity. The children developed an affinity with the wonder of the creation and recreation of life which would not have been possible without access to the symbolic language of drama to interpret abstract concepts into a concrete form, and experience and store symbolically to develop understanding.

A drama activity is a sharing process based on relationships of every possible permutation within the classroom. At its best it is a journey of discovery, potent and exciting for both teacher and child, and one that they take together. Journeys play an important part in Bible stories and could be the starting point for an interesting topic in religious education. Joseph's journey, and that of his brothers in the Old Testament and the journey to Bethlehem in the New Testament, are notable examples, Journeys of migration, of returning home, journeys to death and to birth. Distancing children by using material from the past or imagining the future can encourage them to draw analogies with the present. The story of Joseph and his family and their hazardous journey to a new life in Egypt can have a relevance to many children and should aim to create empathy without, thankfully, the real experience. The journey to Bethlehem only to find that there was nowhere to stay could well reflect today's problems of the young homeless in London.

The epic story of Joseph, like 'The Good Samaritan', needs breaking down, and the essence extracted to establish the foci. If this is not done and the story is simply acted out then the distancing is ineffective and the analogies insignificant. The events of Joseph's dramatic life lend themselves to a wide variety of drama activities. Initially quite a tightly structured session would look particularly at family relationships, individuals being singled out or ostracized. Situations could be set up through which children can explore a range of permutations and combinations, taking on different roles from ones that they play in their real life. Dreams play an important part in Joseph's fortunes and these could be the next focus using a movement strategy and creating the need for children to talk about their dreams and undertake some research into their significance. The conspiracy of the brothers, the plotting and planning, lends itself to language work and has to pose questions about conscience and the complexity of motives. Buying and selling people as opposed to things needs to be firmly placed in a historical context, and yet again carefully considered and structured. It could so easily be superficial, funny for some, painful for others. Set, however, in the right context, worked on slowly, starting, as advocated by Dorothy Heathcote,[4] from 'where you are', helping children and teacher to realize what they already know, providing a springboard from which to progress to higher cognitive levels, schematic learning in practice. Famine and starvation, driving people to leave their native land to find a new, and hopefully better, life has featured throughout history, and is no less applicable to today's world. It might be necessary to help deepen awareness and understanding to look at another period in history which has more real evidence about the kind of momentous decisions that had to be made, the agonies of separation and the hazards of the journey. The early Victorian migration to the New World is well documented and could serve as a means to reflect back to Genesis, chapter 45, and develop empathy with the thousands of refugees undertaking such journeys today.

The uniqueness of drama enables us to bring into the here and now events which are not in the here and now, working as if the fictional were real. It is real because it is happening, but we know it is 'as if'. With this safety valve the imaginative experience allows the child the best of both the fictional and the factual worlds. Teaching in role is an exciting and effective strategy which can focus on a variety of relationships within group dynamics. Primary teachers use it all the time, often without knowing, in the home corner, in the game, as visitor, intruder or counsellor. To be in role is to be highly privileged because the teacher is included in the drama, part of a cohesive group, and this creates a different kind of teacher-learner relationship in which the learner has equal status to the teacher. When teacher and class are in role together, they are 'working as' instead of learning about, and this strategy can be used when it is appropriate. Working as journalists in Jerusalem they can put together a programme about Jesus Christ, assess His newsworthiness, and follow His trial and subsequent journey to Calvary. Working as space scientists in the year 3000 they can track space ships on Christmas

Day visiting countries and planets, going backwards and forwards in time to Bethlehem, past, present and future. Working as Roman soldiers they can experience the harshness and discipline of the military life. Working as undercover agents they can devise their own ways of testing loyalty and handling betrayal, and know what it is like to depend entirely on someone else.

Drama as a teaching strategy in religious education is highly effective. There is a strong bond betweeen the two areas because the concepts and literature discrete to religious education are excellent material for drama, so the relationship is mutual. The experiential nature of drama gives children the opportunity to learn by experience. Moralizing is useless! With the emphasis in drama on understanding and empathy, in creating awareness and the necessity for children to view issues from different standpoints, its vital role in our multicultural society must be realized. There is no one set way to approach drama, it is a wide ranging strategy that integrates easily with other art forms and spans the whole curriculum. It is up to us as teachers to find the way in, to encourage children to work beyond what they already know, to make relationships, and work together to solve problems. It is this type of experience which can change attitudes, develop understanding, and give children the opportunity to come to terms with the society in which they live.

Notes

1 Courtney, R. (1974) *Play Drama and Thought*, London, Cassell.
2 Davies, G. (1953) *Practical Primary Drama*, London, Heinemann Educational, p. 62.
3 *New English Bible*, St Luke, chapter 10.
4 Heathcote, D. (1980) *Drama as Context*, Huddersfield, NATE.

12 Worship in the Primary School

Alan Brown

> The intention behind all these amendments is the avoidance of damaging divisions within a school and its surrounding community. Differences of worship within a community need not divide a community; but they can do so, if, on the one hand, they are overemphasised or, on the other hand, suppressed or ignored. Sometimes the maintenance of harmony within a multifaith school will be best achieved by expression of the differences that exist through provision for different forms of worship. There will also be occasions where common expression of common concerns and interests should be sought.

It was with these words that the Bishop of London presented his amendments on collective school worship to the House of Lords in 1988. The total package of amendments on RE and school worship was forged as the conclusion of many hours of debate in the Lords as well as some urgent discussions in other places. However, it is the clauses on worship that have proved to be the most controversial, raising doubts, concerns and anxieties in the minds of teachers as well as members of religious communities.

We will look at the specific provisions of the Education Reform Act regarding school worship a little later but it is as well to bear in mind that the provisions themselves are quite detailed and therefore, unfortunately, complex. This has resulted in much poor and ill-informed reporting in the national press with many teachers having a false understanding of what is required of them. Baroness Hooper, speaking on behalf of the Government, expressed the concern that many teachers feel:

> First, we wish as far as possible to ensure that the act of collective worship provided for in statute is indeed collective. It is because such an act of worship can perform an important function in binding together members of a school and helping to develop

their sense of community that we in this country make collective worship in schools a statutory requirement although other equally Christian countries do not do so. *This educational value of worship must be clearly distinguished from confessional acts of worship which are properly pursued by practising Christians and members of other faiths.* (my emphasis)

It is not the intention of this chapter to rerun the House of Lord's debate but it is important to understand a little of the background, a little of the intention behind the words of the statute if teachers are to look positively at the place of worship in the primary school.

What New Requirements Does the Education Reform Act Make?

Firstly, collective worship may mean *either* a single act of worship on the part of the whole school *or* separate acts or worship in 'age groups' or 'school groups'. It may now take place at any time in the school day.

Secondly, for county schools, not voluntary-aided or voluntary-controlled schools, school worship will be expected to 'reflect the broad traditions of Christian belief' and be 'wholly or mainly of a broadly Christian character'. However, *not every* act of school worship has to comply with this requirement, provided that in any one term, the majority or such acts of worship do so.

Thirdly, in providing worship in schools headteachers, who are responsible for its organization, must have regard to the age and aptitude of their pupils as well as their family backgrounds.

Fourthly, a headteacher may, after consulting the governing body, apply to the local education authority's Standing Advisory Council for RE (SACRE) which can modify the requirements for all or part of the school. In doing so it can only agree to the request if the 'broad traditions' of another faith other than Christianity are substituted i.e. all the requirements in paragraphs 1–3 above must be adhered to except in paragraph 2 another religion may be substituted for Christianity.

What this means in practice is that while since 1944 an unwritten rule has been accepted that the content of school worship was totally at the discretion of the headteacher, the 1988 Act tightens the law to some extent though, as we shall see, there is still enormous flexibility available.

Clearly the influence of the SACREs in helping schools to find appropriate models for worship will be vital, for if they will be prepared to draw up broad guidelines, schools, particularly primary schools, will find the 1988 Act to be helpful rather than prescriptive.

The intention of the Bishop of London was fivefold in drawing up his amendments and as a final comment before looking at the practical implications for the primary school it would be helpful to be familiar with them.

> We have sought to provide a framework for worship which,

> first, maintains the tradition of worship as part of the process of education, giving proper place to the Christian religion;

> secondly, maintains the contribution of the collective act of worship to the establishment of values within the school community; yet,

> thirdly, does not impose inappropriate forms of worship on certain groups of pupils;

> fourthly, does not break the school up into communities based on the various faiths of the parents, especially in that it makes some groups feel that they are not really part of the community being educated in the school; and

> lastly, is realisable and workable in practical terms of school accommodation and organisation.

No one could deny the breadth of these intentions, but can intentions be put into practice? Or was the Bishop of London, an educational administrator in the Church in his younger days, simply engaging in wishful thinking?

The Implications

One of the most interesting developments of school worship in primary schools over the last couple of decades has been the increasing use of 'assembly' to create an understanding and awareness of which values should be encouraged within the school. Indeed it may be that 'worship' came to be dropped in common usage in schools because it was felt that worship implied an object worthy of worship but how could schools make worship a compulsory requirement when they were not religious institutions? It is, however, a more correct interpretation of the 1944 Education Act to recognize that the 'compulsory' requirement was laid solely upon the school to ensure the provision and not upon the pupils to attend; the pupils only attended if their parents choose not to exercise their right of withdrawal.

However, 'assembly' has become an acceptable term probably because it releases teachers (and pupils) from the implications and consequences of worship; but this should not be regarded as a solely negative response. The importance of assembling is not lost on educators, nor is it lost on the religious. Virtually every religion finds occasions when its followers gather together to share their commonality in some way. It would be unfortunate if the assembling aspect of worship did not find a full and proper expression in the life of a school. Whatever meanings SACREs or individual headteachers place upon the Education Reform Act's requirements on school worship the coming together of staff and pupils (or perhaps parents and governors too from time to time) should be regarded as one way of contributing to the religious experience of the pupil. Not perhaps religious in a narrow liturgical sense but in the sense of sharing common values and recognizing that one is an individual within a social framework. We need to remember again the words of Baroness Hooper which stressed the educational value of school worship and link that with these wise words from Bedfordshire:

> Assembly can be more than a secular activity. Where worship is understood in a broad sense, assembly can be an activity that:
>
> fosters a sense of fellowship by bringing pupils together;
>
> brings pupils to the threshold of worship;
>
> creates an atmosphere in which those who wish to worship can do so;
>
> encourages a reflective approach to life;
>
> increases sensitivity so that pupils are more aware of the search for meaning in the face of life's mysteries;
>
> introduces pupils to aspects of religious worship in an open and honest atmosphere;
>
> encourages pupils to express their responses in a variety of different ways: music, dance, drama, movement, art and craft, poetry and prose.
>
> If school assembly is not an explicit act of worship but an enjoyable educational experience, closely integrated with the life and work of the school, focusing on what is 'of worth', and aware of some of the vital elements of worship, then the problem of the two opposing requirements — educational and legal — can be reconciled. If worship is understood in this broad sense it has a right and proper place in school assembly. (*Bedfordshire RE series: 'Assembly'*)

How May an Individual School Approach School Worship in the Light of the Above?

One of the major problems regarding worship is that there is little unanimity among Christian theologians as to how worship may be best defined. Add to this debate the diverse religious views on what is meant by 'worship' and the humanist concern regarding worship in any sense of the term, together with the huge diversity of pupils and staff within our schools, and it becomes clear that definitions of worship may be less helpful and even more confusing.

It may be more fruitful for headteachers to think about the range of activities that take place when people worship. Each activity in itself would not be worship but in many religions worship involves one or more of the following; prayer, praise, silence, a sense of community, the power of the spoken word, ritual and an awareness of the important.[1] The Education Reform Act does incorporate school worship as an *educational* activity, part of the curriculum of the school and it will be a relief for schools that this educational emphasis releases them from the 'full-blown' activity of formal worship.

As a general means to interpreting the Act, it would be useful for school staffs not to think initially about the content of school worship but to plan together a series of themes which will have general agreement in the school, removing the need for teachers to exercise their right of withdrawal. As a little in-service activity it may be helpful to try the following little exercise.

1   Regardless of *school* worship and what you feel you should do or not do in the classroom, write down, in *one* minute, as many words as you can that you associate with *worship*.

2   When it is completed, depending on the size of the staff, share your list with a colleague. Then using an overhead projector draw up a composite list. The following is such a list drawn up by one group of teachers

prayer	kneeling
love	adoration
wonder	thanksgiving
deep thought	celebration
singing	gathering
communion	strong feelings or beliefs
praise	petition
mystery	God
friendship	special place
gratitude	reflection
devotion to a deity	

3   Some of these, and some of your list, will be more appropriate to school worship than others. However, depending on the age, aptitude and family background of the pupils in your school you may feel able to select some as being particularly appropriate for your school.

4 With one list of possible concepts and themes you might wish to repeat the one-minute exercise. This time in *one* minute write down what you connect with *Christian worship*.

5 As under 2 above, share your list with a colleague and then draw up a composite list. The same group of teachers as under 2 above drew up the following:

togetherness	commitment	forgiveness
attitudes	consideration	peace
caring	honesty	celebration
sharing	self-awareness	examples of Christian life
moral code		

6 Finally, looking carefully at both lists you will probably find that some terms complement each other.

In addition, you probably have quite a long list of important themes which can be used as 'worship topics' or 'assembly themes' during the year. Of course it is likely that your 'Christian' list will contain many words which may be relevant to Christianity but not specifically or exclusively Christian. They will however be *characteristic* of Christianity.

In a NFER/RE Council questionnaire to all RE LEA advisers the following were included in their list on what themes would be pertinent to Christianity:

compassion	conviction	corporate responsibility
self–sacrifice	humility	tolerance
trust	mercy	self–reliance
forgiveness	self–knowledge	perseverance
cooperation	respect	consideration
integrity	concern	

When one looks at these lists it will probably become apparent that the 'wholly or mainly Christian' requirement has a broad interpretation. Of course the themes chosen may well be important for other faiths but if parents or governors who visit the school are shown your list very few of them would deny the importance of children reflecting on such values. It will be helpful for headteachers to keep a log of what happens in assembly but, in general, if parents can understand that such a list of themes will be explored, in a variety of ways, during the pupils' time in school, they will be reassured. Of course, one can never please everyone the whole time but planning and resourcing will be an important feature of the educational approach to school worship.

This is probably a surfeit of lists and words but it does indicate that the Education Reform Act may focus the headteacher's mind on what should be done in worship. It also indicates that many of the above already reflect common practice in primary schools, and while each word may have a definite 'religious' context, it also has a moral and a value content and so contributes, along with the other words, to the creation of acceptable, even desirable, values within the life of the school. Whatever one's religion, or life stance, there are few words in the above collection which would not be seen as making an important contribution to the individual, the school and society.

> For the educational possibilities of assembly to be realised basic approaches will include experiencing and expressing the excitement, delight and wonder of many childlike responses. There will be a place for celebration and for reflection for human experiences, both joyful and sad. The aim will be to invite full participation, of staff and pupils, and to integrate the contribution of assembly with that of the rest of the curriculum, the whole life of the school, and the local community.[2]

What Content will be Suitable?

If so far we have concentrated (i) on the variety of activities associated with worship; and (ii) on which themes and concepts are characteristic of worship and also Christian worship in particular, this is because unless we can build a framework which reflects our aims and objectives it is not really possible to look for the content which might fill the chosen themes.

There are many, many assembly books and resource packs containing stories, songs and activities from various religions and cultures. It should be possible for a member of staff to have responsibility for school worship and to ensure that the school is properly resourced. There will still be scope for the class presentation of work, for the collective celebration of special days and special events.

> The school assembly provides a unique opportunity for all pupils and staff to learn together. It is essentially an occasion for sharing common values and experiences. Some aspects of the school's work, the achievement of a group of pupils or an individual effort may provide suitable themes for assembly with presentation by staff or pupils as appropriate. School events, religious occasions and festivals of the various faiths, local news, music, drama and art can all be used when appropriate to exemplify how the benefits and values presented in the school may be shared and reported. There may then follow a time for quiet and personal reflection. Subsequently, when invited, some pupils may wish to express thanks and gratitude by joining in a short prayer; others may not. Prayers that are specific to any one faith and which

assume commitment on the part of all those involved should be used with care. For example, the presenter might say, 'this is a prayer that means a lot to me. I hope you will enjoy listening to it and thinking about it' ... It is important that schools should make use of the stories and prayers from the major world faiths. In these ways assembly becomes ... an extension of work done in the classroom.... Neither hymn nor songs always have to be sung in assembly and sometimes simply listening to music is a more appropriate and effective activity. When they are used, however, they should be chosen carefully so that they can be sung with feeling and understanding by the whole age-range of pupils present. (*Religious Education in Warwickshire Schools and Colleges 1985*)

In its guidelines to schools on the place of worship in schools after the Education Reform Act the Hertfordshire LEA builds on the above:

The Act requires that collective worship be of 'a broadly Christian character' and by concentrating on those characteristics which are shared by Christian and other traditions, the school act of worship can become a purposeful collective spiritual act which sets the tone for all of its pupils for the school day ...

In achieving this meaningful act of worship it is important to distinguish between worship and ritual. Rituals such as prayer, hymns, readings from scripture are means to worship not worship in themselves. Schools may feel that other means of worship are as valid. Such as:

stories and readings	sacred/secular readings
dance and drama	artefacts and natural
prayer/meditations	materials
creative silence	children's contributions to
songs/hymns/music	visual arts

but the authors add important advice 'The use of some of the above means of worship may not be appropriate to some faith communities.'

These long quotations are important because they reflect much of the professional concerns of the teacher. No one would argue that the complexity of issues that surround school worship could ever be easily resolved or ever will be. However, the Bishop of London's amendments may well have dragged school worship out of its rather traditional and hide-bound format for it is now clearly a part of the curriculum. As other subjects have developed and particularly in the primary school cross-curricular practices have become common-place, the act of worship has often been treated as a separate entity. Surely most schools will now discuss the implications of school worship for their pupils, staff, governors and the local community. There is an opportunity, as demonstrated by the above, to use both the flexibility of the Act and the quoted intentions of the Bishop to begin a new 'era' for school worship.

Notes

1   This is argued in 'School Worship: A Memorandum' available from the National Society, Church House, Great Smith Street, Westminster, London SW1P 3NZ, 40p + postage and packing. It also considers the whole range of issues connected with School Worship. A new booklet 'School Worship' which sets out the implications for the new Act for headteachers and governors is also available from the Society.
2   WRAGG, I. (1981) 'The purpose and nature of school assembly', *Resource*, **3**, p. 2, spring.

References

School Worship

I = Infant, J = Junior, S = Secondary, + = General

Readings, stories, anthologies
J   ALLEN, L. (1984) *Stepping Stones*, London, Batsford.
       A collection of stories with ideas for follow-up in the classroom. Each story is subtitled with the moral theme it is trying to put over, for example 'The Terrible Traffic Jam (Consideration for Others)'. Little attempt has been made to take into account the multicultural nature of many schools today.
JS   BAILEY, J. (1981) *Themework*, London, Stainer and Bell.
       This may well be in many staff libraries — worth resurrecting and using selectively. A trigger for ideas of newer material.
J   BANKS, H. (1987) *Bright Ideas — Assembly*, Leamington, Scholastic.
       Ideas for primary assemblies previously published in *Scholastic* magazines.
IJ   BARRATT, S. (1982) *Tinder Box Assembly Book*, London, A & C Black.
       Suggestions for integrated assembly and classroom activities. Themes explored are 'self', 'others', 'surroundings', 'times of difficulty' and 'celebration'.
IJ   BIRCH, B. (1985) *Assemblies Round the Year*, London, Ward Lock.
       A systematic look at the school year with stories and ideas for particular days. It includes musical arrangements.
IJ   BOARD OF EDUCATION *Together for ... Christmas, Easter, Harvest, Holy Week, Festivals ...*, London, Church House Publishing.
S   BUTLER, D.G. (1975) *Many Lights*, Leominster, Fowler Wright.
       One of the few multi-faith assembly books that sets out to take all faiths seriously and to see how their insights can be used and developed.

S   CAMPLING, C. and DAVIS, M. (1969) *Words for Worship*, London, Arnold.
     Themes and ideas for assemblies.
JS   CAUSLEY, C. (1982) *The Sun Dancing*, London, Kestrel.
     A wide-ranging collection of readings under subject headings.
     This series is based on material which first appeared in *Together* magazine. A
     useful quarry of ideas.
S   *Celebrating One World*, London, CAFOD/St Thomas More Centre.
     For *any* secondary school trying to help pupils to make Christian sense of a
     world where conflict and injustice seem to be overwhelming. A personal
     resource for teachers in primary schools. One of the best of its kind.
JS   COPLEY, T. (1989) *Worship, Worries and Winners*, London, National Society/
     Church House Publishing.
     A look at the implications for school worship in the light of the Education
     Reform Act with ten kinds of assemblies tried and tested in schools. Amus-
     ing and practical.
JS   DARGUE, W. (1983) *Assembly Stories from Around the World*, Oxford, Oxford
     University Press.
     Useful as a teacher resource.
JS   DARGUE, W. (1985) *Heroes of the Faiths*, Oxford, Oxford University Press.
     A useful teacher resource although most of the stories are unsuitable for
     reading aloud to primary school children as they stand. It is also a pity that
     there are no heroines.
S   DAVIS, M. (1980) *More Words for Worship*, London, Arnold.
     Themes and ideas for assemblies.
S   DE GRUCHY, J. (1986) *Cry Justice*, London, Collins.
     Prayers, readings and music from the embattled Christians of South Africa.
     If you or you pupils do not see how Christians can get involved in matters
     of social justice, this will make it clear.
JS   EGAN, P. (1986) *The Christmas Road*, London, Church House Publishing.
     An anthology of poetry and prose for Christmas.
J   FISHER, R. (1984) *Together Today*, London, Bell and Hyman.
     A wide-ranging series of assembly themes showing how they can be related
     to all aspects of the curriculum. Useful resource lists at the back of the book.
J   FISHER, R. (1985) *The Assembly Year*, London, Collins.
     This book is divided into five sections; Calendar of festivals and anniversar-
     ies; Festivals (multifaith); Stories (multifaith); Poems and Prayers (multi-
     faith); Resources.
S   FRANCIS, L. and SLEE, N. (1983) *A Feast of Words*, London, Collins.
     Useful collection of poems, prayers, and readings to use as a quarry and
     resource.
+   GILBERT, J. (1986) *Festivals*, Oxford, Oxford Universtiy Press.
     Published as part of an English series, this contains stories, poems and
     sayings. Helps get at the heart of festivals, leaving people concerned with
     RE to develop the dimensions of prayer and worship. An excellent resource.
IJ   GRIFFIN, W. (1984) *Exploring Primary Assemblies*, London, Macmillan.
     An absolute must for all primary schools. Invites teachers to rethink the
     whole assembly procedure, including coming in, going out, seating and so
     on, as well as examining content and method.

S   HAYLOCK, D. (1988) *Acts for Apostles*, London, Church House Publishing.
Thirteen sketches on Biblical themes.

S   HERBERT, C. (1986) *This Most Amazing Day*, London, Church House
Publishing.
Easter in Christian traditions ranging across the denominations and through
time.

S   JASPER, T. (1986) *The Secondary Assembly Book*, London, Blandford.
Tony Jasper is both a Methodist lay-preacher and a disc jockey with a big
radio following.

JS MOSS, D. (1986) *A Word for Your Year*, London, Collins.
A book of year assemblies for secondary schools. Could be a springboard
for your own assemblies.

IJ PROFITT, R. and BISHOP, V. (1983) *Hand in Hand*, Harlow, Longman.
Multicultural rather than inter-faith assemblies for infants and juniors. Not
particularly religious, but quite moral!

S   PROSSER, B. (1984) *Gathered Together*, Amersham, Hulton.
Biblically-based and rather conventional.

JS PURTON, R. (1979) *Assemblies*, Oxford, Blackwell.
Daily themes and suggestions. Mostly predictably Christian and western/
cultural.

JS PURTON, R. (1983) *Spring and Summer Days*, and *Autumn and Winter Days*,
Oxford, Blackwell.
Collections of information about births, deaths, events, sayings and customs
for every day of the year. Useful teacher resources.

S   SELF, D. (1982) *Anthology for Assembly*, London, Hutchinson.
A useful collection, both as a quarry and as a trigger for your own ideas.

IJ TAYLOR, D. (1981) *Exploring Red Letter Days*, London, Lutterworth.
A book of themes for assembly. Each chapter has a number of ideas for
stories, poems, prayers, music and activities. There are also suggestions for
follow-up work in the classroom.

I   VAUSE, D. (1985) *The Infant Assembly Book*, London, Macdonald.
A term-by-term collection of ideas for assembly with a special section on
festivals. Ideas include classroom work, discussion points, songs, hymns,
activities and a children's book list.

J   WARD, C.M. (1984) *Assemblies A–Z*, Oxford, Blackwell.
Assembly themes/stories with suggested prayers and hymns. Some reference
to other cultures and faiths. A source of ideas rather than something to be
used as it stands.

Music

IJ CLARKE, H. and KNEALE, P. (1984) *A Time to Sing*, London, Macmillan.
A hundred hymns and songs, traditional and modern, with instrumental
parts available.

IJ CROSS-BEGGS, B. (1983) *A Musical Calendar of Festivals*, London, Ward Lock.
Folk songs of festivals from around the world with music. There are very
few hymns as such.

IJ GADSBY, D. and HOGGARTH, J. (1980) *Alleluya*, London, A & C Black.
Very general, some semi-religious, assembly songs. A few suitable for
worship.

JS *Their Words, My Thoughts* (1981) Oxford, Oxford University Press.
A collection of hymns and prayers.

Prayers

+ APPLETON, G. (1985) *The Oxford Book of Prayer*, Oxford, Oxford University Press.
A collection of prayers across many countries and many traditions, including prayers of faiths other than Christianity. An adult book — but some great prayers can be used in primary schools as words to listen to and think about.

IJ DONEY, M. (1981) *The Piccolo Book of Prayers*, London, Piccolo.
A mixture of ideas about how to pray and prayers, together with children's comments.

+ *Leaves from the Tree of Peace* (1986) London, URC.
An anthology of prose, poetry and prayers, beautifully illustrated with photographs and embroideries on the theme of peace.

J *The Lion Book of Children's Prayers* (1977) Tring, Lion.
A useful resource book of prayers which children can use easily to find suitable prayers for their assembly.

J PURTON, R. (1984) *Dear God*, Oxford, Blackwell.
Useful teacher resources. Prayers are categorized under subject headings and are suitable for young children.

JS RUNCIE, R. and HUME, B. (1987) *Prayers for Peace*, London, SPCK.
An adult book compiled by the leaders of the Roman Catholic and Anglican churches in Britain — for adult pondering and use in secondary assemblies.

Prayer books

Book of Common Prayer
Should be in schools for its language and tradition — and such things as an alternative version of Psalm 23! The collects can be 'prayers to listen to'.

Alternative Service Book (1980)
A book for reference — especially where children watch worship on TV etc. Has the modern versions of great prayers. A source of prayers and readings for secondary schools.

SILK, D. (1980) *Prayers for Use at Alternative Services*, London, Mowbray.
Prayers in modern English arranged thematically.

SIMPSON, W.W. (1965) *Jewish Prayer and Worship*, SCM.
Source of prayers, especially for secondary schools.

Audio visual

BEDFORDSHIRE *Assembly Line*, tape/slides.
A useful aid for promoting constructive staff-room discussion about assembly.

CHURCH SCHOOL GOVERNORS TRAINING PROJECT *School Worship*, video.
Written as part of a series of training tapes, this would be a good discussion starter, although many would not consider the assemblies shown to be particularly good!

CHURCH OF SCOTLAND *It's OUR Assembly!*, video.
Another discussion starter, emphasizing the importance of children's participation.

HOUSETOP *Prayer in the Home*, video.
Although about prayer within the family, this video could be useful as a guide to the circumstances and experiences which help prayer to develop as a corporate activity.

HOUSETOP *Seven Circles of Prayer*, video.
Can be shown in small 'doses' to secondary and possibly top junior pupils. Imaginative, meditative, beautifully photographed. Very good discussion and teaching starter. Teaching notes available.

For Teachers

BEDFORDSHIRE LEA (1985) *Assembly: Bedfordshire RE Series*, Bedford.

CHURCH OF ENGLAND BOARD OF EDUCATION (1984) *School Worship: A Discussion Paper*, London, National Society.

DIGEST IN EDUCATION (1988) 'Teaching Religious Education', London, Longman, 18 November.

GRIFFIN, W. (1984) *Exploring Primary Assemblies*, London, Macmillan.

HERTFORDSHIRE COUNTY COUNCIL EDUCATION DEPARTMENT (1989) *Guidelines for School Worship*, Hertford.

HULL, J.M. (1975) *School Worship: An Obituary*, SCM Press (now out of print but worth reading if a copy can be found).

HULL, J.M. (1989) *The Act Unpacked*, London, CEM.

NATIONAL SOCIETY FOR PROMOTING RELIGIOUS EDUCATION (1988) *Religious Education and School Worship in the 1988 Education Act*, London, National Society.

NATIONAL SOCIETY FOR PROMOTING RELIGIOUS EDUCATION (1989) *School Worship*, London, National Society.

NORTHAMPTONSHIRE LEA (1987) *School Assembly and Worship: Towards a Policy for Good Practice*, Northampton.

TAYLOR, M.J. (1989) *Religious Education: Values and Worship*, NFER/REC.

WARWICKSHIRE LEA (1985) *Religious Education in Warwickshire Schools*, Warwick.

13   Attainment in RE: An Exploration

Derek Bastide

The Education Reform Act is concerned, among other things, that children should have an entitlement to a 'balanced and broadly based curriculum which promotes the spiritual, moral, cultural, mental and physical development of pupils at the school ...' (section 1.2). To promote this end it requires that pupils study during their school careers, a wide range of specified subjects which together comprise the basic curriculum, consisting of religious education and the ten Foundation subjects (English, mathematics, science, technology, history, geography, music, art, physical education and, in key stages 3 and 4, a language — plus Welsh in schools in Wales. More than this, to ensure some similarity of experience among school pupils, each of the Foundation subjects will have a nationally laid down content of skills, knowledge and understanding. The responsibility to impart this to their charges is placed on all schools in the maintained sector.

That the content of the school curriculum should be so closely defined indicated a radical change of direction in the educational system of England and Wales and was, at least initially, a disturbing development for most schools. Strong feelings were expressed over a period of time about the feasibility of some of the new requirements and the Secretary of State has used his powers under the Act to introduce modifications. In January 1991, for example, he removed the requirement that pupils in Key Stage 4 (14–16 years) should have to follow all the Foundation subjects. This modification does not seriously affect the general principle that all pupils have the right to a common educational experience, similar in the range of subjects and in the required content.

For this to be a reality the Education Reform Act requires both that the levels which children are expected to attain be clearly defined and that their progress should be assessed. A concomitant of the principle of entitlement is assessment in that it is clearly of little use specifying the curriculum, with its skills, knowledge and understanding, to which each child is entitled and the levels which they are expected to attain, if there is no way of ascertaining that it has been delivered. If education purports to impart skills, to increase knowledge and understanding and to develop competencies then it is essential that teachers, pupils and their parents should know to what extent this happening. Teachers have, of course, always assessed children's work and made judgments about both their ability and progress, though it has to be said that often it has been done in an intuitive and unplanned way; what has now changed is that the Education Reform Act has highlighted assessment, formalized it and built it clearly into a legal framework. The type of assessment which primary school teachers are generally used to is what is now described as *formative* assessment so the requirement to produce a summative assessment of each child at the ages of 7 and 11 in several areas of the curriculum using a prescribed method has come, in many cases, as an unwelcome challenge.

In the terms of the Education Reform Act the teaching and learning process involves a number of key ideas: attainment targets, statements of attainment and programmes of study.

Attainment Targets

Attainment targets indicate the knowledge, skills and understanding a pupil is expected to achieve between the ages of 5–16 (the ages when the National Curriculum applies). These targets provide in each subject the goals towards which both pupils and teachers are working. Within the period covering the ages 5–16 years, there are ten attainment *levels*, and each of these levels corresponds roughly to age group. Hence Level 1 relates to school year 1 (5–6 years), Level 2 to school year 2 (6–7 years) and so on.

Statements of Attainment

Each of the ten levels of attainment has its own statements of attainment. These statements of attainment lay out the knowledge, understanding and skills required for each of the ten levels of attainment.

Programmes of Study

Programmes of Study provide the subject content, skills and processes which must be taught to pupils and it is within the Programmes of Study that the Attainment Targets and Statements of Attainment must be met. There is no implication that the teacher should just teach to the targets — the Programmes of Study are broader than the targets.

Assessment is usually perceived to have four main interlocking purposes:

(i) *informative* — assessment finds out what progress has been made and this information can be conveyed to pupils and their parents;

(ii) *formative* — in this way pupils can be helped to be involved in the assessment process;

(iii) *diagnostic* — assessing pupils' progress identifies strengths and weaknesses and enables teachers to act accordingly;

(iv) *summative* — assessment makes it possible to present a record of attainment at a particular stage.

If these are appropriate, helpful and normal for other areas of the basic curriculum there is no good reason why they should not be the same for RE. Since the appearance of the Education Reform Act a number of working parties have been established to consider how best arrangements could be made to assess RE. Notable among these are the Westhill group which has produced *Attainment in RE: A Handbook for Teachers* and the University of Exeter project on Forms of Assessment in RE, *A FARE deal for RE*.

Assessment Arrangements

The Education Reform Act divides the years of compulsory schooling into four key stages: 5–7 years, 7–11 years, 11–14 years and 14–16 years. At the end of each Key Stage pupils will be assessed to discover their attainment level. Each pupil will be placed on one of the attainment levels and this will be reported to parents and the overall achievement in each school to the general public. Initially the Education Reform Act required that each pupil should be assessed in each National Curriculum subject at the end of each Key Stage. However, this has been modified so that at the end of Key Stages 1 and 2 assessment of pupils will be required in only the core subjects of the National Curriculum (English, mathematics and science). The purpose of the assessments is to provide evidence of achievement. Assessment will be by a combination of teacher assessment and observation and Standard Assessment Tasks (SATs) which will be laid down nationally.

What Should RE do?

RE is the one subject which the Education Reform Act requires to be taught which it does not require to be assessed and reported upon at the end of each Key Stage. The Secretary of State for Education and Science has no power under the Act to set attainment targets in RE — though neither does the Act prohibit local education authorities from doing so.

Since the Education Reform Act became law, a vigorous debate has raged within RE circles about the propriety of introducing a form of assessment with attainment targets and associated programmes of study into RE.

At a meeting of teachers, college tutors and RE advisers to consider this question there was a lively discussion on both attainment targets and on the idea of assessment in RE. On attainment there was considerable agreement. Many present felt that RE tended to be unplanned and hapha-zard in many primary schools. As one teacher put it:

> A teacher plans a topic on 'Water' and adds the story of Noah's Ark so that RE is included along with science, geography and so on on the topic web. How is that going to help the children's understanding of religion to grow and develop? For all we know the children could do Noah's Ark every year in topics like 'Ani-mals' or 'Boats'!

Other teachers quoted further examples which underlined the situation in very many primary schools where RE was left to the discretion of each individual teacher to include or not and where there was no overall school policy which provided a plan for progression and development in the subject. Attainment targets were seen as a much needed move in the right direction as they would provide identifiable objectives for teachers. As one teacher who confessed that RE was one of her weak areas said:

> I would personally welcome attainment targets with programmes of study because it would give me some structure to work in. I find RE very difficult to get hold of; it seems so broad and the aims laid out in our Agreed syllabus are so general that they are no help!

There was wide agreement in the group that primary school class teachers and their pupils would all benefit from RE having attainment targets and programmes of study which reflected the different aspects of religion. There was also a call that these programmes of study should be, to use the language of education, *content centred* rather than *process centred*.

> It would be so lovely just to know what we ought to be doing — something a bit firmer than the Suggestions' we have had in the past. I'm sure I speak for all teachers who didn't do RE as a main subject.

It was acknowledged that there would inevitably be disagreements about what these attainment targets ought to be but 'it's inevitable that not all will agree — look at the proposals for history and geography — but that's for the Standing Conference to work out in consultation with every-body'.

There was much less agreement over assessment. Those who supported assessment for RE tended to do so because they could see no good reason why RE should be different in this respect from other subjects which make up the basic curriculum. This was countered by the argument succinctly put by one teacher:

> If teachers see assessment and measurement in the form proposed
> as a wearisome imposition, then why introduce it to yet another
> area of the curriculum if it is not actually required by law?

Supporters of assessment, however, argued back that if RE was not to be assessed in the same way as other subjects in the basic curriculum then they feared that many schools would use the excuse of an overcrowded curriculum to ignore it. The principle was likely to be in practice — if it isn't tested, forget it!

A second objection which was frequently raised to assessment in RE was that there are many aspects of RE (as in other areas such as the expressive arts) which are to do with understanding and empathy and are not therefore so accessible to the sort of measurement proposed in the Education Reform Act. There might be a danger, it is argued, that if assessment in this form were introduced, of encouraging RE teaching to focus upon those areas which are more factual, and therefore more easily measured and this would be a disservice to RE. If it is not required by law and if it is not going to aid the pupils' understanding of religion, then why do it?

The overall consensus of the meeting was that there were no relevant reasons for treating RE differently from other subjects in the basic curriculum in this respect and while there was apprehension about the form that SATs could take and an awareness of the danger to affective aspects of RE, there was a conviction that assessment in some form or other was an essential element in the process of teaching and learning. It is an interesting footnote that since this conference, the Secretary of State for Education and Science has used his powers under the Act to reduce the number of subjects which must be assessed and reported upon at Key Stages 1 and 2 to the three core subjects, English, mathematics and science only. It is no longer required that the other Foundation subjects be assessed and reported upon at these first two Key Stages although non-statutory SATs will be provided for those who wish to use them. All the Foundation subjects will still have their programmes of study and attainment targets at Key Stages 1 and 2. It is likely that this modification in assessment arrangements will reduce the desire of some SACREs to devise their own SATs for RE.

Establishing a Firm Base for RE

If Agreed Syllabuses are to contain attainment targets then it is essential that there is a sound basis upon which to build. The Education Reform Act itself gives some guidance as to the breadth of this basis when it states that any new Agreed Syllabus must:

> reflect the fact that the religious traditions in Great Britain are in the main Christian whilst taking account of the teaching and practices of the other principal religious traditions represented in Great Britain.

From this it is clear that the content of RE must be drawn from a number of religious traditions though, as was discussed in chapter 3 'Religious Education and the Education Reform Act', the Act does not lay down the proportion of time for each one nor give guidance as to whether this breadth must be represented at infant as well as secondary school level. However, it is clear that under the law, any new syllabus which decided to omit the study of Christianity or did not take account of Hinduism, Islam, Judaism or Sikhism would be unacceptable.

Beyond this, however, in establishing a sound basis for an RE syllabus it is necessary to look into the nature of religion itself. If RE is principally about, as the Hampshire Agreed Syllabus expresses it:

> The principal aim of religious education in schools within the public sector is to enable pupils to understand the nature of religious beliefs and practices and the importance and influence of these in the lives of believers.

Then we have to explore carefully what *religion* actually is. It is the answer to this question which will begin to form the basis of an RE syllabus within which attainment targets can be established.

In very many primary schools RE is often taught in a haphazard way. Frequently it consists of a series of stories about Jesus along a theme such as the miracles of Jesus or it focuses upon a festival such as Christmas or Diwali or it is an aspect of a general topic such as water or transport. In mathematics, for instance, every school gives considerable attention to coherence, progression and development in the subject. This rarely happens in RE though in their respective chapters Hazel Waddup and Liz Collis show how this has been done for RE in their schools. If we are to give serious consideration to what children ought to know about religion at different stages then it is important that we do have (to use the language of the Education Reform Act) attainment targets and programmes of study. But how do we approach this? What basis do we adopt?

A preliminary to any approach to good practice in religious education must be a consideration of the meaning of the *religious* in religious education. Much popular usage of term 'religious' tends to centre around morality (for example, 'it means leading a good life') or belief (for example, 'it means believing in God'). While it would be wrong to deny that ethics and belief are essential aspects of religion it would at the same time be grossly unfair to religions to regard these as a full and complete account. Many philosophers have over the years attempted to *define* religion with little success in reaching a broad agreement. Perhaps a more fruitful path would be to attempt to *describe* it.

This is an essential activity because it demonstrates how broad is that activity which we call religion. If teachers are to present it to children in a balanced form then it is important that they have a broad basis from which to work. Ninian Smart's seven dimensions of religion provides an efficient and effective account of religion and therefore serves as a comprehensive and balanced *base* upon which teachers can structure their work. These seven dimensions of religion could form the basis for programmes of study and attainment targets for RE.

Religion as a Seven-Dimensional Activity

There is a considerable amount of activity going on in the world which is commonly described as 'religious'. Many, many millions of people claim to belong to one religion or another and over most of the world there is extensive evidence of religious practice and devotion. To observe both closely and widely that phenomenon called religion in its various forms and then to attempt to describe it is likely to give a helpful picture of religion for our purposes. This was the approach adopted by Ninian Smart and the result of his analysis of his observations was summarized firstly in his six dimensions of religion (Smart, 1968) and more recently (Smart, 1989) in his seven dimensions of religion. There is nothing sacrosanct about Smart's account of religion; others might well do it differently. It is, however, described here because many have found it to be a very helpful tool in understanding religion, so helpful, in fact, that it has been used as the basis for a number of approaches to religious education. Smart's seven dimensions of religion are:

> the practical and ritual dimension;
> the experiential and emotional dimension;
> the narrative and mythic dimension;
> the doctrinal and philosophical dimension;
> the ethical and legal dimension;
> the social and institutional dimension;
> the material dimension.

Although Smart has identified these seven dimensions, he would still see a religion as a unity. Although the dimensions can each be identified and studied separately, they are all facets of the same activity and, as such, are interrelated and interconnected indissolubly.

The Practical and Ritual Dimension

The practical and ritual dimension encompasses all those actions and activities which worshippers *do* in the practice of their religion. It ranges from the closing of the eyes in prayer to the once-in-a-lifetime pilgrimage to a holy place. It includes services, festivals, ceremonies, customs, traditions, clothing, symbols. In many ways this dimension is the shop window of a religion. Illustrations of what would come under the heading of the practical and ritual dimension are: the celebration of festivals: Diwali, Christmas, Passover, Eid-ul-Fitr, Guru Nanak's birthday and so on; acts of worship: the eucharist in Christianity, the daily prayers in Islam, the worship of the synagogue, the temple and the gurdwara; the making of pilgrimage to holy places such as Lourdes, Makkah, Jerusalem, Amritsar, Benares. Customs and postures in worship, distinctive forms of dress, initiation rites and many, many other matters would be classified in this dimension.

It is important not to be misled by the use of the word *ritual*. In every day speech this has come to be used in the pejorative sense of something which is empty and mechanical, devoid now of any real meaning or significance. While it is certainly true that religious ritual acts can, like all other acts, degenerate into this state, in this context ritual is merely a neutral descriptive term for the activities in a religion which are significant to its followers. Rituals provide the framework both for sustaining and deepening the worshipper's faith.

The practical and ritual dimension is very closely related to the narrative and mythic dimension (i.e. the stories). Very often the rituals are enactments of the stories. In Judaism an historical event of tremendous significance is the Exodus when the Jews saw the hand of God in rescuing them from from their slavery in Egypt. The Passover meal, celebrated annually in the home, re-enacts this great act of salvation and, during the course of the meal, the ancient story is recounted and made real in the present. On Good Friday Christian pilgrims in Jerusalem regularly retread the Via Dolorosa, the way of sorrow, the path which Christ trod on the way to his crucifixion. As they stop at the various stations of the cross they remember the times that Christ stopped on that journey. The ritual re-enacts the stories and so makes it real and alive to the pilgrims.

The Experiential and Emotional Dimension

At the core of religion is *feeling* and the experiential and emotional dimension bears witness to this. Most, if not all, religious believers would claim that at the centre of their religion is an experience, however fleeting or dim, of the divine. The religious traditions record significant examples: Moses on Mount Horeb when he saw the burning bush, Isaiah of Jerusalem in the temple, St Paul on the road to Damascus, Muhammad in the caves around Makkah, Arjuna as recorded in the Bhagavad Gita. In most religions too, there are mystical traditions in which individuals claim to have had direct and searing experience of the divine. There are also the startling feelings of awe and wonder, what Rudolph Otto described as the 'numinous', in the face of the majesty and wonder of creation which people, and not only believers, experience at certain moments and which are essential to an understanding of the religious impulse.

The experience of most religious believers can be described in much less dramatic and much more homely ways — but none the less significant to them for that. This could be described as a feeling of being in tune with creation, a feeling of being given inner strength in times of difficulty, a feeling as John Wesley expressed it, of the heart at times being strangely warmed.

This dimension was described at the beginning as being the core of religion. This is because it provides the motivation for the believer and makes the practice of religion worthwhile. It is this experience, this feeling, which makes the performing of the rituals a living and satisfying experience rather than a participation in an historical curiosity; it brings the stories to life; it encourages the believer to follow the often difficult ethical path which the religion lays before its adherents; it gives the reason for believers to commit themselves to the credal statements. It is this dimension which is the inner heart of religion.

The Narrative and Mythic Dimension

This dimension, in simple terms the 'story' dimension, is the means of conveying the teaching of a religion through stories, poems, legends, hymns and so on. Every religion has a mass of stories which has become one of its essential elements. These stories are of different kinds. Some will be based on historical events, some are about a time before history, some are about the future, some are about significant people within the religious tradition. In Christianity, for example, crucial stories centre around the life, death and resurrection of Jesus Christ as recorded in the Gospels. Other significant stories involve 'heroes' of the Christian faith, accounts of men and women who have lived out their Christian vocation within their own era. Such 'heroes' who could be drawn from the full sweep of Christian history might include the Apostles, St Augustine, St Benedict, St Francis of Assisi, St Teresa of Avila, Martin Luther, Father Damien, St Maximilian Kolbe and, in our own age, Mother Teresa of Calcutta, Helder Camara of Recife and many, many more. In fact, there are so many significant figures that each individual will have his or her own list! In Islam the key stories centre round the life of the Prophet and the message he delivered. Also of great importance are the accounts of the other prophets from Adam down to Muhammad and the story of the tremendous growth of Islam both in its early years and in the present age.

Most religions have scriptures, sacred writings, which are key documents, written down in many cases after a long period of oral transmission. These scriptures are recognized by the religious community as having authority. Many would see these scriptures as in some sense inspired by God. The Bible, as the sacred book of the Christian religion, is a collection of stories, history (though history with a special interpretation), prophecy, letters, law, poetry and gospels which gained authority within the early church and was finally accepted by the Church as canonical. Most Christians accept the central authority of the Bible and would acknowledge that it is divinely inspired, though they might interpret this in different ways. Islam, Sikhism and Judaism also acknowledge one sacred book, the Qur'an, the Guru Granth Sahib and the Jewish Scriptures respectively and, of course, Christianity and Islam both draw very heavily upon the Jewish tradition. Hinduism is different in that it has a number of sacred books, which it divides into two categories: the *scruti* — that is, scriptures directly inspired by God (the Vedas, the Brahmanas and the Upanishads) and the *dmriti* — that is, books by holy men or prophets (Epics, Puranas, the Bhagavad Gita). The most popular of the Hindu scriptures is the Bhagavad Gita.

A word of clarification is needed. In his earlier account of the six dimensions of religion, Smart (1968) called this dimension the mythological dimension, and although the title has now been adjusted, writers often use the term 'myth' for these stories. This can be unhelpful as in everyday usage the word 'myth' means an untrue story. However, in its more technical sense, the term derives from the Greek *muthos*, which means, literally, 'story'. To describe the sacred stories of the world's religions as mythological is not to pass any judgment upon their truth. The term is completely neutral.

The Doctrinal and Philosophical Dimension

All major religions have a set of doctrines or beliefs which form part of its foundation. In Christianity, the doctrinal dimension is expressed in the creeds which have been defined in church councils in the early centuries of the Church's existence. The most frequently used creed is the Nicene Creed which focuses upon two basic doctrines: the Trinity (the belief in one God in three persons, Father, Son and Holy Spirit) and the Incarnation (the entry of God into humanity in the Person of Jesus Christ). This creed is recited each Sunday when the eucharist is celebrated and the worshippers present subscribe to it. Within Judaism there is great stress upon the oneness of God and in His loving kindness. In Hinduism there is a central belief in Brahman, the life force, and in the millions of gods who are but manifestations of the 'One'. Within Islam there is a strict emphasis upon the uniqueness of God. These doctrines are binding upon the believer. Five times each day the Muslim professes 'There is no God but Allah and Muhammad is His prophet' and this frequency of recitation is a binding rule of Islam.

Just as the ritual dimension draws upon the narrative dimension and in turn brings it to life in the experience of the believer, so the doctrinal dimension arises from the stories and proceeds to systematize and codify them. In the Christian tradition the doctrines of the Trinity and of the Incarnation, referred to earlier, were attempts by the church to explore the relationship of Jesus who in the narratives appears to be in some sense God (which conviction seemed to be reflected in the experience of the first Christians) with the monotheism of the Jewish faith in which they had been raised. The very early Christian affirmation was 'Jesus is Lord'. But what exactly did this mean? The desire for an intellectual statement of belief, allies with a desire to refute interpretations which seemed to be erroneous, led to a increased concern to clarify formal beliefs. And so the creeds arose.

There will inevitably be different levels of understanding between educated and simple followers and there will be different interpretations of the doctrines, some being more literal or more symbolic than others. Nevertheless the doctrinal and philosophical dimension of any religion is an attempt to give greater substance and clarity to the beliefs which are enshrined within its traditions.

The Ethical and Legal Dimension

All religions give guidance to their followers on how to conduct themselves in this world. Judaism, for example, has always placed great emphasis upon the Torah, the Law, revealed by God and required of all those who follow the tradition. The Torah consists of a vast array of legal requirements of which the best known are the Ten Commandments. The importance of the Torah is demonstrated in the ritual dimension by a Jewish boy's bar mitzvah (and in Liberal or Reform Jewish circles also by a Jewish girl's bat mitzvah). When a Jewish boy reaches 13, he comes of age and demonstrates this by reading from the Torah in the synagogue. By so doing he becomes bar mitzvah (literally, son of the Law) and so takes upon himself the responsibility of keeping the Law and so of living by it. Christianity has tended to replace a system of legal requirements with a central ethical attitude, sometimes called the law of love: 'You shall love the Lord your God and your neighbour as yourself'. This ethical notion is deeply rooted in the doctrinal dimension where the Godhead is proclaimed as a Trinity of three persons co-existing in love. Christians look too to the stories of Jesus as an example for living and there they see him giving his life to the world out of love.

In the modern world religions are being challenged to develop and express ethical attitudes towards such issues as ecology and nuclear weapons. Although the problems are new the process is not as religions have always had the responsibility of applying their ethical principles to the issues of the day.

The Social and Institutional Dimension

The social dimension of religion is concerned with the expression of that religion in society or how, as Smart puts it, it is incarnated. Every religion expresses itself in human society and all religions assume a corporate nature. In Judaism, for example, it is important to look closely at the organization of the synagogue and its relationship to the home and family which have a very special place in the Jewish tradition. In Christianity, the Church, as the body of the faithful, is of central importance and within that the role of the bishop in the unity of the church and of the priest in the work of the individual parishes. Religious communities with their monks and nuns are highly significant in most religions and there are also the gurus, the prophets and the seers, the charismatic people who are highly influential in religious movements (and often perceived by those in a formal position in the religious structure to be a nuisance!) but who are not part of the formal structure of the religion. It would include also social structures emanating from a religion such as the caste system within Hinduism.

The Material Dimension

This is the seventh dimension of religion, the one which Smart added to his original six. As the social and institutional dimension indicates how religions are incarnated in institutions and in human society, so the material dimension shows how they are incarnated in *material* form. These incarnations in material form can be either in the form of human creations — buildings or works of art — or in natural phenomena upon which special significance has been placed by religion traditions. Although puritanical groups show suspicion of such forms of outward symbolism, for most people in most religions they have been and are powerful and evocative aids in the approach to God. A visit to the Cathedral of the Assumption of the Virgin in Smolensk on its patronal festival with the huge dimensions of the building, the majesty and beauty of the icons in the iconastasis and the haunting quality of the music provides an arresting example of the material dimension.

In addition to these human creations, which are present and powerful in all religious traditions, there are the natural phenomena which again are powerful evocations of the divine. The sacred River Ganges, Ayers Rock, Mount Sinai are all holy ground to different religious traditions. Sometimes these sacred places merge with the human creations described above. Supreme examples of these are the city of Jerusalem, Benares, Lourdes, Amritsar and Makkah.

The material dimension has very clear links with the ritual dimension which in many cases is a response to it. Christian pilgrims to Jerusalem will, as a response to the sacredness of the place, retrace the steps of Jesus on his journey from his trail to his crucifixion: the ritual dimension is responding to the material dimension.

Establishing Attainment Targets

Ninian Smart's dimensions of religion provide as good a basis as any for constructing an RE syllabus for pupils aged from 4 to 16 (or 18). If Smart's account is accepted as the foundation then pupils will receive a balanced and broadly-based understanding of religion. The next question is how one moves from this position to constructing a syllabus with identified attainment targets. The following account written by a head-teacher of a primary school shows how she with her staff planned RE coherently for the age range 4 to 11, using Smart's dimensions of religion as a base and building in what they considered to be appropriate state-ments of attainment. In addition to this it shows too the process through which the staff went and something of the principles which they estab-lished. The school is a large two-form entry primary school with about 400 pupils serving a suburban area of mainly, though not exclusively, private housing. Apart from a small number of Jewish children, there are no ethnic minorities represented in the school. The school is well re-garded both by parents and by LEA advisers. The headteacher had been concerned for some time about what she considered to be the tenuous nature of RE in the school curriculum and had persuaded the school governors to appoint a curriculum consultant in RE on an incentive allowance. She was fortunate in securing an energetic postholder who

was enthusiastic to accept the challenge of establishing RE firmly in the
school curriculum.

> This school is my second headship and I was very pleased to be
> appointed. No school is ever perfect but I was delighted to find,
> when I arrived, what a happy, well run school it was. One area,
> however, I did feel was ripe for improvement was RE. Before I
> had any time to do anything about it the National Curriculum
> was upon us and we began the process, familiar in all schools, of
> reading the documents as they poured out and then beginning to
> look at their implications for us as a school.
>
> As we began as a staff to plan our responses and to devise
> schemes of work and balanced topics, I did not want RE to be left
> to the end and so become an afterthought. I therefore met with
> my recently appointed RE consultant and arranged an inservice
> day for the whole class to consider ways of developing it as part
> of the overall curriculum of the school. My RE consultant under-
> took to arrange the day, in consultation with me, and we invited
> an RE tutor from the local teacher training establishment to lead a
> key session in the morning on Professor Ninian Smart's dimen-
> sions of religion as a basis for religious education. After that we
> planned in-house discussion for the rest of the day. I was quite
> clear that the purpose of the day was not just a general enlighten-
> ment of the staff about the nature of RE but rather to agree a
> school approach to RE and a strategy for implementing it.
>
> It proved to be a very interesting and useful day. The key
> lecture was very clear and to the point and many of the staff had
> never conceived of RE in such wide terms as this before. They
> could see that here was a broad basis for approaching RE. The
> in-house time was very positive and constructive: the staff is quite
> a mixed group religiously, as, of course, are most staff rooms,
> but no one wished to exercise his/her right to withdraw from the
> teaching of RE which was a relief to me! The points of agreement
> which arose from the discussions were as follows:
>
> 1   It was widely agreed that Smart's dimensions of religion pro-
>   vided a good practical basis for teaching RE but that some of
>   the dimensions were more significant for different age groups.
>   The narrative and mythic, the ritual and practical, the social
>   and institutional and the material dimensions were felt to be
>   particularly relevant to the primary school. On the other
>   hand, the doctrinal and philosophical dimension was felt to be
>   less appropriate in its own right at this stage but it was
>   recognized that doctrines and beliefs were bound to arise from
>   the other dimensions.

2   RE was seen as developmental and the RE curriculum as spiral. Any planned RE curriculum would involve children returning to the same issues but at a deeper level of complexity. The festival of Christmas was referred to frequently as an example of an item which children returned to each year and could be understood at different levels of meaning. This made a whole school policy essential.

3   It was felt that the religious and cultural composition of the school would inevitably affect the content of its RE. The younger the child the more important it is that what he/she studies should be related to his/her first hand experience in the immediate environment. In a school such as ours, it was likely that with the infants most, though not all, of the explicit religious content would be drawn from Christian sources although this would widen in the junior department.

4   Staff all shared the view that if the subjects of the National Curriculum were all to have attainment targets at 7 and 11 years, it would be sensible for RE to have them also as this is becoming the way in which we approach teaching. As these will not be laid down nationally and as our local Agreed Syllabus does not provide them we would have to formulate our own. It was further agreed that we would not want to see ourselves merely teaching to those targets as this would be very limiting.

5   Because RE involves more than just knowing facts about religions and seeks to develop such qualities as empathy and tolerance, staff acknowledged that any attainment targets which we devised will need to reflect the breadth and diversity of the subject. They could see that it would be much simpler to determine attainment targets which merely reflected the factual aspects but this was seen as a temptation to resist!

6   There was an extensive discussion for part of the day as to how RE could be delivered most effectively — through topics or on its own as a separate subject. In the end it was agreed that whereas many of the attainment targets could be met through carefully planned general topics — for example, a topic on water could be very helpful in exploring the symbolism of water in religious thought and practice — it was likely that part of RE would need to be taught separately from other subjects in the curriculum.

7   In many ways this was just the beginning. We had reached the important point of coming to a common mind and we were agreed in principle. We agreed to continue the development of RE through a smaller group chaired by the RE curriculum

> leader. This group, it was stipulated, must represent the different age groups within the school so that we could ensure that the notion of progression and development was built into the planning. The brief given to this group was to prepare a draft RE syllabus with built-in attainment targets which would be presented for consideration by the whole staff. I was very insistent that what was produced would be a proposal and not something written in tablets of stone because it seemed to me essential that what was produced as the final form should represent the mind of the whole staff and not just those who perhaps had a stronger interest in the subject.

This account gives a clear picture of how a staff collectively approached the creation of a whole school policy for RE and it illustrates the importance of collaboration in planning if the staff as a whole is to feel some degree of ownership of the syllabus. So far though the principles only of the exercise have been established. What came next was to provide an example of how such a syllabus might look.

Making a Start

If the layout and approach of the National Curriculum is used, then it would be sensible to take the seven dimensions of religion of Smart's account and to see each one as a *profile component*. Each of these profile components would then be separated into *attainment targets* which in turn would be broken down into more specific *statements of attainment*. The content of the teaching and learning would be laid out in the *programmes of study*. To illustrate this we might take the first Profile Component: The Ritual and Practical Dimension.

Profile Component: The Ritual and Practical Dimension
Attainment Targets: AT1 Festivals and Celebrations
AT2 Forms of Worship
AT3 Rites of Passage

AT1 Festivals and Celebrations — Key Stage 1

Programme of study
Pupils should have the opportunity to explore special times of joy and celebration and the rituals and activities which accompany them (for example, birthdays).

They should have the opportunity to share in some of the celebratory traditions of some major religious festivals such as Diwali,

Christmas, Easter, Passover, Guru Nanak's Birthday and Eid-ul-Fitr and to hear stories associated with them. There should be an emphasis upon the social aspects of the festival — giving presents, special foods etc.

Statements of attainment
Pupils at the end of Key Stage 1 should:

    (i)   be able to describe the rituals of a special day in their own life (for example, birthday);

   (ii)   be aware of the main stories associated with the festivals of Easter and Christmas and some of the traditions associated with them;

  (iii)   be aware of festivals in other world religions and some of the stories associated with them.

AT1 Festivals and Celebrations — Key Stage 2

Programme of study
Pupils should have the opportunity to investigate the festivals and fasts of different religions and to respond to them *empathetically*. They should have access through artefact, video and printed material and, if possible, through first-hand contact to the ways in which major festivals are celebrated and with the associated symbols and stories. There should be an opportunity to study the Christian year focusing upon the major festivals of Easter, Christmas and Pentecost and the seasons of Lent and Advent. Pupils should consider the significance of penitence and fasting with special reference to Ramadan and Yom Kippur.

Statements of attainment
Pupils at the end of Key Stage 2 should:

    (i)   be able to describe the ways in which a number of festivals are celebrated;

   (ii)   be familiar with festivals in a number of religions;

  (iii)   be aware of the chief symbols associated with major festivals;

  (iv)   show some understanding of the significance of festivals for those celebrating them;

   (v)   to show some awareness of the significance of fasting in religious practice.

What has just been described is merely an example of how profile components, attainment targets, programmes of study and statements of attainments might be applied to RE. A full scheme would, of course, be much more extensive than this. What we have here are the programmes of study and the statements of attainment at Key Stages 1 and 2 for one of three attainment targets arising from one of seven profile components! It is described in this way in the hope that it might provide school staffs with a way into thinking and planning RE in their schools in this way.

Assessment

The Education Reform Act intended that each Foundation Subject should be formally assessed at the end of each Key Stage and the results of individual children should be available to themselves and their parents and that the overall results for each school should be available to the general public. Full assessment would be made from a balance between a teacher's own internal assessment and external assessment by standard assessment tasks (SATs). Since then there have been considerable modifications and it now seems that at Key Stages 1 and 2 only the three Core Foundation subjects are to be assessed and reported upon in this way. The other Foundation subjects will be assessed internally and there may even be non-statutory SATs for teachers who wish to use them. This modification will no doubt remove any demands there might have been for LEAs to draw up SATs for RE.

This does not remove the need for thought to be given to assessing RE. The purpose of assessment is laid out very clearly by the Secretary of State for Education and Science for *Science 5–16 in the National Curriculum* (August 1988):

> The purpose of assessment is to show what a pupil has learned and mastered, so as to inform decisions about the next steps, and to enable teachers and parents to ensure that he or she is making adequate progress. In making our recommendations we are concerned that assessment should be seen as part of the teaching process and made in such a way as to give valid information. (6.1)

Much discussion about forms of external testing and about the reporting of the results has tended to cloud the issue and to bring the notion of assessment (wrongly) into disrepute. This statement about assessment demonstrates that it is not only appropriate for all areas of the curriculum, including RE, but essential for any serious teaching.

In RE most of the assessment of the pupils' work will be through *observation* and *discussion*. In the primary classroom teachers inevitably spend considerable time working alongside their pupils in the classroom, either individually or in groups. There they have the opportunity to observe them at work handling material and listening to their discussions and to their questions. The teacher will also be active in assessing, talking to pupils about their understanding of their work and asking key questions. Some teachers will feel it appropriate with older pupils to ask questions in a written form. Many teachers will want to consider keeping folders of children's work and of devising ways of recording pupil progress. It is important to reiterate again what was said earlier in the chapter: that assessing pupil progress is not new in the primary school. The effect of the Education Reform Act has been to place assessment at the centre of educational concern and to encourage teachers to be more systematic in assessing their pupils' progress and to devise more effective ways of recording it and of using that recording in their forward planning.

The purpose of this chapter is *not* to present *the* way to tackling attainment in RE in the primary school. No one is yet in a position to do that; the idea is too new for there to be any extensive agreement. What it has attempted to do is to raise some of the issues which are present in the debate and to look at an approach to the situation which may be of help to teachers in the primary school who are attempting to get more to grips with RE in the context of the National Curriculum. At this stage in the evolution of thinking about approaching attainment and assessment in RE the process is perhaps more important than the content.

Two useful publications in this area are:

A FARE deal for RE produced by the FARE Project, University of Exeter (1990);
Attainment in RE produced the Regional RE Centre (Midlands) (1989).

Notes on Contributors

Vida Barnett is a freelance writer and lecturer. Author of *A Jewish Family in Britain* (RMEP) she contributes to a number of educational journals. After fourteen years teaching in schools, she became Head of Religious Studies at a Liverpool College of Education, where she founded one of the first multifaith RE centres. As an Associate Secretary of the Christian Education Movement she is heavily involved in in-service education. She is a member of the editorial team of *RE Today* and the SHAP Mailing and Advisory and Information Officer for the SHAP Working Party. She works part time for the IQRA Muslim Educational Trust.

Derek Bastide has taught in both primary and secondary schools. He is at present Principal Lecturer in Education at Brighton Polytechnic and Course Leader for the BEd (Hons) Early Years of Schooling. He is involved in in-service work both locally and nationally and is author of *Religious Education 5-12* (Falmer Press). He is Chairman of Chichester Diocesan Schools' Committee and a member of the East Sussex SACRE.

Dennis Bates has taught RE in secondary and primary schools and lectured in RE in colleges of higher education, most recently Humberside Polytechnic, where he had major responsibility for INSET including a curriculum project on topic work in primary schools. He is a member of Humberside SACRE and has contributed articles to a number of journals including the *British Journal of Religious Education*.

Elaine Bellchambers is Deputy Head of a Hampshire primary school and has been an RE primary school consultant for the past fifteen years. She is currently Primary Advisory teacher for Religious Education in Hampshire and very much involved in INSET and is a contributor to both *Paths to Understanding* and *Following the Path*. She is a member of Hampshire's SACRE.

Alan Brown is Director of the National Society's RE Centre in Kensington, London and Schools' Officer (RE) of the Board of Education of the General Synod of the Church of England. He is currently Vice-Chairman of the SHAP Working Party and Director of the Chichester Project. He has written a number of textbooks on RE as well as contributing to a variety of educational journals in Britain and elsewhere on the Continent.

Liz Collis has taught for many years in primary schools both here and abroad. She now teaches in a Hampshire junior school where she is Curriculum Coordinator and the consultant for RE. She has contributed to county in-service training and to the CEM topic packs *Exploring a Theme*. She is currently a member of the county working party set up to review the agreed syllabus and to consider assessment advice.

Kate Fleming graduated from the Rose Bruford College of Speech and Drama. After working in the theatre, she had varied primary school experience and is now Senior Lecturer in Drama at Brighton Polytechnic. She makes regular contributions to in-service courses in London and the South East. The daughter of a country parson, her interest in RE began at an early age.

Carole King has specialist interests in language and religious education. She has worked for many years within the area of primary RE, as a Curriculum Consultant, as a contributor to county in-service work and as editor of the county RE magazine. She has also been as consultant to, and scriptwriter for, BBC schools' radio programmes in RE. She has now moved into teacher education, where she is lecturing in language and literacy. She feels strongly that many teachers do not realize the very strong positive links between language and RE, especially in the realm of story.

Erica Musty trained as a primary teacher and spent several years working with children with English as a second language. She has worked in Special Education for the last thirteen years with responsibility for curriculum development, PSE and RE. She is currently Coordinator for RE and Special Educational Needs based at the West London Institute of Higher Education where she also lectures. She is involved nationally in in-service education and has lectured in Europe. She contributes regularly to *RE Today* and has had articles published in several RE journals and books.

Hazel Waddup is headteacher of a large infants school in East Sussex. She has lectured and given workshops in local colleges as well as in

France and Germany. She has been very active in primary RE in the county and has been a contributor to *RE Today*. She is particularly interested in the links between the arts, especially drama, and RE. She has been a practising Buddhist for several years.

Index

Advent, 37, 132, 157–8
Agreed Syllabuses, 6–7, 15, 18, 81,
    104, 107, 114
    see also Hampshire Agreed Syllabus
Aims of RE, 5ff, 11–12
Anansi, 147
Artefacts, 3, 26, 29, 48, 93, 131–142
    list of, 140
    see also Resources
Assembly
    see Worship (collective)
assessment and evaluation, 4, 30–31,
    63, 86, 100, 118, 185ff, 202
attainment targets, 13, 22, 116,
    186–190, 200–203
Attitudes in RE, 113–114

Baisakhi, 75–76
Barmitzvah/Batmitzvah, 195–6
basic curriculum, 1, 13, 117, 189
Bible, 20, 100, 156
    stories, 55, 58, 93–94, 100, 169
Bruner, J., 103, 108, 113
Buddha, The, 77
Buddhism, 34, 35, 36, 138

Charlotte's Webb, 144
Chris and the Dragon, 149
Christianity, 17, 18, 20, 98, 101, 108,
    138, 162, 190, 192, 196
Christian Aid, 26, 39
Christian Education Movement, 48
Christmas, 35, 39–41, 73, 132, 137,
    152–154, 157–159, 192, 199

confessional approach to RE, 1
Cowper-Temple clause, 11, 16–17
Curriculum from 5–16, 68

Dance, 34
depth themes, 106, 109, 112, 113
determinations (collective worship),
    16, 19, 21–22, 173
Discovering an Approach, 10, 113
Display, 48
Diwali, 37, 132, 137, 192
Drama, 33–34, 43–44, 164ff
Durham Report, 9, 12

Easter, 52, 55–56, 81, 82, 132,
    160–161
Education Act (1870), 11
Education Act (1944), 6, 11, 25, 174
Education Act (1981), 65–66
Education Reform Act (1988), 2, 14,
    20, 23, 95, 173–175, 176, 179, 189
    see also National Curriculum, RE,
    worship collective, SACRE and
    Foundation Subjects
Eid-Milad-ul-Nabi, 77, 78
Eid-ul-Fitr, 192
Equal Opportunities, 33–34

FARE Project (Exeter), 116, 125
Festivals, 70ff, 132, 192
    see individual festivals
Fiddler on the Roof, 136
Following the Path, 26, 28, 31
Foundation Subjects, 13, 185